3-27-97

Mr. Macananny...

We appreciated doing
business with your organization,
and also getting to know you.
We hope this book
will be a blessing to you. May
the Lord continue to bless
you in ALL your ways!

Sincerely,
Gordon & Denise
Marth

TOWARD

A

RENEWED MIND

TOWARD

A

RENEWED MIND

Richard F. Gottier, Ph.D.

TOWARD A RENEWED MIND

Library of Congress Catalog Card Number: 90-92937

ISBN: 0-9625671-0-8

Published by: Dr. Richard F. Gottier, President
Zion Ministries of the East Coast, Inc.
P.O. Box 737
Kitty Hawk, North Carolina 27949

Printed in the United States of America

DEDICATION

TO

CAROL

Whose rock-like faith and quiet confidence proved to be the mooring cables when my own mind was adrift toward humanism. She almost instinctively grasped the need for a Renewed Mind, and made my own pilgrimage back ever so much more certain—and pleasant.

ACKNOWLEDGMENTS

Only in the prolonged labor and birthing of a book does one discover how much he really owes to others. Of many who could be mentioned, I thank especially:

Carol, who encourages, counsels, transcribes, types, reads, cooks, entertains and, in the midst of all, remains a joyful and loving wife.

John and Lisa Archer, whose careful reading, editing, proofing and shepherding of this manuscript produced a much purer copy.

Bill and Reneé Norton, whose patient instruction in computer techniques and assistance in manuscript typing aided greatly in producing this book.

Gordon and Denise Marth, for their encouragement, prayers and grasp of the Renewed Mind.

Dad and Mom, whose love, prayers and confident expectations quite literally kept us pressing on.

Jay Colle, whose artistic abilities made the cover possible and the book more appealing.

Melissa Abbott, for her design of the teaching charts and her ability to interpret the writer's intentions.

Good Shepherd, patient students of the Word, faithful prayer partners and beloved friends. Always eager to hear the next teaching series preparing the end-time army, they immediately set about implementing God's most recent word!

CONTENTS

PREFACE

Nearly a dozen years ago the Lord spoke very directly to me and said that the great end-time battle would be for the minds of men. Far more important than the battle with communism and all the countries associated with it; far more critical than the fight against drugs, alcohol and other addictive substances; far more crucial than all the medical struggles with cancer, heart trouble and related diseases; far more urgent even than the current battle that is raging with AIDS and other sexually transmitted diseases; and far more pervasive than even the economic struggles about to descend upon our world, the battle for the mind controls every area of life. Christians in particular are so vulnerable, so naive and so easily deceived by the arguments of our enemy Satan that every aspect of our Christian life is involved in this battle for the mind.

This is full-scale war—no holds barred! Yet so subtle is this battle that the vast majority of Christians are virtually unaware that they are being caught up in the throes of it. Before we venture far down this journey toward a Renewed Mind, it will become obvious to everyone that there is no matter of greater urgency in all the discussions of Christian living than the matter of pursuing a Renewed Mind.

If it is true that the teaching most worthy of our attention is the teaching born deep in the furnace of personal affliction, then you may want to ask the Lord to prepare your heart for the teaching that follows. For the teaching on the Renewed Mind as it is recorded in this book grows out of a long and bitter struggle in the author's own heart. While I accepted Jesus as my personal Savior at the age of nine and served Him faithfully during my college days and beyond, the ensuing ten years of graduate education seemed almost diabolically contrived to destroy all the faith I ever possessed.

During the years of theological seminary my confidence in the authority of the Word of God and in His power to intervene in the affairs of men was quite thoroughly and almost totally undermined. In the years of graduate education that followed, day after day humanistic and rational teaching hammered away at what few shreds of faith I had left; finally the day arrived when the PhD was in hand but skepticism and humanism were really the order of the day for my own thinking.

Space does not permit me here to trace in detail the agony of those years in the spiritual wilderness. Suffice it to say that in early 1974, God in His goodness saw fit to draw me back to Himself and in one of the most dramatic moments of my life led me to reaffirm my faith in the authority of the Word of God. For many months following, I spent many hours a day quite literally in the school of God. During this period, He taught me the things of His Spirit, filled me anew with His Spirit and opened the Word afresh.

All of this might lead you to the conclusion that I had arrived spiritually! Nothing could be further from the truth. Suddenly I began to realize the great and crying need to have virtually all of my thinking, education, as well as the deepest assumptions of my mind retrained in the light of God's Word. That struggle has been going on for much over a decade now and continues. One of the most important truths growing out of many hours in the Word is the more He has revealed to me of His ways, the more I realize how really distant our natural human thinking is from the mind of the Lord.

Thus the purpose of this present manuscript is not to illustrate all the ways in which our thinking varies from His thinking and our ways fall short of His ways; rather, in the simple steps in which He has instructed me, my objective is to help you understand how we come to achieve a truly Renewed Mind. Once you begin to discover the thrill of having a mind that thinks within the framework of His ways, you will find with every turn of the page in the Word of God new ways in which your mind needs to be challenged and restructured to agree with Him and His Word.

Ever since my earliest boyhood memories, Christians have had a love-hate relationship with "knowing." Many groups prided themselves on having an uneducated clergy. In some extreme instances, spirituality and knowledge seemed to be the opposite ends of the continuum; the more one avoided any evidence of being educated, the more spiritual one was perceived to be.

In fairness, such fears were not entirely groundless. Many cults were springing up which taught, much like the Gnostics of New Testament times, that what one knew really was determinate of one's salvation. Further, the historical-critical approach to the Scriptures, birthed in Germany in the mid-nineteenth century, was in the first half of this century reaching into theological seminaries all across America. Pastors in many denominations were being turned out with no clear understanding of the authority of the Word of God and His willingness and power to intervene in the affairs of men, and frequently with no commitment to the deity of Jesus Christ and the saving power of His blood shed on Calvary. Young people from our churches went off to colleges just beginning to be ravaged with the early stages of humanism; they came home with many new ideas plainly contradictory to the Word of God. The resulting attitude of most Bible-believing Christians all across this country for nearly half a century was the rejection of all knowledge, even in most cases any deep understanding and teaching of the Word of God.

The outcome of this love-hate relationship with "knowing" has been that the vast majority of Christians all across our land are literally sitting ducks for the humanism that has come so openly to the fore in the seventies and eighties. The assumptions and perceptual framework in which the evening news is presented night after night is virtually 100 percent antithetical to the principles of the Word of God. Situation comedies on television mock every moral standard that we know, mock the basic principles of a strong family with a godly father at its head and glorify every kind of illicit sexual relationship, including homosexual relationships. Talk shows of every kind applaud humanistic and New Age principles and dismiss the basic Judeo-Christian precepts with a sneer.

So subtle is this satanic strategy for the mind that multitudes who sincerely name the name of Christ and intend to be obedient to Him would on any test of Christian beliefs score as rank humanists rather than Christians. My entire life has been spent in the world of academic community, and I honestly believe that I number among my friends hundreds of men and women who go to church on Sunday and worship Christ with a great deal of sincerity but who

11

step into the classroom on Monday morning and teach humanism with a naivete that is appalling.

Unfortunately the great renewal movement of the sixties and seventies has in many ways only exacerbated this situation. With the rediscovery of the indwelling presence of the Holy Spirit and the gifts that He brings, there has been a great willingness to live with the excitement of the moment but a strong hesitancy to get into the deep things of the Word of God. Hosea focused on this plight when he said, "My people are destroyed for lack of knowledge" (4:6).

In Isaiah 55:8-9, we read:

> *"My thoughts are not your thoughts, neither are your ways My ways," declares the Lord. "For as the heavens are higher than the earth, so are My ways higher than your ways, and My thoughts than your thoughts."*

And in Isaiah 55:11, God says:

> *"So shall My word be which goes forth from My mouth; it shall not return to Me empty, without accomplishing what I desire, and without succeeding in the matter for which I sent it."*

The important point here is that God's ways are revealed in His Word, and the Word must go out if it is to accomplish the purpose for which it is intended.

Praise the Lord, I can report to you with confidence that I believe the indifference toward the deep things of God's Word is changing. For months the Lord has been witnessing to my spirit that He is beginning to create a great hunger for the teaching of the Word all across this land. He urges upon me the eleventh verse of Amos 8:

> *"Behold, days are coming," declares the Lord God, "when I will send a famine on the land, not a famine for bread or a thirst for water, but rather for hearing the words of the Lord."*

In the third week of March 1979, I had set aside several days for prayer and fasting, seeking the will of the Lord in a major new direction for our lives and ministry. In the midst of a very beautiful communion and fellowship with the Lord, He spoke very clearly to me: "I have called you to be a teacher to the end-time army." Closely linked to that prophetic word, He led me to a passage of Scripture that is the foundation of what is now Zion Ministries. In Habakkuk 2:14, God gives a thrilling promise: "The earth will be filled with the knowledge of the glory of the Lord, as the waters cover the sea."

There are three reasons why this passage of Scripture has become central for me. First, it became a great driven stake, an anchor if you will, to my wife, Carol, and me in the midst of days of severe testing that would come upon us. Second, no matter how much it looks as if our world is totally engulfed in the rolling tides of humanism sweeping over us, here is our Lord's testimony of the fact that the day will come when men shall know Him and His kingdom in a dimension as great and as evident as the waters of the ocean. Third, only if men's minds are totally renewed is it conceivable that the knowledge of the glory of the Lord can cover the earth; therefore, the message that follows in whatever form must get out and men must turn to the renewing of their minds.

At the risk of claiming too much for the words that follow, I stand firmly convinced that if you will sincerely pursue the Scripture passages cited and give yourself to the discipline of acquiring a Renewed Mind, it will change your relationship to the Lord, make you more sensitive to the voice of His Spirit, lead you into victorious faith, bring you to a new understanding of the ways of the Lord and give you victory over numerous temptations. Quite simply, it will be a thoroughly life-changing event in your life.

INTRODUCTION

Have you ever struggled within yourself as you read the Word of God, part of you longing to be obedient to every command you find there, but another part of you rising up in rebellion at every turn? Have you ever felt your spirit resonating with the apostle Paul as he said, "I joyfully concur with the law of God in the inner man, but I see a different law in the members of my body, waging war against the law of my mind" (Romans 7:22-23)? Have you ever found anger, bitterness, envy or jealousy rising within you while every effort at controlling it seemed to be fruitless? Have you ever found yourself drifting off to sleep at night only to discover that your mind was entertaining frightfully lustful thoughts? Have you ever wanted desperately to believe the promises of God as found in His Word but found yourself waging a losing battle with unbelief?

In short, is there a vast gulf between what you already know to be His perfect will for your life and the reality of your daily living?

Then you are a candidate for a Renewed Mind!

Have you had a major victory in your spiritual battles—perhaps a physical healing—and then right before your eyes the enemy of your soul stole it away? Have you begun to grow spiritually and seen miracles in several areas of your life, and yet there are one or two areas over which you simply cannot get the victory? Have you ever cried out to know the Lord's perfect will in your life—cried out to be led by the Holy Spirit and to flow in His perfect will—and yet there is that ever-gnawing uncertainty about whether you heard the voice of God or the voice of the enemy? Have you ever cried out, "Lord, I want to be more like You, more spiritual, more like Jesus," and yet every spiritual battle seems to be a battle of externalities.

In summary, are you aware that God's Word promises an overcoming, victorious Christian life—in fact you have seen full evidence of it in others—but the reality of it seems just beyond your grasp?

Then you are a candidate for a Renewed Mind!

A Renewed Mind! I am fully convinced that no teaching is more central to living an overcoming Christian life. No teaching is more central to a disciplined end-time army. There is no greater secret to standing against the wiles of the devil in the great end-time temptations and persecutions. And yet the simple fact of the matter is that we have had virtually no teaching on the matter of the Renewed Mind within memory of the present church. A couple of works have been printed describing the subtle battle between the Christian mind and the deceits of humanism in the New Age. Virtually nothing has been written on how one takes the proverbial bull by the horns and gets hold of the deepest struggle within a man and comes out victorious.

How we praise God that at least within the evangelical church teachings concerning the rebirth of the spirit, of coming to know Christ as Savior, have been widespread and continuous for many years. Further, for at least the last forty years there has been widespread teaching about the possibilities of the healing of our physical bodies, as we have come to understand that this healing was included in the cross of Christ. Yet the mind, caught as it is between the spirit and the flesh, has enjoyed virtually no sustained and focused teaching on the possibility of renewal. I trust that the Scripture passages and teaching that follow will be helpful in this endeavor.

One final thought before we move on. I believe there are only two kinds of preaching and teaching. The first type is comprised of those who begin with the circumstances of life as they perceive them to be, rationally analyze the problems about them through sense knowledge, and then cut and fit the Word of God to suit life as they see it on a rational level. Their breed seems ever to increase.

The second type of preaching begins with a thorough saturation in the Word of God—a grounding in His principles and His ways— knowing that His ways are not our ways and His thoughts are not our thoughts. From that vantage point, the circumstances of life are brought into conformity with the Word of God and His ways.

As for me and my house, we choose the latter course.

CHAPTER ONE

CREATED MAN: THE MIND AS GOD INTENDED

In order to grasp something of the full potential of a Renewed Mind for today's Christian, we must first see it cast against the broad canvas of man as God intended he should be at the first creation. There is a simple assumption in the Word of God that the creation as God spoke it and formed it in the beginning was perfect. By satanic deception and intervention, sin entered that creation through man and his disobedience, and God's once perfect creation has been in a state of constant deterioration from the moment of the Fall until this day. Yet an understanding of God's original creation and His intent for man is mandatory if we are to understand something of the potential before us today.

All of this hinges upon a second assumption, not developed at any length in this book. The very purpose of the incarnation of Jesus Christ, God come in the form of man, and of His death on Calvary's cross was to reverse the effects of the Fall. With that hope of full restoration through Calvary constantly before us, then a close look at God's creation becomes exciting indeed.

In the Image of God

In the opening chapter of the Genesis account we read:

> *Then God said, "Let Us make man in Our image,*
> *according to Our likeness; and let them rule over the*
> *fish of the sea and over the birds of the sky and over the*
> *cattle and over all the earth, and over every creeping*
> *thing that creeps on the earth. And God created man in*
> *His own image, in the image of God He created him,*
> *male and female, He created them.* (Genesis 1:26-27)

The Genesis writer renews this theme in the fifth chapter: "In the day when God created man, He made him in the likeness of God" (Genesis 5:1). And yet again he writes: "Whoever sheds man's blood, by man his blood shall be shed, for in the image of God He made man" (Genesis 9:6). Think of it! There is something in the very being of man that the moment you see him you think of God. That is a far cry from the Darwinian notion of an ever-improving species and the belief that man is simply the extension—and a slight one at that—of the animal kingdom in general and of the primate species in particular.

David the psalmist, certainly speaking under the anointing of the Holy Spirit, offered this magnificent picture of man:

> *When I consider Thy heavens, the work of Thy fingers,*
> *the moon and the stars, which Thou hast ordained;*
> *what is man, that Thou dost take thought of him? And*
> *the son of man, that Thou dost care for him? Yet Thou*
> *hast made him a little lower than God, and dost crown*
> *him with glory and majesty!* (Psalm 8:3-5)

In a similar vein, the apostle Paul described man as "the image and glory of God" (1 Corinthians 11:7).

In the image of God! Just a little lower than God! How are we to view man in light of such profound statements? Jesus revealed the key to this matter as He visited with the Samaritan woman at the well:

But an hour is coming, and now is, when the true worshipers shall worship the Father in spirit and in truth; for such people the Father seeks to be His worshipers. God is spirit, and those who worship Him must worship in spirit and truth. (John 4:23-24)

Therefore, man, created in the image of God, must be like the very nature of God. Jesus has revealed that nature to us clearly, saying that God is spirit.

It is worth noting here that the very reason for the creation is revealed in this passage, for the Father seeks those whose spirits are alive and able to worship Him. The desire of the Father's heart for fellowship and worship is central to the entire understanding of the universe, and will be developed further later in this study.

So man is spirit! The essential part of man, that part on which God has stamped eternal, is spirit. That part of us that lives forever and spends eternity with or without God is the very central essence and nature of man—his spirit.

The Tripartite Nature of Man

A more comprehensive understanding of the biblical view of man is found in the New Testament. Paul in particular has a clear grasp of the full nature of man, for he writes to the Thessalonians:

Now may the God of peace Himself sanctify you entirely; and may your spirit and soul and body be preserved complete, without blame at the coming of our Lord Jesus Christ. (1 Thessalonians 5:23)

Hebrews 4:12 tells us that "the Word of God is living and active and sharper than any two-edged sword, and piercing as far as the division of soul and spirit." Luke writes of the new believers in Acts: "The congregation of those who believed were of one heart and soul" (Acts 4:32). Earlier Luke records Mary's exaltation as she visits with Elizabeth: "My soul exalts the Lord and my spirit has rejoiced in God my Savior" (Luke 1:46-47).

Chart 1 (on page 109) is one attempt to diagram the very complex biblical understanding of the nature of man. The Bible rather consistently uses either of two terms for each of the three parts of man. These six words are found quite consistently in the Old Testament Hebrew as well as the New Testament Greek.

In the center is the very essence of man, his *spirit*. But the Bible also uses the word *heart*, which carries the connotation of middle, among other meanings. The Old Testament speaks of the heart of man as being desperately wicked (Genesis 6). But say whatever you will, it is the spirit—the heart, the very essence of man—that is eternal.

Now to the spirit of man God has given two more parts. First, He has given the *soul* or the *mind* as you note in the second circle. There are those who would divide the mind and the soul into two parts and come up with a description of man's nature having four parts; I find this unwarranted in the biblical account. The mind is that part of us that can learn, remember, recall, will, emote, choose, and think. The concept of the soul varies just slightly from that of the mind in that it speaks more of the mature personality, the total personhood involving the accumulated experiences of the mind.

Third, note that the Lord gave to our spirit and our soul a body of flesh in which to dwell while living in this mortal span of time. More on the body in a moment, but note in passing that apparently the body is our ticket into this world, the vehicle that allows the spirit to live in this mortal world. Several kinds of evidence are apparent: The moment our physical body perishes, our soul and spirit goes to be with the Lord. Further, though Christ was pre-existent with the Father, when He came to earth to bear our sins on the cross, He took upon Himself the form of a man; He was born into human flesh. Also, even the spirits in the Gadarene demoniac requested permission to enter the swine, perhaps an indication of the need for some fleshly form in order to continue to inhabit this earth.

Space does not permit an intricate detailed study behind all of these concepts in the nature of man. However, a very brief look at the six Greek words behind the six words on the chart may prove instructive.

First, *pneuma* refers to spirit, breath, the very vital principle of life itself by definition. Parallel to this is *kardia*, the heart, that which is in the middle, such as the heart of a tree. We derive some familiar

English words from these Greek words: for example, relative to breath or air we have pneumatic tires, and relative to heart we have cardiac arrest.

Second, *psuche* refers to soul, sometimes called the animal sentient principle. From it we get the study of psychology. The parallel Greek word is *nous*, meaning intellect, mind, thought, will, understanding.

Third, *soma* refers to the body in its totality or wholeness. It gives us such words as psychosomatic. And parallel to this, *sarx* means primarily the flesh, especially the flesh or the meat of an animal, but also referring to the frailty of human nature and our carnal fleshly self.

All of this is to illustrate one simple point: The biblical languages have three pairs of words to identify the three parts of man's nature. Within each pair of words, the two words are used virtually interchangeably to indicate one aspect of the tripartite nature of man. These concepts—spirit/heart, soul/mind and body/flesh—will be found throughout this book, and if I use the words interchangeably, it only reflects that Scripture does so as well.

Let me illustrate this a bit more clearly for you. If you and I meet for the first time, the initial thing that we notice about each other is the physical appearance. I would notice the basic characteristics of your body: the color of your hair and eyes, your size and several of your other features.

The moment we begin to visit and fellowship together, however, I am soon past any thought of your outward appearance, and I am visiting with your soul or your mind. We probably compare notes on the sizes of our families, our occupations, where we live and other mundane matters as we are visiting mind to mind, or soul to soul.

Most human conversations never progress beyond this level of communication—for reasons that will be very apparent in a couple of chapters. But if in the process of our visiting, you and I discover that we both know Jesus as Savior, our fellowship proceeds on to a communion of spirit with spirit. I will explain the reasons that this is possible momentarily, but for now consider the deep fellowship that you have with a beloved Christian friend. Or a better illustration is a husband and wife who both know the Lord and who have had fellowship together in Him for years. The communion between them goes far beyond the communion of mind to mind, as spirit with spirit they fellowship together. In fact, I suspect there is a communion between spirit and spirit that is not dependent upon the fleshly communication of spoken word at all.

Created Man

With a fuller understanding of the biblical nature of man, let's return for a closer look at that first man, Adam.

What do we know about him?

We know that he was perfect in every way as a creation of God. He was created in the very image of God; certainly God is perfect. Or as David put it, he was created just a little lower than God.

We know that God was willing to entrust to him great responsibilities. In the opening chapter of the Word it is written:

> *And God blessed them; and God said to them, "Be fruitful and multiply, and fill the earth, and subdue it; and rule over the fish of the sea and over the birds of the sky, and over every living thing that moves on the earth.* (Genesis 1:28)

Note again, subdue—rule—have dominion over the earth.

I believe that God saw the perfection of the man He had made and fully intended for him to rule—have dominion—over the entire universe, all of God's creation. In fact, thousands of years later the writer to the Hebrews described God's design for man:

> *For He did not subject to angels the world to come, concerning which we are speaking. But one has testified somewhere, saying, 'What is man, that Thou rememberest Him? Or the son of man, that Thou art concerned about Him? Thou hast made him for a little while lower than the angels; Thou hast crowned him with glory and honor, and hast appointed him over the works of Thy hands; thou hast put all things in subjection under his feet.* (Hebrews 2:5-8)

How then might we describe this perfect creation of God?

Man's spirit was in direct fellowship with the Father. Upon his spirit God had stamped eternal; he was designed to live forever. That first man was spirit-led, spirit-taught, spirit-infused, and he thrived on direct communion with his Creator and Lord. I fully believe that though they could have spoken verbally as you and I speak today, between God and Adam there was no need to speak. They simply communicated Spirit to spirit, the Spirit of God speaking with the spirit of man as they communed in the garden. All of this need not seem far-fetched if you simply realize that Jesus Himself told the Samaritan woman that those who worship God must worship Him in spirit and in truth. If we who have fallen through the very sin of Adam are called by God today to worship Him in spirit, is it difficult to believe that the first man of perfect creation could fellowship with the Father directly, spirit to spirit?

Man's mind was powerful enough to comprehend the Father's very creation. In fact, Genesis 2:19-20 records that God brought each of the beasts of the field and the birds of the sky by Adam to see what he would call them, and whatever the man called that living creature, that would be its name. This suggests that man not only saw the animals but that he could comprehend the very nature and function of each creature, and thereby out of its functions provide a suitable name for the beast.

Even today the impaired mind of man has twelve billion cells. Couple this with the fact that each cell has ten thousand synaptic connections to adjacent cells, and you have the fact that the brain of man even today has the possibility of one hundred and twenty trillion synaptic connections for storing and remembering experiences and bits of knowledge.

You can understand why it is so frequently mentioned that we use only a very small fraction of the capacity of the brain even today. Now if Adam, before the Fall, had the capacity to utilize all of that brain capacity, you begin to understand why it must have been a delight to God Himself to come down and commune with man in the cool of the evening. It must have been a challenge even to God Himself to converse with this magnificent creature He had made.

His body was designed to live forever. Death was the furthest thought from him. He was strong, handsome, robust, healthy. Unravaged by genetic deterioration, disease and all the consequences of sins, his body must have been something to behold. Without sin he would have been unacquainted with anything remotely close to what we know as the aging process today, and there was no reason but to believe that this powerful body would go on living eternally.

The Cool of the Day

Genesis 3:8-9 gives us a glimpse of the former glory of Eden. Following Adam's sin, it is recorded that Adam and Eve heard the sound of the Lord God walking in the garden in the cool of the day, and that the man and his wife hid themselves from the presence of the Lord among the trees of the garden. The Hebrew here suggests that this was a very usual walk that they took in the cool of the day, as if it had been done many, many days past. Further, there is the implication that the man and his wife were expecting God, knew when to expect Him, and were hiding from Him because of the gravity of their sin. There is the final inference that God Himself expected man to be waiting for Him, to greet Him, for He cries out, "Where are you?"

It takes only a small flight of fantasy to imagine the former glory of the Creator of the universe and these two created beings walking together in the cool of the day. One can almost imagine their conversation as they walked and talked, fellowshipping spirit with spirit: the voice of the Father saying, "What did you see today, Adam?" and Adam's response as he pours out all the things that he has observed—new discoveries, new fields, new mountains, new animals, new aspects of the creation that were fresh to him that day. As man the son expresses his thrill and adoration of the Father at the greatness of His creation, one can imagine the mighty fellowship that they knew.

Perhaps Adam says, "I discovered this strange-looking beast You made, Father. It was way over beyond the second mountain, and it has a very long nose." The Father replies, "Tell me about it. What do you think, Adam?" Adam says, "I don't understand it fully. Why did you make it that way?" Then the Father stops to explain why the elephant has a long trunk.

I think that one evening they climbed the highest peak in Eden, and just as the sun was setting the Father says, "Adam, let me tell you about the refraction of light: When the light beams are broken apart, the colors of the spectrum are visible, creating that beautiful golden-reddish hue as the sun goes down. Let me explain to you about light and color and atmosphere and humidity and refraction. Let me explain to you the beauty that you see."

I think that evening Eve heard them coming down the mountain as the last rays of light were disappearing over the horizon, laughing and fellowshipping together, God the Father still teaching Adam, His son, filling that brilliant mind with all kinds of divine knowledge as Spirit spoke to spirit.

Evening after evening they walked in the garden, Adam in his own way adoring the Father and the Father in His own inimitable way encouraging His son; the Father expressing the very desires of His heart and Adam understanding the very heart of God.

Luke 2:47 records of our Lord that as a boy of twelve he sat amidst the elders and teachers in the temple listening and asking them questions. All who heard Him were amazed at His understanding and His answers. This ought not to surprise us as this sinless child with a mind uncontaminated by the Fall would astonish the most brilliant minds of His day, although only a boy of twelve.

If you have ever visited an old friend now ravaged by cancer and looked upon that emaciated form of one who had once been so robust and healthy, you may have walked out of the hospital room to comment, "I would never have recognized him!" If you look at man today, ravaged by sin, he must appear to be but a shadow of that first beautiful, perfect creation. So too we must comment, "We would never have recognized him!"

Two Ways of Knowing

If you turn now to Chart 2 (on page 109), you will note that it is really an elaboration of the earlier chart. Let me point out one of the most crucial qualities of the mind, one that is frequently overlooked by those who are instructing us on how we ought to think: The mind is totally isolated from any form of knowledge or sensory input in and of itself. Stated differently, the mind is trapped between the body and the spirit and has no access to the world around it in any way. One way of illustrating this is the fact that we now have technology to keep the human brain alive almost indefinitely apart from the body. However, that brain apart from the body and any sensory input could not possibly be getting new information, nor could it respond to the world around it.

Many years ago Plato grasped this and described the mind as a white clay tablet. Centuries later John Locke would describe the mind as a white paper. While the technology developed from clay tablets to paper, they both grasped one central truth: The mind waits to be written upon but does not write of itself. It is most urgent that you get hold of this concept early in this book, for it will determine the extent to which you can appropriate a renewing of the mind in your own life.

Since the entire focus of this book is on the mind, Chart 2 is an attempt to portray graphically the experience of Adam before the Fall. Note if you will from the diagram that the mind of Adam had two basic sources of input and knowledge. First, with information coming from the Father—Spirit teaching spirit—his mind could be instructed by his spirit. As God spoke to him through his spirit, his mind could be taught through direct communion with the Father; for as God spoke through His Spirit to the spirit of man, He would be sharing information, knowledge, wisdom. Adam would be knowing from God through his spirit; this constitutes revealed knowledge.

Of course, the world simply denies the very existence of revelation knowledge. Evidence the fact that if you are so bold as to suggest that God "speaks" to you, everyone who is at all skeptical and rationalistic will look at you askance as if to say, "Oh, come on." However, the entire Christian faith is built around the central concept that God reaches out to us in salvation through faith in His Son Jesus Christ and speaks to us—reveals Himself—through His Word and through His Spirit. Therefore, everything related to the matter of the renewing of our minds must be built on the concept of revealed knowledge.

Next, note that much information comes into the mind through the body or through the flesh. This means only that we get much information through the proverbial five senses. (While psychologists will identify at least a dozen senses, let us continue to refer to the five basic senses—seeing, hearing, touching, tasting and smelling—as the basic sensory input for the purposes of this book.) As Adam wandered through the garden, he saw the animals, heard their cries, smelled the flowers, tasted the fruit, touched the plants. He was constantly learning, even as a small child might today, through his senses. This sense knowledge or observation we call rational knowledge.

The apostle Paul speaks frequently of sense knowledge as the flesh or fleshly knowledge. In our culture we have so often taken the flesh to refer to sexual desires and all of the connotations associated with this concept. However, I believe that if you reread Paul, you will discover that what he refers to as the flesh frequently refers to the mind being focused on the things of the flesh, and the knowledge and information coming in through the senses of the flesh.

Now this next observation is crucial to understanding the whole matter of a Renewed Mind. The great advantage that Adam had as he communed with the Father was that if he made any errors in the rational knowledge coming in through his senses, it was readily corrected when God came down and spoke to him in the course of the evening through revealed knowledge. If Adam misunderstood the purpose of one of God's creatures or the complexities the Father had incorporated into His created work, it was readily corrected as God and Adam communed together. "That is a good idea but this is really the reason that it is made that way," we can hear the Father explain.

For want of a better term, I have chosen to call this *course correction*. This means that as you experience God's created world and begin to misunderstand what you are observing, the still small voice within you says: "No, this is the way that works," or "Look at it from this perspective and you will understand." Obviously, I have borrowed the term from the experience of a pilot and his crew flying a plane across country. If the navigator receives triangulated radio signals from at least two different points and discovers that the plane is actually several degrees off-line of the intended destination, he relays the message to the pilot, who makes the appropriate correction in the guidance of the plane.

Now let me carry the illustration to the ridiculous: The pilot could sit there and say, "Feels to me like we are going in the right direction." The navigator could agree, "Yes, I think we are doing fine." But they are operating without external knowledge or feedback coming into the plane. When that radio signal comes in and overrides their "seat of the pants" information, the flight course must be corrected.

The important point to understand about the knowledge Adam received from God is simply this: At any point in which he made a mistake through his senses interpreting rational knowledge, this was at once corrected as the Father spoke through the Spirit, adding revealed knowledge to Adam's rational knowing.

Before we come to a fuller understanding of the plight of man apart from revealed knowledge, let me leap ahead and note that the great problem of rational knowledge today is that it knows nothing of the spiritual world; in fact, it denies that the spiritual world exists. Given this, rational knowing not only has no hope of being corrected by revealed knowledge, it rejects such knowledge when confronted by it.

However, man is still pressed, either by forces within himself or by pressure from his peers, to make decisions for which he has absolutely no adequate information—decisions that absolutely require revealed knowledge, without which he will come to totally erroneous conclusions. All of this does not deter the rational mind, however. Every man, scholar and layman alike, presses on to opinion and pronouncement on any number of subjects, whether or not he has any basis for knowing. In fact, when man comes to the very limits of his knowledge and begins to make educated guesses beyond all bounds of his knowing, we honor him with the title of philosopher.

As an illustration: Imagine an island in the middle of the Pacific inhabited by people who for generations have had all of their senses except the sense of sight. No one, as far as they can remember, could ever see; for that matter, no one ever thought about the possibility of sight. Then one day a man arrives by ship, walks onto their beach and begins to speak to them. Suddenly they become highly suspicious of the man for he knows a great many things about them that he ought not to be able to know. He begins to describe their appearance in detail, but from a distance. He describes many unusual features, details and characteristics that they did not even know about themselves. Having never had the sense of sight, their immediate reaction is to reject this man and all that he is telling them. And so with the rational mind, having never experienced revelation knowledge, the ultimate recourse is to reject the messenger of revealed knowledge and his message.

So great is the world's explosion of knowledge in recent years that the Library of Congress in Washington D.C. now contains approximately 100 million volumes. Here is more information than any of us could assimilate in several lifetimes. The discouraging problem is this: All of this wealth of knowledge is almost totally the result of rational knowing. Consequently, much of the accumulated wisdom that this age is so confident of, that we teach our children from kindergarten through the Ph.D., is really the product of rational knowledge. As a result, humanism holds sway, and mankind is doomed to know nothing of revealed knowledge.

By Way of Illustration

Let us pause here long enough to insert three brief diagrams that further illustrate the two ways of knowing. Chart 3 (on page 111) is simply a contrast of revealed versus rational knowledge. You will note that the channel of revealed knowledge is the spirit, while rational knowledge comes through the flesh to the mind. The source of revealed knowledge is God; rational knowledge is open to fleshly and ultimately satanic influence. Revealed knowledge is spiritual while rational knowledge is soulish or fleshly. Revealed knowledge glorifies God; rational knowledge frequently questions or blames God. Revealed knowledge comes by faith; rational knowledge demands that we be "reasonable." Revealed knowledge agrees with the Word of God; rational knowledge unwittingly contradicts the Word.

Chart 4 (on page 111) carries the illustration further. The Word of God not only understands the difference between divine truth and the knowing of this age (John 8:31-47), it also contrasts heavenly and human wisdom. James clearly draws this line for us;

Who among you is wise and understanding? Let him
show by his good behavior his deeds in the gentleness of

29

wisdom. But if you have bitter jealousy and selfish ambition in your heart, do not be arrogant and so lie against the truth. This wisdom is not that which comes down from above, but is earthly, natural, demonic. For where jealousy and selfish ambition exist, there is disorder and every evil thing. But the wisdom from above is first pure, then peaceable, gentle, reasonable, full of mercy and good fruits, unwavering, without hypocrisy. (James 3:13-17)

The message of this little chart is simply to demonstrate that if we depend on knowledge that is rational, soulish, secular, fleshly, then the wisdom derived from such knowing will be impure, earthly, deceptive.

In Chart 9 (on page 119) we introduce a concept that will receive much more attention as we go along: Spiritually restored man is really parallel to created man, man as God intended. God's concept of authority permeates His Word—whether it is authority within the body of Christ, authority within the family or authority within the individual person. As this chart indicates, God intended that our created spirits should hear from Him and rule our minds, and the spirit and the mind together should rule the flesh. Where this concept prevails, sin and rebellion do not have a chance. However, the ultimate result in natural man today, as we shall see in next chapter, is that the flesh rules the mind and there is no perception of an existing spirit. Paul would describe this as "sin reigning in our mortal bodies," and the simple truth is that rebellion is characteristic of such an individual.

Three Kinds of Human Beings

The following three chapters will center on Paul's concept of three kinds of men, designated by the condition and orientation of their minds. We shall devote most of this book to his understanding. Just here, however, I want to suggest that all human beings can be divided into three categories based primarily upon which part of man's tripartite nature controls his being.

In the flesh-dominated man, the body rules the mind and the

spirit. One can imagine almost endless illustrations here. A new-born is only concerned about enough to eat, the absence of pain, comfort for the flesh, and sleep. Some people, obsessed with the importance of bodily health, imagine every kind of disease for themselves—we call them hypochondriacs. The sad frequenters of the crack houses in our cities live only for the next fix of drugs. Alcoholics and other chemically dependent persons allow the demands of the flesh to control their lives. Many in our culture are so oriented toward sexual gratification that the fleshly desires dominate. Some cults, particularly Eastern religions, capitalize on this weakness and offer unlimited fleshly gratification in an effort to attract followers. In this country such an aberrant religious cult as EST comes to mind. Whether one speaks of hedonism, being a reprobate or a barbarian, the central fact is that the body and its pleasures rule this kind of man.

In the second kind of man, the mind dominates the body and the spirit. To a greater or lesser extent, this individual is rational and intellectual in every aspect of his being. He wants a reasonable, rational answer for all things. The rule of such individuals becomes the very epitome of what our scholars call civilization. Perhaps an easier way of visualizing this person is to consider the "proper English gentleman." For this individual the answer to the world's problems is always the same, more education. If society and government would simply be willing to fund more education, we would one day find that man has solved all known problems. Humanism is the obvious outgrowth of all of this. One can readily understand why the Christian Science cult is so popular with intellectuals, and even why it was birthed in the university culture of Boston. While the individual who is ruled by bodily passions will face a lifetime of problems related to the flesh, the person who is ruled by rational knowledge will find that most of his struggles relate to his ego.

In the third instance a person's spirit rules his mind and his body. Even this early in our studies, you can recognize the utter impossibility of spiritual rule apart from a Renewed Mind. The burden of this book is to define the spiritual man and discover God's plan for his restoration.

The Reign of Rational Knowledge

Even a cursory look at contemporary American culture should convince even a skeptic that every aspect of life as we know it is dominated by rational knowledge. The age of reason has held sway in this country for nearly a century and a half, and in every corner of our culture, the humanist perspective is evident. Whether on television, on radio or in the print media, the gatekeepers of knowledge in this country are virtually to a person thoroughgoing rationalists. Our public educational system from kindergarten through graduate school is utterly and thoroughly rationalistic. Unfortunately most of the fine institutions related to the Christian church have followed the fashion of the day and are as completely humanistic as are the public institutions.

Sadly, many of our churches and pastors, even those claiming a personal relationship with Jesus Christ, have fallen prey to decades of rational arguments. I have heard well-meaning pastors state that our God is a reasonable God and you can be certain that He will never do anything that is outside the realm of our reason. In other words, if what occurs does not fit the reasoning of my mind, it is not God.

We have been so schooled to trust what we can "know" with our senses that we are literally victims of the wisdom of this age. Even the most mature Christian has often been subtly and imperceptibly influenced in his thinking, absorbing the world's rationalism by osmosis. Is it any wonder that Christians—even those who wish to believe in the promises of the Word of God—find faith so very difficult?

And so we head for a spiritual bomb shelter every time a so-called professional makes a pronouncement relating to matters of God's kingdom. If he has a Ph.D. and teaches at an Ivy League school or one of the great German universities, we are that much more intimidated. If he is labeled a research scientist, his arguments become that much more formidable. I have seen entire rural communities cowed by a local medical doctor who prides himself on being a spiritual skeptic; simply because he was perceived to be the most educated man in town, the entire community was shaken by his arguments. The reasoning goes: "He must be right for he has the education. What do I know?"

One of the saddest products of a century and a half of rationalistic imperialism in America is the harvest the church is now reaping of several generations of pastors who are the culmination of the apostasy of the great theological schools, first in Europe and more recently in America. Jeremiah, Ezekiel, Zechariah and other Old Testament prophets have harsh words for the hireling shepherds who cry, "Thus saith the Lord," when God has not spoken through them. Unfortunately, the pew in many of our churches is largely undiscerning and totally intimidated by the rational knowledge that is offered as being the Word of God.

We would hardly select a man who was totally blind to judge the great oil paintings of master painters. Neither would we select a man who was stone deaf to be the music critic for a newspaper. Yet when a spiritually unreborn man, whose mind is totally unrenewed, takes mocking shots at God's Word and divine revelation, Christians cower with arms shielding their heads and worry that the church is about to be buried.

Conclusion

Let us take inventory of what we have learned about man as he was created:

First, man was created in the very image of God—"a little lower than God," according to David. Note carefully that this is not a "spark of divinity" as some liberal religionists would have it, proposing that man becomes better and better each day, more and more godlike—with the end result that he rejects the authority of the Father and worships himself. Not at all! Rather, man was created with such a heavenly image that he had the capability of constant communion and fellowship with the Father. In fact, Jesus confirmed man's essential purpose when He said to the woman at the well that the Father seeks men of spirit and truth to worship Him.

Second, the Scriptures indicate that man is tripartite in nature. (This three-part nature is depicted in Chart 1 on page 109.) Jesus revealed to us that God is spirit, and we found that the very nature of man is his likeness to the Father. It is on the spirit of man that God has stamped eternal. His spirit is alive, the very essence of his being, and intended for continual communion with the Father. Further, God gave man a mind that is so powerful, with such capacity, that it could grasp the complexities of His creation: a mind that can know as God knows, think as God thinks, choose as God chooses, decide as God decides, will as God wills. God also fashioned for man a magnificent body—strong, robust, healthy, designed to live forever.

Third, man's primary assignment was to rule over all of God's creation. He was entrusted with a charter for dominion that was as great as the universe itself, so long as he was obedient to his Creator. Such dominion included authority over Satan and his evil realm, as we will explain in the next chapter.

Fourth, sense knowledge in created man was subject to correction by revealed knowledge received by the spirit in communion with the Father. We have already pointed out that the mind itself has no direct access to reality, either the things of God's kingdom or of this world. The mind of man has two basic ways of knowing: It must receive direct input through the five senses, which report on the natural world around us, or it must be taught by the spirit of man, which is attuned to the things above. Succinctly, God intended for rational knowledge to be constantly subjected to the correcting influence of revealed knowledge. I have called this "course correction." (A diagram of this appears in Chart 2 on page 109.)

And so we have found man created in the very image and glory of God. His spirit was alive, in constant fellowship and communion with his heavenly Father. His highest purpose in life was to know and worship the Lord. His mind was powerful, with a vast capacity to know even as the Father would instruct him. His splendid body was designed to live forever. He was given the responsibility and the authority to rule over God's created universe.

Man as God intended: in constant fellowship with his heavenly Father, taught of God, Spirit-led, flowing in the knowledge of the kingdom above! Man was created to be a great joy to his Creator and Friend as they walked in the cool of the day.

About now I suspect that you, dear reader, are asking, "Just a minute! That is so far from the men I see about me—so far from the reality of life I experience myself—what hope is there for me?" I can

ear another saying, "Why waste our evenings reading this; it is only
iry tales."

My answer to you, my friend, is look at the possibilities. If even a
limmer of hope exists that man can be restored to his created
ation, the effort is worth life itself. It cannot be accomplished in and
f ourselves through some "inner strength" as the possibility think-
rs would have it. Restoration will come through the power of Christ
1 us—the power of His Spirit, living and working in us; the power of
1e living Word of God, remaking our spirits and minds.

The simple thesis of this book is that you and I, my friend, can be
s God intended because of Calvary.

CHAPTER TWO

THE NATURAL MIND: SUBTLE
RESULT OF THE FALL

Subtle result of the Fall: why subtle? A person acquainted with God's Word may find it quite simple to identify the effects of Adam's disobedience in much of the world around us: disease, sickness, pain, human suffering, hostility of the animals, weeds, storms, natural disasters, and the evil, wretched heart of man. The very perverseness of the heart of man is the subject of Old Testament history and prophecy. In addition, the impact of the Fall on the body is visible about us every day. If you have ever watched just one close friend die under the ravages of cancer, you can never doubt the fall of man.

But to most people, including most Christians, the mind seems largely untouched. It serves us reasonably well in solving life's daily problems. We can grasp new learning in a wide variety of instructional settings. We apparently function rather normally in the routine of life. So we tend to reject any thought that the mind was damaged in Adam's treacherous deed. How subtle!

This misconception has even affected our theology. The evangelical Christian world has for several centuries held to the need for a reborn spirit—apart from new life in Jesus Christ there is no hope of heaven. In other words, the heart of man is wicked and only through Christ's shed blood can man receive new life. Moreover, the last half-century has witnessed a growing acceptance of the reality of divine healing for the physical body, concluding on a wide scale that such healing was included in Calvary.

Yet few Christians have any grasp of the tragic warping that has taken place in the thinking of all men. A few teachers have taught that the Renewed Mind is an automatic by-product of a reborn spirit—a teaching based upon a most superficial reading of God's Word. Clearly we are made new creatures in Christ Jesus and our spiritual natures are born anew. But the fact remains that when a person comes to know Jesus as Savior—after perhaps twenty, thirty or even fifty years of programming by the world's way of thinking—he may be totally unaware that he still thinks as this world thinks! This subtle problem is at the very core of this book.

Man Commits High Treason

Webster defines treason as a betrayal of allegiance owed to one's sovereign state; treachery or a breach of faith; a betrayal of trust. Recently in Norfolk, Virginia, three members of one family, all trusted officers in the U.S. Navy, were found to have betrayed some of the highest secrets of the American government. For a relatively small amount of money these men had sold to an enemy government plans of naval vessels, strategies for submarine encounter, and codes that would unlock the most secret messages in a time of battle. Had these acts of treachery gone undetected, the safety of the American people could have been jeopardized in a time of war, and the entire course of world history could have been rewritten. No matter how much revulsion we feel toward such a dastardly act, it pales into insignificance when cast alongside the betrayal of faith that occurred in the Garden of Eden. The very nature of man and his place in the economy of God would be altered for all time.

This story begins with God's instruction to man concerning his garden home:

And the Lord God commanded the man, saying,
"From any tree of the garden you may eat freely; but
from the tree of the knowledge of good and evil you shall
not eat, for in the day that you eat from it you shall
surely die." (Genesis 2:16-17)

"You shall surely die": Such a concept must have been as foreign to Adam as one can imagine today. He was a creature of life, ongoing life, but here his death is certainly assured if he is disobedient.

It is worth asking the question: Why would God forbid the eating of the fruit of the tree of the knowledge of good and evil. The answer: He knew there was no need for man to be exposed to the source of evil.

Man was created in the image of God, and God is good, righteous and holy. Man had perfect communion and fellowship with the Father, so all he knew and all he was exposed to was good. Only two sources of all events exist in the universe about us, good being from our heavenly Father and evil from the enemy of our souls. Since man had constant access to the greatest example of good in the entire universe, he had absolutely no need to be exposed to the source of evil. By his insistence on partaking of the tree of the knowledge of good and evil, he was actually saying to his Creator Father: "Don't think that You can withhold from me anything that is rightfully mine. I might like the evil better."

That fictitious argument rears its ugly head again and again in life today. One instance is the often-promoted child-rearing principle that we ought to let our children sample everything there is in life—good and bad—and when they are older they can choose for themselves. Another example is the argument: "I have got to try everything there is in life at least once, and then I can come back and serve the Lord with greater knowledge of Him." As Jesus would have commented, "Wisdom is justified of her children" (Matthew 11:19, KJV).

Satan's Fourfold Lie

One of the fascinating things about the story of the temptation in Genesis 3 is that in many ways it reads as if it were a chapter stripped from the humanistic writings of the late twentieth century. Perhaps the writer of Ecclesiastes was right: There really is nothing new under the sun. At any rate, when the enemy of our souls is involved, you can count on the arguments being the same. The four basic propositions presented to Eve in the garden are the same basic half-truths that he presents to us today.

The serpent's first word to Eve is a devious question: "Indeed, has God said, `You shall not eat from any tree of the garden'?" (3:1). We note first Satan's basic tactic: He rephrases the Word of God to produce the opposite of God's intent. God, of course, has prohibited eating the fruit of one tree; Satan twists God's Word to say that they could not eat of any or every tree of the garden. But the deeper, and far more damning, statement here is: "Indeed has God said?" Satan's one strategy for undermining our faith and for destroying the integrity and effectiveness of the Christian walk is to question the authority of God's Word. He will again and again question not only the authority and the truthfulness of God's Word, but the very right of God to say it.

Satan's second word to Eve is a brazen lie: "You surely shall not die!" (3:4). There is an array of challenges to the heavenly Father in this statement. First, Satan was calling God a liar. And if the enemy can get you to listen to him very long today he will be offering you that lie very early on. But the more ominous aspect of Satan's proposition is his denial of the difference between divine life and satanic death. What Satan is saying is that this earthly, fleshly life—not divine, godly life—is really all that matters. There is then only a very small step to doubting the very existence of God and the agnosticism/atheism that is so prevalent in our world about us today. Satan's second word to Eve is exactly what it appears at face value, a lie, 180 degrees opposite the truth—he says that our God is not holy, pure and true, but a liar.

The serpent's third word to Eve is an enticing deception: "For God knows that in the day you eat from it your eyes will be opened, and you will be like God" (3:5). Here again is the old satanic strategy of telling you a half-truth, with just enough truth in it to get you to bite, never showing you the ultimate consequences.

I am reminded of much of the advertising that goes on in today's world. Television portrays for you a glamorous cocktail party, socializing with good friends, all benefiting your personal career. The central ingredient of this inviting scene is liquor. But this vignette never tells you the ultimate consequences: ruined lives, wrecked bodies, destroyed careers, dashed hopes, and even death.

So Satan offers to Eve the enticing possibility of eyes that are opened, of knowing much beyond her little parochial world, of being like God! Implicit in this argument is that God has ulterior motives. If He were really the good God that He says He is, He would offer you that fruit and let you in on the secrets that He knows. There is the implication that God is jealously guarding His position and His turf; He really doesn't want any other "gods" about Him. The further implication is—and here the arguments of modern-day humanism come home again—that man is of supreme worth. No matter what God says, if it looks appealing and enticing, do it. Again there is only one final small step to full-blown humanism: With man as his own god he is free to worship the creature rather than the Creator.

The enemy's fourth word to Eve is an intellectual appeal: Disobeying God would result in "knowing good and evil"—something "desirable to make one wise" (3:5-6). The seeds of rebellion seem to be born in the heart of the youngest child today. Tell him that he cannot cross the road because a car might hit him, and he is instantly convinced that there is something wonderful across the road that you are trying to keep from him. And so Eve in her own way saw the cunning cleverness of it all: God really was keeping something from her and here was the possibility of knowing good and evil. Not only that, but now one can be wise!

The cunning arguments of Satan today can be seen in this dialogue. You can rule the universe better than God. And so we have here the glorification of human reasoning, the glamorizing of human intellect. One of our own U.S. presidents said a number of years ago in a State of the Union message: "Man has now arrived at that position in time when he can by his own intellect solve every problem facing mankind." And there you have it: the glorification of the rational mind over the spirit, the elevation of reasoning and rational knowledge over revelational knowledge, and the notion that man released to his full potential can run the universe better than God.

These same four arguments that brought about the fall of man in

Eden are the same four propositions on which the satanic end-time religion of humanism is pillared. The first doubts the authority of God's Word. The second questions the veracity of God and even His existence, proposing that this mortal life is all that matters. The third states that man is of ultimate worth and with him as god we are free to worship the creature rather than the Creator. The fourth claims that we really have no need of God in the world because man can by his own creative genius solve all of his own problems through the elevation of the human intellect and the rational mind to the point of being all-wise. (Note that if you substitute science, scientific method and research methodology for human intellect in the fourth statement, you will have an even fuller understanding of the intent of humanism.)

The Result of Man's Treachery

The deed is done! Genesis 3:6-7 reads: "She took from its fruit and ate; and she gave also to her husband with her, and he ate. Then the eyes of both of them were opened." So it is true! God was right! Satan was right! Their eyes were opened, but Satan's enticement had a fatal flaw!

Their eyes were opened, but notice the first thing that they saw—themselves! Their innocence was gone, their nakedness was evident, and they scrambled hurriedly to assemble a few fig leaves to make a covering for themselves. God was vindicated: Satan was proven to be a liar—but at what a cost!

Genesis 3:8-13 begins the portrait of this awful fallen condition:

> *And they heard the sound of the Lord God walking in the garden in the cool of the day, and the man and his wife hid themselves from the presence of the Lord God among the trees of the garden. Then the Lord God called to the man, and said to him, "Where are you?" And he said, "I heard the sound of Thee in the garden, and I was afraid because I was naked; so I hid myself." And He said, "Who told you that you were naked? Have you eaten from the tree of which I commanded you not to eat?" And the man said, "The woman*

*whom Thou gavest to be with me, she gave me from the
tree, and I ate." Then the Lord God said to the woman,
"What is this you have done?" And the woman said,
"The serpent deceived me, and I ate."*

The most obvious result of the Fall is fear—fear of the very Lord
with whom they had had such sweet communion just the day before;
fear that would drive them to cover, hiding themselves from their
loving Father. But the most significant outcome of this terrible act
was the broken communion with the Father. The intimate fellowship they had known for so long was broken—permanently as far as
Adam knew. Man had suddenly fallen from a Godlike nature to the
very nature of Satan himself.

So the judgment of God is pronounced: The serpent is to be more
cursed than all other beasts of the field and is to crawl on his belly.
The woman would know constant enmity with the serpent, between
her seed and his seed, and her central function in life—the mother-
ing of the human race—would be accompanied by great pain in
childbearing. Adam, so recently the lord of all he surveyed, suddenly found the very ground cursed beneath him. In toil he would
eat, with thorns and thistles as his enemy in his struggle. And the
final pronouncement of doom for the two of them: "As you came
forth from the ground, so to the earth you shall return."

The final three verses of Genesis 3 must be among the blackest of
all the Word:

> *Then the Lord God said, "Behold, the man has become
> like one of Us, knowing good and evil; and now, lest he
> stretch out his hand, and take also from the tree of life,
> and eat, and live forever"—therefore the Lord God sent
> him out from the garden of Eden, to cultivate the
> ground from which he was taken. So He drove the man
> out; and at the east of the garden of Eden He stationed
> the cherubim, and the flaming sword which turned
> every direction, to guard the way to the tree of life.*
> (Genesis 3:22-24)

Adam and Eve were driven out, out from their beautiful home in the garden, out from the sweet fellowship of the heavenly Father, out from the ever-abundant and ever-available fruit, out from the tree of the knowledge of good and evil—most of all, out from the tree of life. The Word of the Lord explains the reason for man's expulsion in verse 22: "lest he stretch out his hand, and take also from the tree of life, and eat, and live forever"—lest in the midst of this awful, godless, sinful condition he reach out and partake of the tree of life and live forever bound in this awful state!

From the point of view of mankind today, there was an equally dismal result in the garden. Earlier we noted in Genesis 1:26-28 that God had chosen to give man rule and dominion over all the works of His hands. And the dominion that Adam handed over to Satan by his act of high treason is the plague of mankind to this very moment. In Ephesians 2:2, Paul calls Satan "the prince of the power of the air." And the authority that was granted the enemy that day as Adam yielded to his intrigue and sinned against the heavenly Father will be one of the central issues throughout this book; for one of the central aspects of the Renewed Mind is the recovery of that wasted authority.

In case you doubt the scope of Satan's authority in the world today, let me refer you to just one passage of Scripture. In Luke's account of the temptation of Jesus we read:

> *And he led Him up and showed Him all the kingdoms of the world in a moment of time. And the devil said to Him, "I will give You all this domain and its glory; for it has been handed over to me, and I give it to whomever I wish. Therefore if You worship before me, it shall all be Yours."* (Luke 4:5-7)

Note what Satan said: "It has been handed over to me, and I give it to whomever I wish." Further observe that Jesus did not contradict him in this but simply rebuked him, saying that we are to worship the Lord our God and serve only Him (verse 8).

What about God's prophetic statements in Genesis 2:17 that the day that man ate of the forbidden fruit he would surely die? I have heard professed scholars assure us that there are many errors in the Bible and one of the surest proofs is that Adam did not die the day that he ate of the forbidden fruit, but as Genesis 5:5 tells us, he lived to be 930 years old.

Adam did die that day. Certainly the death process for the physical body began the day that Adam sinned, and while it may have taken 930 years, he did die physically. Yet there is a much deeper meaning in all this: I am firmly convinced that the day in which Adam sinned against God he died spiritually. We may not be able to comprehend this fully, but one thing is certain: The day Adam sinned, his full fellowship and communion with the Father was broken and his spirit withered and died even as the Word of God attests.

Numerous New Testament passages speak of man's spiritual death. In John 5:24, Jesus assured us that if we hear His words and believe Him who sent Jesus, we pass out of death into life. In John 10:10, Jesus told his listeners, who were certainly very much alive physically: "I am come that they might have life, and that they might have it abundantly." The apostle John wrote, "We know that we have passed out of death into life, because we love the brethren" (1 John 3:14). Paul also spoke of this spiritual deadness when he wrote, "A natural man does not accept the things of the Spirit of God; for they are foolishness to him, and he cannot understand them, because they are spiritually appraised" (1 Corinthians 2:14).

Suddenly man's body was vulnerable to toil and weariness. It was vulnerable to disease, sickness, injury and attack by wild beast. Suddenly he was a victim of the very creation over which he had so recently ruled in absolute dominion. That once robust body, undoubtedly still magnificent in comparison to ours today, began to deteriorate—however gradually—until death would come 900 years later.

As far as Adam's mind was concerned, I believe that if you could have observed him carefully you would have seen no great change in his mind's functioning in the early days following the Fall. And yet just as Helen Keller was a prisoner in her own body without the gift of either sight or sound, in dramatically greater measure Adam was a prisoner within himself without the moment-by-moment fellowship with his heavenly Father.

The greatest change in this pitiable creature was the absence of the Father's voice. With all revelation knowledge cut off, he is abruptly cast upon his own resources and senses. The preservation of life itself now depends upon the keenness of those five senses. The world is hostile—on every side it would close in if he were not alert. The fleshly senses, which were secondary before, are now all important. This sweeping and dramatic change in the mind of Adam would become much more apparent in the centuries ahead, and even more so in generations to follow. Man would become more soulish, more sensual, more dependent on the external senses and on the surrounding world. His worship would approach magic shortly, always dependent on the external objects in his environment. The blind religionists of every age—like the Pharisees of Jesus' time—would find themselves increasingly drawn to the codification of external behavior, for the internal fellowship with the Father was gone.

Chart 5 (on page 113) graphically portrays the Fall as related to the tripartite nature of man. Simultaneously with the Fall came the death of the spirit. The physical death of the first man would come much later. The mind in terms of created man and his ability to know of the Father continues to deteriorate to the very point of death itself.

This is one of the most critical points for understanding the thesis of this book: The loss of the knowledge of God (as portrayed by the declension of the line identifying the mind) begins significantly within the lifetime of Adam. And following the death of Adam, knowledge *of* God becomes knowledge *about* God simply by definition. Put simply, this chart depicts the decline of man's mind: Within a few generations—had it not been for the loving and compassionate intervention of a merciful God in the lives of men—there would have been no knowledge of Him at all.

History's Most Poignant Moment

Come with me for a moment for one last view of Adam, our created man. We find him this evening keeping lonely vigil on a mountain somewhere east of Eden. It is almost impossible in the limited language of finite man to describe the awful, wrenching loneliness and lostness. The fellowship with the Father is not only broken, there is no longer even a glimpse of God. Somehow the voice never comes in the cool of the day. In place of the enormous

46

thrill that used to rush through his spirit at those first footsteps coming at the first sign of dusk, there is now that terrible, aching void. Always there are the questions, those enormous burning questions—but now they have to be figured out on his own. There is such a need to worship, to fellowship, to commune—but all is lost.

This particular evening seems unusually difficult. The sunset is more spectacular than any since the angel was stationed at the garden's eastern gate. The sunset is brilliant, the colors are richer than ever before, and yet the tears stream down Adam's cheeks. Never again will the voice of the Father say, "Adam, let me tell you about the refraction of light." That voice is gone—forever gone!

* * * * * * * * * *

After the first three chapters of Genesis the Old Testament is a picture of man on his own. He doesn't understand his great heritage. He doesn't recognize that he is essentially a spiritual being, created in the very image of God. Worse, he doesn't even know of God's existence. Now he is so focused on this physical world, so completely absorbed in the things his senses tell him, he will spend the millennia ahead asking the same questions over and over: What is the meaning of it all? Why am I here? What is the purpose of it all?

There would be rare instances in which the Holy Spirit would break through to speak to God's prophets, but they seem so very far apart. Man—intended for fellowship with the God of creation, intended to fulfill his entrusted dominion over God's creation, intended to be the very epitome of God's creation—has become a hater of God! With his natural senses he sees evil in every corner of the world now under Satan's control. Not understanding it all, he blames God. Yes, man, intended for fellowship with the eternal God, has become the very enemy of God.

Is This All Overstated?

About now I suspect some of you are asking: "Just a moment, haven't you really exaggerated the impact of man's sin on all creation?" That question is answered throughout Scripture—from Genesis 4 through the end of Malachi. The Old Testament is an ongoing portrait of fallen man and his rebellious heart.

Each generation drifted farther and farther from the knowledge of God. Perhaps in the beginning as they sat around the campfire in the evening, Adam shared with them some of the great experiences of walking and talking with God. But with every passing year and with each new decade, there was increased skepticism about the old man's stories of God. Then there came new generations that had only heard of the stories that Adam told. Finally the skepticism and the cynicism were so great that even in his own waning years Adam quit telling the stories anymore.

Finally, Adam and Eve, the only ones who had ever really walked with the Father, were gone. Now any mention of God around the campfire in the evening was simply to make Him the point of ridicule. "You know, old Adam used to think that he had actually seen God!" one descendant would comment. "Yes," another would reply, "he even had delusions that he had talked with God." Still a third would add, "My daddy always said that the old man was just slightly crazy."

As knowledge of God trickled away, the final lock snapped shut on the mind of man, and to his own destruction he became a captive to the pooled ignorance of those around him.

Again, is this view of Old Testament man exaggerated? Come with me for just a moment through the scattered debris on the landscape of the Old Testament as we see the results of man's spiritual deadness and his captive mind. Genesis 3 closes with the cherubim and the flaming sword guarding the gate to the tree of life. The first tragic consequence of the fall of man and its effect on his family appears in the opening verses of Genesis 4—anger and murder:

> *Abel, on his part also brought of the firstlings of his flock and of their fat portions. And the Lord had regard for Abel and for his offering; but for Cain and for his offering He had no regard. So Cain became very angry and his countenance fell. Then the Lord said to Cain, "Why are you angry? And why has your countenance fallen? If you do well, will not your countenance be lifted up? And if you do not do well, sin is crouching at the door; and its desire is for you, but you must master*

*it." And Cain told Abel his brother. And it came about
when they were in the field, that Cain rose up against
Abel his brother and killed him. Then the Lord said to
Cain, "Where is Abel your brother?" And he said, "I do
not know. Am I my brother's keeper?" And He said,
"What have you done? The voice of your brother's blood
is crying to Me from the ground. And now you are
cursed from the ground, which has opened its mouth to
receive your brother's blood from your hand."* (Genesis 4:4-11)

Anyone who doubts the awfulness of the satanic agenda need look
no further than these verses.

Not very many generations after the Fall, God's verdict on man's
condition is formed:

*Then the Lord saw that the wickedness of man was
great on the earth, and that every intent of the thoughts
of his heart was only evil continually. And the Lord was
sorry that He had made man on the earth, and He was
grieved in His heart. And the Lord said, "I will blot out
man whom I have created from the face of the land,
from man to animals to creeping things and to birds of
the sky; for I am sorry that I have made them."*
(Genesis 6:5-7)

*Now the earth was corrupt in the sight of God, and the
earth was filled with violence. And God looked on the
earth, and behold, it was corrupt; for all flesh had
corrupted their way upon the earth. Then God said to
Noah, "The end of all flesh has come before Me; for the
earth is filled with violence because of them; and
behold, I am about to destroy them with the earth."*
(Genesis 6:11-13)

Amazing! Those verses sound as if they were written to the
twentieth century instead of several millennia before Christ. The

final end of man in rebellion against God is corruption and violence.

In the midst of this sinful generation, God found a man righteous in his time. Through Noah and his family and the ark that they were instructed to build, God saved His creation and the human race for another attempt at achieving righteousness on the earth.

Once again, the ark had barely settled on Mount Ararat when the wickedness and rebellion of man reared its ugly head. Within the lifetime of those who had been spared the destruction of the Flood, the ensuing generations rebelled once again against God: "Come, let us build for ourselves a city, and a tower whose top will reach into heaven, and let us make for ourselves a name" (Genesis 11:4). God had entered into covenant with Noah, vowing never again to destroy the earth by flood; so He visited the plain in Shinar, there confusing their speech and scattering abroad the rebellious tribes. Babylon has been synonymous with pride, blasphemy, insurrection and a mutinous heart against God to this very day.

A number of generations later, the stench of man's sins arose once again and even the long-suffering mercies of our God were exhausted:

> *The Lord said, "The outcry of Sodom and Gomorrah is indeed great, and their sin is exceedingly grave. I will go down now, and see if they have done entirely according to its outcry, which has come to Me; and if not, I will know."* (Genesis 18:20-21)

> *Now the two angels came to Sodom in the evening as Lot was sitting in the gate of Sodom. When Lot saw them, he rose to meet them and bowed down with his face to the ground. And he said, "Now behold, my lords, please turn aside into your servant's house, and spend the night, and wash your feet; then you may rise early and go on your way." They said however, "No, but we shall spend the night in the square." Yet he urged them strongly, so they turned aside to him and entered his house; and he prepared a feast for them, and baked unleavened bread, and they ate. Before they lay down, the men of the city, the men of Sodom, surrounded the*

house, both young and old, all the people from every quarter; and they called to Lot and said to him, "Where are the men who came to you tonight? Bring them out to us that we may have relations with them." But Lot went out to them at the doorway, and shut the door behind him, and said, "Please, my brothers, do not act wickedly. Now behold, I have two daughters who have not had relations with man; please let me bring them out to you, and do to them whatever you like; only do nothing to these men, inasmuch as they have come under the shelter of my roof." But they said, "Stand aside." Furthermore, they said, "This one came in as an alien, and already he is acting like a judge; now we will treat you worse than them." So they pressed hard against Lot and came near to break the door. But the men reached out their hands and brought Lot into the house with them, and shut the door. And they struck the men who were at the doorway of the house with blindness, both small and great, so that they wearied themselves trying to find the doorway. (Genesis 19:1-11)

The book of Job starkly portrays the dependence of rational man on sense evidence. Notice how the words of Eliphaz betray his absolute reliance on knowledge acquired by the senses: "According to what I have seen, those who plow iniquity and those who sow trouble harvest it" (Job 4:8); "Behold this, we have investigated it, thus it is; hear it and know for yourself" (Job 5:27).

In the time of Moses and then perhaps two centuries later in the midst of the period of the judges, the same summary judgment on the nature of man was made: "Every man did what was right in his own eyes" (Deuteronomy 12:8; Judges 17:6). In the days of the boy Samuel, at the close of the period of the judges, even Israel had fallen to such evil depths that the Bible says: "Word from the Lord was rare in those days, and there was no frequent vision" (1 Samuel 3:1). Even God's chosen priesthood fell into the depths of debauchery under Eli and his sons. When Israel was defeated by the Philistines after removing the ark from the Holy of Holies and taking it into battle (almost as a magical charm), the wife of Phineas would call her newborn son Ichabod, saying: "The glory of the Lord has departed from Israel."

The clearest portrait of man at the very depths of his infamy comes in 2 Kings 17. King after king had rebelled against God and mocked the prophets whom God sent; the mighty judgment of God could be restrained no longer. The king of Assyria swooped down from the north and the ten northern tribes are carried into captivity to be lost forever. Few more tragic words have ever been penned than those that follow:

Now this came about, because the sons of Israel had sinned against the Lord their God, who had brought them up from the land of Egypt from under the hand of Pharaoh, king of Egypt, and they had feared other gods and walked in the customs of the nations whom the Lord had driven out before the sons of Israel, and in the customs of the kings of Israel which they had introduced. And the sons of Israel did things secretly which were not right, against the Lord their God. Moreover, they built for themselves high places in all their towns, from watchtower to fortified city. And they set for themselves sacred pillars and Asherim on every high hill and under every green tree, and there they burned incense on all the high places as the nations did which the Lord had carried away to exile before them; and they did evil things provoking the Lord. And they served idols, concerning which the Lord had said to them, "You shall not do this thing." Yet the Lord warned Israel and Judah, through all His prophets and every seer, saying, "Turn from your evil ways and keep My commandments, My statutes according to all the law which I commanded your fathers, and which I sent to you through My servants the prophets." However, they did not listen, but stiffened their neck like their fathers, who did not believe in the Lord their God. And they rejected His statutes and His covenant which He made with their fathers, and His warnings with

*which He warned them. And they followed vanity and
became vain, and went after the nations which sur-
rounded them, concerning which the Lord had commanded them not to do like them. And they forsook all
the commandments of the Lord their God and made for
themselves molten images, even two calves, and made
an Asherah and worshiped all the host of heaven and
served Baal. Then they made their sons and their
daughters pass through the fire, and practiced divina-
tion and enchantments, and sold themselves to do evil
in the sight of the Lord, provoking Him. So the Lord
was very angry with Israel, and removed them from
His sight; none was left except the tribe of Judah.* (2
Kings 17:7-18)

Before we leave this biblical portrait of the nature of fallen man,
let's look at two New Testament passages that are appropriate. First,
the apostle Paul speaks of the whole creation groaning, longing to
be set free from its slavery to corruption.

*I consider that the sufferings of this present time are not
worthy to be compared with the glory that is to be
revealed to us. For the anxious longing of the creation
waits eagerly for the revealing of the sons of God. For
the creation was subjected to futility, not of its own will,
but because of Him who subjected it, in hope that the
creation itself also will be set free from its slavery to
corruption into the freedom of the glory of the children
of God. For we know that the whole creation groans
and suffers the pains of childbirth together until now.
And not only this, but also we ourselves, having the first
fruits of the Spirit, even we ourselves groan within
ourselves, waiting eagerly for our adoption as sons, the
redemption of our body. For in hope we have been
saved, but hope that is seen is not hope; for why does one
also hope for what he sees? But if we hope for what we
do not see, with perseverance we wait eagerly for it.*
(Romans 8:18-25)

Paul grasps so clearly the fact that not only man fell in the garden, but the entire creation came under the corruption of satanic rule.

Finally, Jude warns of the danger of false prophets who would creep in. He portrays so eloquently those who trust only in the flesh:

> *But these men revile the things which they do not understand; and the things which they know by instinct, like unreasoning animals, by these things they are destroyed.* (Jude 10)

And so man in his awful act of treachery is changed in an instant from the nature of God to the nature of Satan. This beautiful creation of the Father has become corrupt, violent, a rebel, a murderer, a hater of God! By biblical account there seems to be no deed, however foul, of which he is incapable.

Paul's Natural Man

Perhaps no other biblical writer so grasps the problems of the human mind and the urgency of acquiring a Renewed Mind as did the apostle Paul. Indeed we are indebted to Paul for the vast majority of the Scripture passages on which this book is based. By the very depths of his understanding of the things of God, Paul demonstrates that his is an exemplary Renewed Mind. He fully comprehended that the thinking of God is as far above our own thinking as the heavens are above the earth.

Paul visualized the human mind existing in one of three states, which he described in terms of three men: natural man, carnal man, spiritual man. Carnal man and spiritual man will be defined in the two chapters that follow. Let us turn our focus to natural man, the term Paul used to describe fallen humanity in its lowest state:

> *Now we have received, not the spirit of the world, but the Spirit who is from God, that we might know the things freely given to us by God, which things we also speak, not in words taught by human wisdom, but in those taught by the Spirit, combining spiritual thoughts with spiritual words. But a natural man does*

not accept the things of the Spirit of God; for they are
foolishness to him, and he cannot understand them,
because they are spiritually appraised. (1 Corinthians
2:12-14)

The natural man (or as the NASB margin has it, the unspiritual
man) cannot understand and cannot accept the revelations that
come from the Spirit of God; they seem like foolishness to him,
because they must be discerned spiritually. There you have the
subject of this chapter: The mind of the natural man is the most
subtle result of the Fall.

The natural man has never been born again. He is spiritually
dead. He has no inner witness or evidence of the existence of God.
He has never been made alive in Christ. He is without God and
without hope. Spiritual truths pass him by like a ship in the night,
because without the indwelling Spirit he is incapable of compre-
hending them. Further, he can listen to the finest teaching of the
Word of God and it will appear as sheer nonsense to him. Spiritual
discernment is as foreign to him as culture to a barnyard animal.

Go back with me a moment to our created man. The essential
characteristics of his nature were the life in his spirit and the
constant communion and fellowship with the heavenly Father.
Natural man is dead toward God in his spirit: There is no possibility
of spirit communing with Spirit nor of his hearing and recognizing
the voice of the Father. If we as Christian believers could get this
into our thinking once and for all, then we would not be intimidated
by every blasphemous pronouncement that comes forth from the
natural mind.

To the Ephesians Paul wrote:

You were dead in your trespasses and sins, in which
you formerly walked according to the course of this
world, according to the prince of the power of the air, of
the spirit that is now working in the sons of disobedi-
ence. Among them we too all formerly lived in the lusts
of our flesh, indulging the desires of the flesh and of the
mind, and were by nature children of wrath, even as
the rest. But God, being rich in mercy, because of His

great love with which He loved us, even when we were dead in our transgressions, made us alive together with Christ (by grace you have been saved), and raised us up with Him, and seated us with Him in the heavenly places, in Christ Jesus. (Ephesians 2:1-6)

Note specifically God's assessment of the characteristics of natural man and the natural mind:

1. Natural man is dead in trespasses and sin.
2. He walks according to the wisdom of this age (this world).
3. He is ruled by the prince of the power of the air.
4. He is no different from all other men of disobedience.
5. He is driven by the lusts of the flesh and indulges in such regularly.
6. His mind is likewise a slave and carries the baggage of the flesh.
7. His very nature makes him a child of wrath even as other unregenerated men.

Paul wrote that our gospel is veiled to those who are perishing, for Satan has blinded the minds of the unbelieving (2 Corinthians 4:3-4). It hardly seems possible to describe more vividly the plight of the natural mind. With the spirit dead toward God, revelation knowledge is impossible. The mind is fully oriented to the senses and the flesh, and without the spirit's help, the mind is largely dominated by the lusts and the desires of the flesh. The truths of God are foolishness to such a mind. He lives day by day as a captive of this age, enslaved to the god of this world.

God's Warning to the Unrenewed Mind

Since the Lord began to open this area of study to me more than a dozen years ago, I have been amazed at the multitude of references to the plight of the natural mind, as well as the possibilities of our knowing as God knows. In repeated readings of the Word of God, I have identified more than two thousand verses related particularly to this matter. At the risk of seeming to belabor the point, I want you to be aware of some of the most crucial passages cautioning the unrenewed mind.

In Paul's magnificent theology that we call the letter to the Romans, we have the classic portrait of the man who arrogates unto himself the authority and truth that belongs only unto God:

The wrath of God is revealed from heaven against all ungodliness and unrighteousness of men, who suppress the truth in unrighteousness, because that which is known about God is evident within them; for God made it evident to them. For since the creation of the world His invisible attributes, His eternal power and divine nature, have been clearly seen, being understood through what has been made, so that they are without excuse.

For even though they knew God, they did not honor Him as God, or give thanks; but they became futile in their speculations, and their foolish heart was darkened. Professing to be wise, they became fools, and exchanged the glory of the incorruptible God for an image in the form of corruptible man and of birds and four-footed animals and crawling creatures. Therefore God gave them over in the lusts of their hearts to impurity, that their bodies might be dishonored among them. For they exchanged the truth of God for a lie, and worshiped and served the creature rather than the Creator, who is blessed forever. Amen.

For this reason God gave them over to degrading passions; for their women exchanged the natural function for that which is unnatural, and in the same way also the men abandoned the natural function of the woman and burned in their desire towards one another, men with men committing indecent acts and receiving in their own persons the due penalty of their error. And just as they did not see fit to acknowledge God any longer, God gave them over to a depraved mind, to do those things which are not proper, being filled with all unrighteousness, wickedness, greed, malice; full of envy, murder, strife, deceit, malice; they are gossips, slanderers, haters of God, insolent, arrogant, boastful, inventors of evil, disobedient to parents, without understanding, untrustworthy, unloving, unmerciful; and, although they know the ordinance of God, that those who practice such things are worthy of death, they not only do the same, but also give hearty approval to those who practice them. (Romans 1:18-32)

Note carefully the step-by-step degeneration of the unrighteous man who rejects the truth of God:

1. Man intentionally rejects the truth of God.
2. Through His creation, God reveals enough of His invisible attributes and His eternal power to make Himself known.
3. Though he cannot escape the fact that he is a product of a higher power, man still does not honor God nor give Him thanks.
4. God's response is dire: He turns man over to his own futile speculation and to a darkened heart.
5. Proud in his own professed wisdom and speculation, man becomes a fool.
6. Refusing to submit to the glory of an incorruptible God, man chooses to worship man himself or the creatures around him. (By definition humanism is born at this point.)
7. With the mind thoroughly corrupted, God gives man over to the lusts of his heart and the immorality of the flesh.
8. Because man has intentionally rejected the truth of God for his own lie and worships the creature rather than the Creator, his doom is sealed.

9. From this point on, degradation follows degradation in rapidly descending order. Women burn in the passion of their lesbian relationships, while men do likewise in their homosexual liaisons.
10. God's judgment is swift: He gives them over to a depraved or reprobate mind to do the things that are not proper.
11. Now the floodgates are open: unrighteousness, wickedness, greed, malice, envy, murder, strife, deceit, malice, gossip, slander, hatred of God, insolence, arrogance, boasting, inventing new evil.
12. Ultimately, there is the rejection of one's own parents and of all close relationships; this pitiable creature becomes unloving and unmerciful.
13. In the final depraved scene, man not only participates to the limit in all of these perverse activities, but he is actively engaged in recruiting others to his godless way of life, cheering them on as they participate.

Paul takes a slightly different tack in his first letter to the Corinthians:

Christ did not send me to baptize, but to preach the gospel, not in cleverness of speech, that the cross of Christ should not be made void. For the word of the cross is to those who are perishing foolishness, but to us who are being saved it is the power of God. For it is written, "I will destroy the wisdom of the wise, and the cleverness of the clever I will set aside." Where is the wise man? Where is the scribe? Where is the debater of this age? Has not God made foolish the wisdom of the world? For since in the wisdom of God the world through its wisdom did not come to know God, God was well-pleased through the foolishness of the message

*preached to save those who believe....Because the fool-
ishness of God is wiser than men, and the weakness of
God is stronger than men.* (1 Corinthians 1:17-25)

Once again we have a picture of the worldliwise man, depending
on his own reasoning and wisdom while missing the very heart of
life itself—eternal life through the cross of Jesus Christ. Most of us
have probably had the experience of observing this pathetic man,
caught up in his own wisdom, trying to reason his way into righteousness. Such a man misses not only eternal life, but also the very
elite truth for which he seeks. God says He will destroy such wisdom
and nullify such cleverness.

Paul pursues nearly the same matter in the next chapter:

*When I came to you, brethren, I did not come with
superiority of speech or of wisdom, proclaiming to you
the testimony of God. For I determined to know nothing among you except Jesus Christ, and Him crucified.
And I was with you in weakness and in fear and in
much trembling. And my message and my preaching
were not in persuasive words of wisdom, but in demonstration of the Spirit and of power, that your faith
should not rest on the wisdom of men, but on the power
of God. Yet we do speak wisdom among those who are
mature; a wisdom, however, not of this age, nor of the
rulers of this age, who are passing away; but we speak
God's wisdom in a mystery, the hidden wisdom, which
God predestined before the ages to our glory; the
wisdom which none of the rulers of this age has
understood; for if they had understood it, they would
not have crucified the Lord of glory.* (1 Corinthians 2:1-
8)

Here we have the man who comes to hear Paul share the simple
message of Christ crucified for our sins, but who is willing only to be
argumentative in the realm of rational knowledge. This man, too,
misses Christ. Sadly, as Paul points out, had this man been willing to
listen to the Spirit and accept Christ, he would then have been

admitted to the wisdom of God, which is the wisdom of the ages.

This is the tragic condition of natural man: He does not because he cannot—he does not accept spiritual truths because he cannot accept the things of the Spirit of God. In his very quest to master all knowledge, the natural man rejects the very tools that would have unlocked for him the great mysteries of the universe.

Paul takes all of this one step further in the following chapter:

> *Let no man deceive himself. If any man among you thinks that he is wise in this age. let him become foolish that he may become wise. For tne wisdom of this world is foolishness before God. For it is written, "He is the one who catches the wise in their craftiness"; and again, "The Lord knows the reasonings of the wise, that they are useless." So then let no one boast in men. For all things belong to you, whether Paul or Apollos or Cephas or the world or life or death or things present or things to come; all things belong to you, and you belong to Christ; and Christ belongs to God.* (1 Corinthians 3:18-23)

These words remind us of the words of Christ, who said that unless we become as little children we will never get into the kingdom of God (Matthew 18:3). Paul's requirement of the natural mind seems to border on the impossible: He must become foolish in order that he may become wise.

Paul was well aware of the spiritual blindness of natural man. Before his experience on the Damascus road, Paul passionately persecuted the Christians, convinced he was doing a great service to God. Only God's sovereign interruption of his frenetic pursuit of believers jolted Paul out of his naturalistic thinking. In two very powerful passages in 2 Corinthians, Paul seems to be reaching back deep in his own experience to illustrate the blindness of heart characteristic of the natural mind:

> *Having therefore such a hope, we use great boldness in our speech, and are not as Moses, who used to put a veil over his face that the sons of Israel might not look*

intently at the end of what was fading away. But their minds were hardened [blinded, KJV]; for until this very day at the reading of the old covenant the same veil remains unlifted, because it is removed in Christ. But to this day whenever Moses is read, a veil lies over their heart; but whenever a man turns to the Lord, the veil is taken away. (2 Corinthians 3:12-16)

Therefore, since we have this ministry, as we received mercy, we do not lose heart, but we have renounced the things hidden because of shame, not walking in craftiness or adulterating the word of God, but by the manifestation of truth commending ourselves to every man's conscience in the sight of God. And even if our gospel is veiled, it is veiled to those who are perishing, in whose case the god of this world has blinded the minds of the unbelieving, that they might not see the light of the gospel of the glory of Christ, who is the image of God. (2 Corinthians 4:1-4)

The Jewish mind, prototype of all natural minds, was and is hardened to this very day in the reading of Scriptures, Old or New Testament. This veil of blindness remains until it is lifted in Christ Jesus. In case you still struggle with the source of this spiritual blindness, Paul clearly points out that the God of this world (or this age) has blinded the minds of the unbelieving that they might not see the light of the gospel (2 Corinthians 4:4). You can see that there can be only one first step to a Renewed Mind: turning to Jesus Christ as Savior and Lord of your life, and having the veil of satanic darkness lifted from your eyes.

Paul further agonizes over his beloved Corinthians:

But I am afraid, lest as the serpent deceived Eve by his craftiness, your minds should be led astray from the simplicity and purity of devotion to Christ. (2 Corinthians 11:3)

The chilling warning here is that though one has begun to walk with Christ and moved into some measure of a Renewed Mind, the appeal of the intellect is always to draw us away from the simplicity of the gospel of Christ. I know from deep personal experience that to choose the rational path once again is immediately to open one's self to doubt, skepticism and the enticing arguments of humanism.

Several key passages in the Pauline epistles to the Ephesians and the Colossians further underscore this crucial passage from darkness into light.

You were dead in your trespasses and sins, in which you formerly walked according to the course of this world [this age, KJV], according to the prince of the power of the air, of the spirit that is now working in the sons of disobedience. Among them we too all formerly lived in the lusts of our flesh, indulging the desires of the flesh and of the mind, and were by nature children of wrath, even as the rest. (Ephesians 2:1-3)

Let no one deceive you with empty words [vain words, KJV], for because of these things the wrath of God comes upon the sons of disobedience. Therefore do not be partakers with them; for you were formerly darkness, but now you are light in the Lord; walk as children of light. (Ephesians 5:6-8)

Let no one keep defrauding you of your prize by delighting in self-abasement and the worship of the angels, taking his stand on visions he has seen, inflated without cause by his fleshly mind, and not holding fast to the head, from whom the entire body...grows with a growth which is from God. (Colossians 2:18-19)

Paul's choice of words may vary, but his understanding is unfailing: The natural man is dead in sin. He walks according to pattern of this age, carried along by the impulses of this present world-system, dominated by the power and influence of the prince who controls the invisible powers of darkness. Such a one indulges in every desire of the flesh and the mind, however sinful.

Paul calls the natural mind utterly futile, darkened in understanding and ignorance because of a very hard heart. As a believer you must recognize empty, vain words for what they are—deceit. Children of the light ought to have no part with the darkness from which such words flow.

The reference in the Colossians passage to the "fleshly mind" has been widely interpreted as the mind set on fleshly desires, particularly sensual or sexual lusts. Certainly there is this element involved in a fleshly mind, but if you follow Paul carefully you will discover that he refers again and again to the flesh as in contrast to the spirit. In this light the fleshly mind refers to the mind set on the evidence coming in through the senses, rational knowledge in contradistinction to revealed knowledge.

Notice in Colossians 2:18 that the person with a fleshly mind, who is vulnerable to every false doctrine, gets there by not holding fast to the head of the body, who is Jesus Christ. The moment he lets go of Jesus Christ, the things of his spirit and revelation knowledge, he is dependent on fleshly knowledge and has a fleshly mind.

From Paul's day to ours, there have always been those who have operated on the fringe of the Christian faith, individuals who are much impressed with their own arguments and the cleverness of their own thinking. There were the Gnostics in Paul's day, as well as many of their ilk in our day. Men who reject the indwelling Holy Spirit and His gentle tug toward brokenness and humility seem particularly vulnerable. Describing such persons, Paul wrote:

> *If any one advocates a different doctrine, and does not agree with sound words, those of our Lord Jesus Christ, and with the doctrine conforming to godliness, he is conceited and understands nothing; but he has a morbid interest in controversial questions and disputes about words, out of which arise envy, strife, abusive language, evil suspicions, and constant friction between men of depraved mind and deprived of the truth, who suppose that godliness is a means of gain. But godliness actually is a means of great gain, when accompanied by contentment.* (1 Timothy 6:3-6)

O Timothy, guard what has been entrusted to you, avoiding worldly and empty chatter and the opposing arguments of what is falsely called "knowledge"— which some have professed and thus gone astray from the faith. (1 Timothy 6:20-21)

Paul's words concerning these men are unusually harsh: conceited, understanding nothing, a morbid interest in controversy, enjoying strife, merchandising the gospel, depraved of mind and deprived of the truth. Paul's advice to Timothy is simply to avoid such vain arguments and false "knowledge." However much you try to reason with such men and lead them to the light of Jesus Christ, they seem, in Paul's words, to be "always learning and never able to come to the knowledge of the truth" (2 Timothy 3:7).

The Peril of the Natural Mind

Let us review the way we have come. The Word has a great deal to say about the natural mind, and the passages we have selected for this chapter are enough to stimulate many hours of thought and provide the content for the making of many books.

We began with created man, made in the very image of God. Being spirit, as God is spirit, the essential characteristic of created man is his ability to know and fellowship with the Father. And so we observed him naming the creatures of God, coming to understand the majesty and greatness of God's power in creation, ruling that creation in all of its far-flung reaches and, most important, communing and fellowshipping with his heavenly Father in the rich bonds of love.

But we have seen in this chapter that all this changes with man's impudent rebellion against the very authority of God. In one act of willful disobedience, Adam ate of the forbidden fruit of the knowledge of good and evil, and death overtook him in a moment. Spiritual death came first, in an instant, as the fellowship with the Father was broken and the instructive voice of the Spirit was silenced. The seeds of death took root in the body of man that same day, and though he would live another 930 years, the vulnerability of the body to the ravages of sin, sickness and disease was soon apparent. The effects on the mind of man were more subtle and less visible; however, it would be but a short time before we would begin to see the futility of man's thinking, captive as it had become to rational knowledge. With the Fall came the loss of dominion, for the rule that man had so enjoyed under the authority of the Father is now given over to the very enemy of his soul, Satan. In a single generation man's great love for God degenerates into contempt and then hatred.

For the sake of our study here, the paramount result of the Fall is seen in the mind's being cut off from the instruction of the heavenly Father and the loss of all revealed knowledge. Man's access to God is gone; he can no longer know spiritual things. Errors in his naturalistic observations can no longer be corrected by his frequent visits with the Father. No matter now how powerful the mind of man, how virtually limitless his capacity for understanding the things of God, the "knowing" he now has through the senses is based upon information coming in from the world around him. That world is now under control of the very enemy of his soul, and deceit is the agenda of the day.

At this point I have heard folks say: "Poor Adam, if he had only known." Nonsense! Adam knew! Adam was not stupid! He had a mind that could grasp the very truths of God, and he knew full well that God had promised him the consequences of his misdeed. I am fully confident that Adam did know what he was doing, but that the arguments of Satan won the day. And they win today, again and again. It is appealing to know all about evil as well as good, to have the wisdom to run the universe on your own and, yes, to be free from the shackles of God's authority on your life.

With access to the Father cut off, it is easy to understand man's almost total obsession with fleshly, physical, sensual, natural "knowing" about the world around him. His very survival and existence in that world is dependent upon the accuracy of the input from his five senses. If he is to avoid the attack of the lion, he must see or hear him coming. He must carefully distinguish between edible and poisonous plants. Every scrap of information his senses can report seems crucial for life itself. And so the bottom-line definition of the natural mind is just that: It is a captive of the natural world around it.

I have been trained as a psychologist, and the central problem of modern-day psychology is simply this: Without instruments to measure and report either the spirit or the soul, present-day psychologists deny the existence of either. In fact, the very term "psychology," based as it is on the Greek stem of the word for soul, is an anachronism itself. So the psychologist, by his philosophical precommitments, is limited to the investigation of physical behavior while virtually denying the other two parts of man.

At the very peak of the behavioristic movement under B.F. Skinner, there was even the suggestion made that the central nervous system did not exist. For a brief period there was an attempt to demonstrate that all learning could be explained by learning stored in the muscular system and the external skeletal system of the body. In an effort to deny the existence of the spirit and the soul, there was actually the denial of the thought processes themselves. While most of psychology has retreated from this extreme position today, the terms spirit and soul are still totally anathema to the secular psychologist.

The philosopher long ago set the task for himself: "Know thyself." Yet assigning such a task to the rationalistic philosopher is like saying to Helen Keller: "Go look at yourself in a mirror" or "Listen to the beautiful music." Man is a spirit with an eternal soul, but neither the psychologist nor the philosopher can know this while rejecting the authority of God upon his life.

And yet so great is the God-shaped void in our lives and the spiritual hunger for fellowship with the Lord, that the modern intellectual or skeptic is caught in the conundrum between two. While he denies the existence of God or the authority of God in his life, his hunger for the spiritual exists. Is it any wonder that astrology, the occult and all related searches run rampant in an academic community? The peril of the natural mind is that without the course-correcting system of revelation knowledge, a man can be off course for a lifetime and never know it!

Finally, let me underscore one point: You need to understand that all men apart from God are ruled by sense knowledge, and thus are captives of their own rationalistic thinking. They cannot know God, they cannot see Him, they cannot fellowship with Him, and they cannot understand His revealed Word. Passages in the Bible that seem so patently clear to the believer are as gross darkness to the unbeliever. Therefore, when they begin to rail against your faith in Jesus, mock the very concept of faith itself, demand "scientific proof" and blaspheme against our Lord, it ought to affect us no more than a mere infant's babbling.

Limitations in Sense Knowledge

About this point in my teaching, someone frequently interjects: "Come now, don't you think you have unfairly impugned the wonderful mind of man?" Without doubt man has made enormous strides in understanding the world around him. Advances in the the sciences, transportation, communication, medicine and many related fields are obvious. We have sent men to the moon and brought them back safely. We have sent reconnaissance satellites past distant planets that have transmitted back amazingly vivid pictures. We have made great strides in the miniaturization of systems, in improved surgical techniques, and even in the conveniences of our homes. However, all of this is but humble testimony of the enormous power and capacity of the mind of man as God created it.

We have experienced a knowledge explosion of gigantic proportions in these end times, just as the Word of God predicted (Daniel 12:4). The Library of Congress today holds something over 100 million volumes, and thousands of scientific journals are issued monthly; even the most brilliant scientist can only hope to keep abreast of perhaps two dozen such journals. And yet scientific methods and scientific facts are not always reliable. So-called "facts" are constantly being corrected; often yesterday's "facts" are today's "comedies" in the laboratory. Further, the very nature of the scientific method is to constantly revise "facts"—yet the academic world seldom remembers such limitations and issues these "facts" as established landmarks for all time.

Yet there is one truth more crucial than all of these. All of the scientific findings, all of the technological advances, all of the "knowledge" we have gained, come from the natural world around us and have been gathered through the five basic senses. All such knowledge has been reported through fallible instruments (the physical senses), has been gathered in a world full of error and deceit under satanic control, and is devoid of course correction through revelation knowledge.

Sadly, all of these limitations never seem to produce the expected humility that they should in the mind of the learner. Man, ever more impressed with his own "knowing," makes ever-greater claims for his reasoning powers. When he comes to the end of what he might reasonably claim to know, he makes great leaps into the unknown, frequently drawing conclusions that are preposterous when viewed from the vantage point of God's heavenly kingdom.

When man reaches the absolute limits of his "knowing" and begins to make unwarranted guesses, we call him a philosopher. He is then entitled to offer wide-ranging speculations concerning matters of origin and destiny; the meaning, purpose and direction of life; and the nature of the universe and man's place in it. He speaks of matters that his mind could never hope to know with an ease and assurance that convinces vast numbers of other people of his "wisdom."

Yet the natural mind can never know the beginning of all things, the reasons for creation, the why of man, his purpose in the whole scheme of things, nor even the basic nature of man himself. Natural man will never understand the origin of life, the origin of man, the origin of matter, the origin of motion, the origin of energy and force. Far worse, he postulates great theories about the origin and nature of evil, the purpose of this life we live, the nature of death and the ultimate destiny of man.

The central problem that few recognize is this: The scientist himself, this wonderful purveyor of all knowledge, is also himself a man. He also was born, lives under the same temptations as all other men, and must die. As natural man with a rebellious heart, he is in no position to issue timeless truths about the eternal destiny of man and his universe.

When man reaches the frontiers of knowledge, he builds theories and postulates that fit his own preconceptions and assumptions. Because natural man is in rebellion against God his preconceptions, and thus his theories, are going to be in direct conflict with divine truth. So, no matter how much he may claim to test his theories, revise them and test them again, bad theory will lead to faulty research, which will support distorted and deceitful conclusions.

Only if man could be open-minded enough to reject the theories that he is testing and begin to subject them to the revealed knowledge of God, could he hope to get at questions of eternal destiny.

Darwin stood at such a frontier of knowing. He rejected all revealed knowledge. He rejected the concept of creation and a Creator God, and the very purpose of man. Refusing what his senses could not perceive, he constructed a "reasonable" theory—a master guess. Within a matter of months, or at most a few years, his theory gained widespread acceptance within the scientific community. Had his theory been on any other subject, it would have been either rejected or else subjected to years of scientific inquiry. Unfortunately, here was a theory that freed man from all indebtedness to divine authority; it would set man loose to determine his own destiny. The proud heart of man quickly embraced a "scientific explanation" for his rebellion. Darwinism won the day.

Men whose minds are open to revealed truth have repeatedly shown how incongruous the theory of evolution really is. Yet in debate after debate all over this nation, men of a natural mind will defend Darwinian theory to the point of stretching credulity. Why of all the theories of knowledge in the world would the matter of creation become such a touchstone for argument? The answer seems so very obvious, and yet it is so largely ignored today. The moment man begins to admit the possibility of a special or higher creation, then he is also admitting that a mind far higher than his formed it all. If a higher being made us, then He has a claim on our lives. We owe Him submission and worship. But if our minds are like all other natural minds and are in rebellion against God, we refuse Him our allegiance and worship. Thus, an explanation of creation with even quasi-scientific evidence will appeal to the natural mind.

I believe this is the central issue of education from kindergarten through graduate school, in this country and throughout the world: Much of what is being taught as well-researched, factual information to our students today is really the camouflage of great spiritual issues. Refusing revelation knowledge and steeped in the darkness of sense knowledge, today's academic mind in virtually every discipline is willing to take great "gulps" of unproven and untested assumptions into his theories. The academic community demands freedom to pursue every thought and idea, no matter where it leads.

I know of no group of people on the face of the earth who are less tolerant of ideas, if such ideas run counter to the accepted wisdom of this age. If anyone suspects that revealed truth based on the Word of God has entered the discussion, then all tolerance of diverse ideas is forgotten.

For the moment, allow me one illustration of this truth. By now you understand that by definition all satanic theories are 180 degrees opposite of the truth of God. For example: revealed truth tells us of an all-powerful, all-knowing, all-loving God who created a universe as a perfect place of residence for created man with whom he desired fellowship. The biblical portrait here is of a perfect creation and a perfect man, all of which has been deteriorating since the Fall. Man wanders farther and farther away from God, growing more and more evil, and would ultimately destroy himself if left to his own devices.

Contrast that with the far-reaching implications of evolution. Not only did all life begin with some obscure amoeba floating around in primeval waters that finally crawled up on the beach. All life itself is getting better and better. The world is improving with each passing year. Man is becoming more moral, more humane in his treatment of his fellow man. In Paul's words, one has to be blinded by Satan to miss the fallacy of this line of reasoning, but it is a perfect portrait of the world of academe in the late twentieth century.

God's Majestic Hierarchy

Our God is a God of order and authority. The Word tells us that He hates confusion (1 Corinthians 14:33). God, through His Word, clearly establishes lines of authority and insists that they be maintained.

It is not within the scope of this book to develop God's hierarchy of authority at any length. However, you will recognize immediately that God the Father is sovereign over all. Christ brings all things together under His reign and submits them to the Father. The church in turn is submitted to the headship or lordship of Christ. Within the church, elders share authority but submit unto the headship of Jesus Christ. In turn, a wife is to be submitted unto the headship of her husband, and children are to be obedient to the authority of their parents.

I say this only to develop the point that in like fashion God's intent for His created man is that he also should be in order in his tripartite nature and be submitted unto God. If you will note Chart 6 (on page 113), you will find a variation of Chart 9 (on page 119). Previously we pointed out that God intended for the spirit of man to rule his mind and for the spirit and mind together to rule his body. Sacrifice this divine order, or take away the rule of the spirit because of man's spiritual death in rebellion against God, and you have chaos—chaos in man and in the world. On the other hand, a man in rightful order—with spirit ruling mind ruling body, and all submitted to the authority of the heavenly Father—has great power with God and with man.

Now look at the second half of Chart 6 (on page 113) and note that reason stands between revelation and passion exactly as the mind stands between spirit and body, as long as man is in his created order. We have already observed that reason holds the same relationship to revelation as the mind does to the spirit in our earlier pages. Reason must constantly be illumined by revelation in the process we have called course correction. Passion reflects the desires of the flesh, and God fully intends it to be subject to the control of revelation and reason within man.

If passion rules, calamity is certain. America in the late twentieth century is a perfect portrait of passion ruling a great host of people. Driven by lust, unbridled sex, heterosexual and homosexual promiscuity, alcohol and drugs, modern man displays the same barbaric propensity that we saw again and again in the book of Genesis. Always there is the element of immediacy in fleshly demands; if the body craves a "fix," it must have it now. If she is attractive and desirable, the flesh wants her now.

Apart from a complete revival of the knowledge of the Lord and righteousness in this country, the only improvement over the reign of passion we can hope for is the rule of reason.

For example, while the rule of reason is widely touted among civilized men, enlightened self-interest is still the very highest possible goal of man. Under the rule of reason the only restraining force in the world is not my God-given compassion and love for you, but my own self-interest in wanting to save my own neck. Therefore, I will not participate in your destruction if you do not engage in mine.

Reason can only appeal to the "reasonableness" of pursuing mutual self-interests; it can never change the heart of man and its evil motives.

If every leader in America (academic, political, business) understands the foolhardiness of the reign of passion and agrees that drug trafficking in this country has to be stopped, then it is still just as true that the proffered solution is the reign of reason.

If all this seems a bit obtuse, let me state it bluntly and directly: Apart from revelation knowledge, rational man can still destroy the world and himself with it just about as quickly as passionate man.

Natural Man's Tragic Truism

I am certain you have heard it a thousand times: Experience is the best teacher. This is the basic assumption of the natural mind. Saying it differently: Seeing is believing. A bit more sophisticated, the humanists say: The scientific method will solve all of our problems.

It is virtually impossible to convince the average person today of the bankruptcy of this simple bit of worldly wisdom. Experience is the best teacher! And yet the average individual does not understand that his experience is gathered in a world open to satanic deceit. He may have the same experience a hundred times and be utterly convinced of its efficacy, yet be blind to the error built into the natural observation. Not to belabor the point further, but I simply urge you to remember that "experience is the best teacher" is the cornerstone of rational knowing in this natural world. Faith is based on the principles of God's heavenly kingdom. The two are as incompatible as the natural mind and the Renewed Mind.

Conclusion

The impact of Adam's fall upon the body of man as well as on the surrounding world is obvious. To the Christian believer, the impact of the Fall on the spirit of man is equally apparent. But the parallel changes in the mind of man are so subtle that even the most astute Christians can find themselves thinking very much as the world thinks and be unaware of the error.

73

The natural mind has been cut off from fellowship with the Father, and can no longer know about God or receive revealed knowledge from Him. The natural mind is hostage to its own senses, and thereby cannot grasp spiritual truths. The natural mind is by definition in rebellion against God, and so natural man does not know about God, does not wish to know about God and rejects revealed truth if it is presented to him. The natural mind is sinful, deceived, and as Paul tells us, set on the flesh and death (Romans 8:5-6).

The mind of man, captive as it is between his spirit and his flesh, has many points of similarity with the electronic computer. A common statement in the computer world is: "Garbage in, garbage out." The same is true of the mind: What the mind knows has to be "input" either through revelation knowledge or through rational knowledge. The common problem for most of us is that we come to know Jesus as our Savior at the age of thirty or forty years, and as a result, we have had just so many years of "sense programming." As new Christians there are enormous amounts of "facts" that have to be unlearned. Worse, there are whole strategies and modes of thinking that have to be unlearned.

The sad fact of the matter is that the vast majority of Christians, being untaught in the things of God, simply never unlearn the thirty or forty years of programming that controlled their thinking before they came to know Christ as Savior. I wish every young child could come to know Jesus as Savior at the age of four or five as I know they are capable of doing. If each one could then be instructed in the ways of God's kingdom, having the "mind of Christ" could be ever so much easier. I also believe that their future potential with God would be infinitely greater, for they would have so very little to unlearn.

Present the truths and promises of God to a child and he has no problem whatsoever accepting them with faith. The reason is simple: He simply has not had the great struggles of being steeped in the rationalism of this age and having his trust destroyed again and again. Jesus understood this; He said that unless we become as little children we will not even get into the kingdom of God.

Let me go a step further in all this. So often I have wished I had access to each new Christian within days of his coming to know Jesus as Savior and Lord. I am discovering that vast numbers of

Christians have come under the tutelage of those who believe that God does not move in the lives of men today, miracles are no longer possible, the gifts and the power of the Holy Spirit were for another age, and anything close to a victorious Christian life is a fiction. Now we are confronted with the individual who must not only unlearn the problems of rational knowledge before he came to the Lord, but the problems of erroneous teaching since he accepted Christ. Frequently, such doctrinal teaching presents a far greater hurdle to a Renewed Mind than the rational knowing of the natural mind.

Is the whole relearning process possible? The testimony of God's Word is a resounding "Yes!" Most of us would be better off never to have had our minds cluttered with much erroneous teaching, both naturalistic and ecclesiastical. However, I thoroughly believe that with God's help and by intentional effort on our part, we can retrain the mind to think as God thinks. I know of no other endeavor that will so completely transform your entire Christian life or pay greater dividends for time and eternity.

INTERLUDE

Let me stop here and speak to you directly for a moment, my reader friend. If you have found your way thus far in this book, and yet you have never had the certainty of having been born again, have never had your spirit made alive in Christ Jesus, have never really accepted Jesus personally as Savior, then I have a special word for you. How I praise the Lord you are interested and have found your way to this point.

First, I want you to realize that every person alive today is alienated from God unless he has come to God through Jesus Christ. Jesus Himself said that He is the door into the sheepfold and anyone who enters by Him shall be saved; but anyone who climbs up another way is a thief and a robber.

You may have seen yourself in reading these opening two chapters and very honestly have to admit that your mind is really in bondage to rational "knowing." You further recognize that you will never understand the things of God and deep spiritual truths until you yield your will and very being to Him and have your spirit made alive. You may have even felt rebellion rise up within you at some of the things you read. This is a sure sign that the enemy of your soul does not want you to come to know Jesus as your Savior. In fact he is extremely upset with you and would love to confuse your mind so that he could keep you in his kingdom.

The next important step for you is to open your heart to Jesus Christ as Savior. Accept Him as your Savior and Lord, confess your sins and cry out, "God, be merciful to me a sinner!"

I invite you to pray the following prayer with me from the bottom of your heart—just turn your attention to Jesus and really mean it— and I know that He will hear you and answer your prayer.

Heavenly Father, I come to You and confess that I need Jesus as my Savior. I confess that I am sinful in my heart and oftentimes rebellious. Though I have tried to lead a good life, I confess that I have failed many times and sinned against You. I now repent of my sins and turn away from them to follow You. I receive Your forgiveness. Right now I accept Jesus Christ as my Savior and Lord, by an act of faith. I ask that You begin to make me more like Jesus. Thank You for Your mercy and Your forgiveness, and for receiving me into Your family. Help me to grow day by day by reading Your Word and by fellowshipping with You in prayer. I thank You in Jesus' name. Amen.

Now since you have prayed this prayer, I want to pray for you. I ask that as you read, you will somehow be aware that in my spirit I am there with you praying for you. Receive the blessing God has for you:

Heavenly Father, I pray for my friend who has just now turned to You and received Jesus as Savior and Lord. I pray that You will begin to strengthen him day by day in his Christian walk. Also, I pray that right now, heavenly Father, You will fill my friend with Your Holy Spirit until he knows the power, the anointing, the teaching and the strength that comes from His indwelling presence. I pray that You will begin to manifest in my friend both the fruit and the gifts of the Spirit, and that he will know the depths of the love, joy and peace that only You can give within. I pray also that You will begin to make him a soul winner; give him the courage to share what has happened in his life with his friends around him and point them to Jesus Christ, the Savior of the world. I thank You, heavenly Father, for hearing me, and I thank You for filling my friend with Your Holy Spirit and causing him to know the great peace and joy that You give day by day. In Jesus' name. Amen.

If you have prayed this prayer with me today, my dear reader friend, I wish you would take just a moment and write to me. Tell me of what the Lord has done for you so that I can rejoice with you in His name. I want to welcome you into the family of God. You will find my name and address on the last page of this book, and if you write, I will answer with several pieces of literature that will help you grow in the Christian faith. In the meantime, I praise God for you, and as the angels in heaven rejoice for your new life in Christ Jesus, so do I.

CHAPTER THREE

THE CARNAL MIND: SNARE TO VICTORIOUS CHRISTIAN LIVING

The carnal mind is easily the number one problem in the Christian church in this age. The mind of the carnal man—the apostle Paul's name for the immature believer—is the key to the inconsistency of his Christian life. The Word of God contains a wealth of material describing the plight of the carnal man; but our study can be no more than a cursory examination of the carnal mind, for our attention must be fixed on the possibility of the spiritual mind, the Renewed Mind.

We began in chapter one by sketching the nature of created man as a backdrop for the rest of our study. When you can picture the unspoiled and majestic nature of God's first creation as a broad canvas of what God intended, then the peril of the unrenewed mind apart from God can be seen in sharper contrast. Man was created in the very image of God and given life of the ages. His spirit was alive and he was in constant communion with the Father. His mind was powerful and alert, grasping the very scope of the creation of God. He was able to know, think, choose, decide and will, even as his

81

heavenly Father. His body was strong, robust, handsome, designed to live forever. God had entrusted him with the rule of His universe, including the dominion over Satan himself. Man was Spirit-led, God-taught, ever pleasing to his heavenly Father.

Then came the saddest day in all of recorded history: Man turned against the loving God who had formed him, rebelled against His will, ate of the forbidden fruit of the knowledge of good and evil, and gambled away his God-given position. Satan, who had been only a tiresome serpent to this point, suddenly was in charge of the world. All the rules of the game were changed in an instant: Adam's spirit, the very eternal essence of his being, was suddenly dead, and his communion with the heavenly Father was broken forever as far as he knew. His body was exposed to unlimited attacks from his adversary through disease, fallen nature and hostile animals.

However, it is the mind of man that is our interest in this study. The impact of the Fall on the mind is much more subtle than its effect on the spirit or body. Our conscious awareness, our rational self, our ego rests in the mind; therefore, an objective analysis borders on the impossible. But the Bible, which always reveals the mind of the Father through the voice of the Spirit, paints a grim picture of the natural mind.

The mind, even in created form, was a captive between the spirit and the flesh. Now with the spirit dead and revealed knowledge from the Father cut off, the mind is indeed a hostage to the five senses. It cannot grasp spiritual things, for it is now in open rebellion against God. Caught in this sinful and rebellious state, the mind is credulous, unsuspecting and open to deceit—readily believing that the only reality is what the senses report. Paul would capsulize it thus: "The mind set on the flesh is death" (Romans 8:6).

The mind has difficulty even with the facts. Left to its own devices, the natural mind would never in a million years figure out the purpose, the beginning, the end and the meaning of life. In fact, the natural mind apart from God will become ever more rebellious, increasingly a hater of God, further from truth and more vulnerable to deception. Through its own suspicions, jealousies and animosities, the natural mind would destroy both itself and all those around it—unless God intervened. Current events bear this out. Nuclear missiles and chemical weapons have been found in the possession of desert chieftains who are apparently little more than fanatical madmen. It takes little imagination to create a scenario in which virtually the entire population of the earth could be destroyed.

But note that I said "unless God intervened." Based on the promises of the Word of God, I am convinced that He will and does even now intervene. He has promised that the knowledge of the glory of the Lord shall cover the earth as the waters cover the sea (Isaiah 11:9; Habakkuk 2:14). And that requires Renewed Minds on a massive scale in this world. Hallelujah! I claim that promise in the name of Jesus!

The Power of Calvary

How we praise the almighty Father that the chapter on the natural mind is not the last chapter. When the fullness of time had come, God sent forth His Son into the world with the expressed mission of undoing the results of Adam's awful deed. Untold volumes have been written on the power of Calvary and the scope of Christ's work on the cross. There is space here only to note the glorious fact of Christ's victory on Calvary and to add a few footnotes selected from the Word of God on the breadth of His redemption.

Chart 5 (on page 113) contrasts the effects of the Fall on the body, the mind and the spirit. Note first the spirit of man. The Bible opens with God's dire warning: The day you eat of the forbidden fruit—the knowledge of good and evil—you shall surely die. As we have seen, man did eat and his spirit died immediately. The Bible presents two basic agenda for the universe—life and death. And there are scores of verses wherein life and death are cited as cosmic opposing forces, diametric themes, conflicting plans: life, the will of God; death, the will of Satan. The culmination of these verses may be in John 10:10 where Jesus said: "The thief comes only to steal, and kill, and destroy; I came that they might have life, and might have it abundantly." The possibility of a reborn spirit and of eternal life through faith in Jesus Christ is the central tenet of the Christian faith.

Next observe the effect of Christ's atoning death on the body. The day that Adam sinned, the seeds of death were planted in his flesh. Though the days of man may have dwindled from nine hundred plus years down to our present three score and ten, nothing has really changed. Death is the most certain fact in our lives. From the moment of birth, death is at work in our flesh. Yet on Calvary's hill, our Savior triumphed over death and bore our sicknesses.

The prophet Isaiah, peered down through the ages and caught a glimpse of the bruised Servant, our Jesus. Speaking under the Holy Spirit's anointing, he cried out: "Surely our pains He Himself bore, and our sicknesses He carried....And by His scourging we are healed" (Isaiah 53:4-5).

Matthew stood one day watching the power of God at work in the ministry of Christ. We can only imagine the thrill of his soul as he wrote:

> *He cast out the spirits with a word, and healed all who were ill, in order that what was spoken through Isaiah the prophet might be fulfilled, saying, "He Himself took our infirmities, and carried away our diseases."*
> (Matthew 8:16-17)

Later Peter wrote: "He Himself bore our sins in His body on the cross, that we might die to sin and live to righteousness; for by His wounds you were healed" (1 Peter 2:24).

Chart 7(on page 115) illustrates some of the central aspects of both the fall of man and Christ's redemption on the cross. (Though space prohibits, this chart should be several times longer so the time lines might be in perspective: The age of the natural mind as portrayed in the Old Testament should be far longer than this chart can show.)

The top line represents life—life of the ages as created man knew it with no comprehension of death. Eternal life, as the reborn man accepts it, is the hope granted through faith in Jesus.

The bottom line depicts death—first death of the spirit and of the body, but ultimately, apart from Calvary, eternal death in the lake of fire. Jesus spoke of this as the second death, which is unending (Revelation 21:8). The great pivotal point of all history is the cross, undoing the dreadful consequences of Adam's rebellion.

Note one crucial matter: The rebirth of the spirit is an immediate matter and brings one from death unto life in an instant. The redemption of the mind of man requires time, discipline and growth.

The impact of Calvary on the minds of men will be discussed in detail in later chapters. The last half of this book focuses on the possibilities of a Renewed Mind, on having the very mind of Christ. But note that were it not for the reborn spirit as a result of Calvary the natural mind would be without hope. The why and how of God's reclaiming of the mind lie ahead.

One matter of great urgency relating to the Fall lies almost beyond the scope of this book. When Adam sinned, not only was his own God-given nature changed completely, but he also squandered away his rule of the universe which God had entrusted to him. The recouping of this lost dominion was one of Christ's greatest victories on Calvary. The messages of instruction to God's end-time army, as the Lord has spoken them to me, nearly all focus on reclaiming our lost authority and rule. God is urgently calling His people to prepare to retake what was lost in Eden.

I have mentioned these studies on dominion to make one crucial point. Any preparation of an end-time army will return again and again to a required first step: Living an overcoming Christian life demands first that we have a Renewed Mind. As audacious as this may appear, I believe the call of God to us today is consistent and clear. A Renewed Mind is foundational to our living a victorious life on the plane of the miraculous.

Let me add one thought before moving on. Frequently, as I speak in seminars and churches, someone will ask some form of this question: "I have seen this individual who apparently lives so victoriously that the miraculous is a normal part of his life. All of this seems so unfair, for I too pray every day. Why don't I see God's miracles on any regular basis?" My answer is direct and simple: "How much time have you honestly spent in the Word of God studying out His ways? Have you found the conditions for your authority that God wants to grant you? Have you studied the life of our Lord to discover there, step by step, the way in which He won victory over Satan? How willing have you been to study, be disciplined and pay the price to understand the basic requisites of His Word?"

Now all of this is not intended to be harsh. The simple fact of the matter is that even as Christians we live in a world dominated by the common wisdom of this age. If our minds are filled with rational knowledge—which is colored often by satanic deceit—then you must understand that our prayers are frequently more filled with the ways of this world than they are with the truth of God. However much our heavenly Father loves us and wants to bless us, He is not going to abridge the rules of the kingdom of God to accommodate our finite thinking clouded by the earthly wisdom about us. There are times, I realize, that God looks past our weaknesses and ignorance, and meets our needs in spite of ourselves. God calls us to victory, and living in that victory demands on a day-by-day basis the discipline of understanding His Word, His ways and His will, and requires us to order our prayers, our faith and our lives after His ways.

Paul's Carnal Man

The goal of this chapter is to understand the carnal man as the Word describes him and to grasp the tragedy that the carnal mind brings to victorious Christian living. Since carnal man occupies the territory between the natural man and the spiritual man, let us fix clearly in our thinking the nature of Paul's natural man.

In 1 Corinthians 2:14 Paul gives his clearest summary of the tragedy of the natural man: He does not accept the things of God, for he cannot understand them apart from spiritual discernment. So herein is the crux of the problem: Natural man is alienated from God, cannot hear the voice of God, cannot receive the things of the Spirit of God. The entire kingdom of God and all of its glorious ways are blocked from his view. As a result, natural man walks according to the wisdom of this age (Ephesians 2:1-3): His mind ruled by Satan, he indulges in lusts of the flesh, and becomes increasingly a child of wrath.

Paul further describes natural men (Ephesians 4:17-19) as those who walk according to the futility of their own mind, being darkened in their understanding, alienated from the life of God because of their ignorance and the hardness of their hearts. The behavioral outcome of such a mind Paul describes as callous, sensual, impure and greedy. In 2 Corinthians 4:4, Paul notes the spiritual blindness of such men:

The god of this world has blinded the minds of the unbelieving, that they might not see the light of the gospel of the glory of Christ, who is the image of God.

In short, the natural man is alienated from God and cannot understand the things of God, so he walks according to the wisdom of this world.

Carnal Man Defined

Paul's piercing indictment of the Corinthian people two millennia ago could as well have been written of the church of Jesus in America in the late twentieth century:

And I, brethren, could not speak to you as to spiritual men, but as to men of flesh, as to babes in Christ. I gave you milk to drink, not solid food; for you were not yet able to receive it. Indeed, even now you are not yet able, for you are still fleshly. For since there is jealousy and strife among you, are you not fleshly, and are you not walking like mere men? (1 Corinthians 3:1-3)

Paul is writing to Christian brethren, men whose spirits have been made alive in Christ. Though they are now spiritually alive, tragically they are not able to grasp spiritual truths. Evidently Paul had to feed them the most elementary truths of the gospel to keep them from straying away.

Three different translations of verse 1 reveal much of the scope of the problem. The King James Version translates Paul's words as: "I could not speak unto you as unto spiritual, but as unto carnal." The suggestion here is that their minds are still fixed on evil, lustful matters. The New International Version reads: "I could not address you as spiritual, but as worldly." The focus of the mind here is clearly still on worldly circumstances. The New American Standard Bible reads: "I could not speak to you as to spiritual men, but as to men of the flesh." With the mind set on the flesh the senses and the knowledge they produce hold the attention of the mind.

A first tentative definition of carnal man offers itself: While his spirit has been made alive, his mind is still fixed on the worldly

87

circumstances about it, paying attention primarily to the sensory input of rational knowledge, and far too often focused on the carnal evil, lustful matters of life.

In verse 3, Paul carries this further when he notes: "You are still fleshly....walking like mere men." He cites as evidence the jealousy and strife so common among them. Now add to our definition a new point: Carnal man is schizophrenic by nature. His spirit is made alive, but his mind and his body are still fixed on the flesh and he walks as a mere man—that is, a mere natural man.

The writer to the Hebrews adds to our understanding:

> *For every one who partakes only of milk is not accustomed to the word of righteousness, for he is a babe. But solid food is for the mature, who because of practice have their senses trained to discern good and evil.*
> (Hebrews 5:13-14)

Holding for the possibility of true maturity in Christ, this writer agrees that it will be the training of the senses, the refocusing of the mind, that will bring about this maturity and a new taste for the things of righteousness.

As Paul writes to the Ephesians, he outlines for us the possibility of rising above the petty quarrels of little children and moving toward becoming mature men of faith:

> *And He gave some as apostles, and some as prophets, and some as evangelists, and some as pastors and teachers, for the equipping of the saints for the work of service, to the building up of the body of Christ; until we all attain to the unity of the faith, and of the knowledge of the Son of God, to a mature man, to the measure of the stature which belongs to the fulness of Christ. As a result, we are no longer to be children, tossed here and there by waves, and carried about by every wind of doctrine, by the trickery of men, by craftiness in deceitful scheming; but speaking the truth in love, we are to grow up in all aspects into Him, who is the head, even Christ, from whom the*

*whole body, being fitted and held together by that
which every joint supplies, according to the proper
working of each individual part, causes the growth of
the body for the building up of itself in love. This I say
therefore, and affirm together with the Lord, that you
walk no longer just as the Gentiles also walk, in the
futility of their mind.* (Ephesians 4:11-17)

The important point in this passage is the possibility for maturation and growth for every one of us in our walk with Jesus Christ.
Apart from that maturation we find ourselves walking just as the
unbelievers do in the futility of their minds. No longer are our minds
to be tossed here and there by every wind of doctrine that comes
along, nor to be open to the deceitful schemes of the enemy of our
souls—there is the real possibility of growing into a firm faith in
Christ.

Paul wrote to Timothy of men "holding to a form of godliness,
although they have denied its power;...always learning and never
able to come to the knowledge of the truth" (2 Timothy 3:5-7). We
know many such men both inside and outside the household of
faith. However, it is especially disheartening to find men who claim
to know Christ yet who are not maturing in the ways of God as found
in His Word and seem always to be learning without being able to
come to the truth. Such ones should have long ago learned enough
about the things of God to stand firm in the faith and to help newborn
Christians in their own daily walk. Yet crises come and they cry,
"Help! What am I going to do?"

I think no other aspect of the carnal mind must be quite as
wearying to the heart of God as the jealousy, strife and quarreling of
which Paul speaks. All over this great nation churches are kept in
turmoil, even split, over the petty ego-strivings of the carnal mind,
bringing much disrepute upon the cause of Christ and giving great
occasion for the enemies of the Lord to blaspheme. Paul's beloved
words in 1 Corinthians 13:4-7 seem more urgent than ever before:

*Love is patient, love is kind, and is not jealous; love
does not brag and is not arrogant, does not act unbe-
comingly; it does not seek its own, is not provoked, does*

not take into account a wrong suffered, does not rejoice
in unrighteousness, but rejoices with the truth; bears
all things, believes all things, hopes all things, endures
all things.

Carnal man: What do we know by way of definition at this point? The natural man walks according to the wisdom of this age because he has no other choice. His spirit dead, his mind darkened, he is a rebel against God and cannot understand spiritual matters.

By contrast, the carnal man has accepted Christ as his Savior and his spirit has been made alive in Christ Jesus. All the possibilities of spiritual man are his: He could hear the voice of the Father, he could let the things of the spirit dominate him and he could begin to grasp the knowledge of God. But sadly, he does not! He still walks, talks and thinks as the natural man. He is still carnal, worldly, fleshly fixed on the circumstances about him; his thinking is just as futile as that of the pagan minds around him.

At the risk of earning your consternation, let me make one observation. If I judge simply by the words that come out of the mouth of the average professed Christian today, the thinking of most evangelical/charismatic Christians is vastly more similar to the thinking of the world about us than to the mind of Christ and His ways.

Most of us have undoubtedly thrilled at hearing the testimony of the newborn Christian—perhaps a young person just recently salvaged from the shipwreck of life. Such a person, having never grown up in church, knows none of the right words or language to express what he is feeling. We rejoice at his testimony and smile to ourselves at his ill-fitting words as he tries to portray what has occurred in his life. There is so much spiritual truth that he does not understand, but we rejoice with him even if we do wince at his confused theology. However, when we hear the testimony of someone who has professed to walk in the faith for over thirty years, but whose every word betrays his lack of understanding of the Word of God and His ways, it is no longer amusing—we weep. We must agree with the apostle Paul that the carnal mind is not a pretty picture.

One more observation. There have been numerous reports in recent years of young girls, still children themselves, bearing babies out of wedlock. Confused, frightened and not knowing what to do, these girls frequently abandon their babies in an empty apartment, a dumpster or a nearby woods. We are revolted and lash out at the awfulness of it. However, shouldn't we be equally revolted at the awfulness of a parallel picture? Immature shepherds of Christ's flocks all over the country, with no semblance of a Renewed Mind, continue to see lambs birthed into the flock. As the child-mothers do, these untaught shepherds abandon the newborn lambs without adequate nourishment or care, never leading them to maturity of mind and spirit or to a victorious Christian life.

Finally, I have an urgent warning. The natural man *cannot* grasp spiritual truths; the carnal man *does not* grasp spiritual truths. But the carnal man is twice vulnerable: Like the natural man he is still reliant upon the rational knowledge of the world around him, which is subject to satanic deception; but worse, as a new child of God, he is now the target of the redoubled efforts of Satan to draw him back into the world. Putting it simply: The natural man, already a rebel against God, is causing Satan no particular trouble. Carnal man, now a reborn child of God, represents a potential threat to the satanic kingdom. Therefore, carnal man is not only missing the things of the kingdom of God and walking in the futility of his mind; he is at the same time a sitting duck for every attack Satan wishes to hurl at him. Do you still marvel when a newly born-again Christian says to you: "I thought when I came to Jesus everything would be perfect. Now everything seems to be falling apart."

The Plight of the Carnal Mind

Let us focus our attention for a moment on the quicksand that tends to engulf the carnal mind. So powerful is this snare that an unbelievably high percentage of new Christians fall by the wayside and are caught in its grasp in the first few months of their Christian walk.

One of the most poignant passages in all the Word of God must be Romans 7. As Paul charts the growth of the Christian throughout the book of Romans, he frequently looks back at his own struggles for Christian maturity. Remember that Paul is writing to believers:

For that which I am doing, I do not understand; for I am not practicing what I would like to do, but I am doing the very thing I hate. But if I do the very thing I do not wish to do, I agree with the Law, confessing that it is good. So now, no longer am I the one doing it, but sin which indwells me. For I know that nothing good dwells in me, that is, in my flesh; for the wishing is present in me, but the doing of the good is not. For the good that I wish, I do not do; but I practice the very evil that I do not wish. But if I am doing the very thing I do not wish, I am no longer the one doing it, but sin which dwells in me.

I find then the principle that evil is present in me, the one who wishes to do good. For I joyfully concur with the law of God in the inner man, but I see a different law in the members of my body, waging war against the law of my mind, and making me a prisoner of the law of sin which is in my members. Wretched man that I am! Who will set me free from the body of this death?
(Romans 7:15-24)

What a comprehensive picture of the mind torn between the spirit and the flesh! In verse 22 Paul says he "joyfully concurs with the law of God in the inner man." The inner man—the heart, the spirit—refers to the new-born nature of Paul as he was made alive in Christ. His spirit joyfully concurs with God and His ways. But the flesh accustomed to having the dominant position for so many years, does not yield readily. So the mind appeared to Paul to be a virtual prisoner between the ways of God and the simple desires of the flesh. From this vantage point Paul cries out: "I am torn, doing the very things I do not wish to do, and not doing the things that I would choose to do. Part of me agrees with the Word of God and confesses that certainly that Word is true; another part of me is still in open rebellion."

Paul continues sketching the great spiritual struggle between life and death in the next chapter:

For those who are according to the flesh set their minds

*on the things of the flesh, but those who are according
to the Spirit, the things of the Spirit. For the mind set
on the flesh is death, but the mind set on the Spirit is
life and peace, because the mind set on the flesh is
hostile toward God; for it does not subject itself to the
law of God; for it is not even able to do so; and those who
are in the flesh cannot please God.* (Romans 8:5-8)

So powerful is that passage that we will return to it again and
again. The first observation to be made here is the frightening
possibility that though our spirits may be truly made alive, our
minds may still be set on the things of the flesh. Remember that
those to whom Paul wrote were all believers, yet some had their
minds set on the flesh and some on the Spirit. Note that the mind set
on the flesh is death. The mind set on the flesh is hostile toward God,
for it does not subject itself to the Word of God, for from that vantage
point it is not even able to do so. Later in this book we will discover
the keys that unlock the mind from this awful prison. But for now
underscore this: The mind set on the flesh, hostile toward God, is
the truest picture of the carnal mind.

Earlier in this chapter we examined 1 Corinthians 3:1-3. There
Paul decries immaturity, calling them carnal, worldly, fleshly, characterized by jealousy and strife. But observe that the central mark
of immaturity is the rejection of the meat of the Word of God. And
that very carnality of mind, that rejection of the Word, is the downfall
of the carnally minded Christian.

Paul pursues this thought in 2 Corinthians:

*I wish that you would bear with me in a little foolish-
ness; but indeed you are bearing with me. For I am
jealous for you with a godly jealousy; for I betrothed you
to one husband, that to Christ I might present you as
a pure virgin. But I am afraid, lest as the serpent
deceived Eve by his craftiness, your minds should be led
astray from the simplicity and purity of devotion to
Christ.* (2 Corinthians 11:1-3)

The betrothal of which Paul speaks indicates that they have come

x

93

to know Christ as Savior. Yet the unrenewed minds of these Corinthian Christians were highly vulnerable to the deceptions of the enemy. The danger is always the same: being "led astray from the simplicity and purity of devotion to Christ." The accompanying danger is that we will be susceptible to every false doctrine that comes along.

Paul writes to the Colossians in a very similar passage:

> *Let no one keep defrauding you of your prize by delighting in self-abasement and the worship of the angels, taking his stand on visions he has seen, inflated without cause by his fleshly mind, and not holding fast to the head, from whom the entire body, being supplied and held together by the joints and ligaments, grows with a growth which is from God.* (Colossians 2:18-19)

The soulish, fleshly mind, always proud of its own accomplishments and experiences, is not careful to hold fast to Christ and so misses the source of truth and ignores the things of the Spirit and the Word.

Paul's first letter to Timothy sheds additional light on the plight of the carnal mind:

> *Guard what has been entrusted to you, avoiding worldly and empty chatter and the opposing arguments of what is falsely called "knowledge"—which some have professed and thus gone astray from the faith. Grace be with you.* (1 Timothy 6:20-21)

How many Christians are so impressed with the cleverness of their own arguments that they get caught up in arguing for the sake of the arguing. Empty chatter, opposing arguments, great knowledge, rational knowledge, sensory input, all lead further and further from the true faith in Christ Jesus.

Two passages in the book of James are among the finest insight into the plight of the carnal mind:

But if any of you lacks wisdom, let him ask of God, who gives to all men generously and without reproach, and it will be given to him. But let him ask in faith without any doubting, for the one who doubts is like the surf of the sea driven and tossed by the wind. For let not that man expect that he will receive anything from the Lord, being a double-minded man, unstable in all his ways. (James 1:5-8)

But He gives a greater grace. Therefore it says, "God is opposed to the proud, but gives grace to the humble." Submit therefore to God. Resist the devil and he will flee from you. Draw near to God and He will draw near to you. Cleanse your hands, you sinners; and purify your hearts, you double-minded. (James 4:6-8)

A double-minded man. What wild interpretations I have read of his passage! Actually, it is very simple.

James clearly identifies the double-minded man with the doubter. e further points out that the doubter is like one driven back and rth on the surface of the sea, tossed by every wind that comes long. What a perfect portrait of the mind caught in the trap between e reborn spirit and the fleshly, rational knowledge of many years f past experience. I know of few better definitions of doubt in the ntire Word of God.

Here is carnal man, double-minded in this sense: His reborn spirit egins to hear of the things of God and wishes to follow; on the other and, his natural mind has been programmed to receive the wisdom f this age through the five senses. Since he has depended on the pparent truthworthiness of rational knowledge for so many years, e urge to trust this sense knowledge seems almost irresistible.

One can readily imagine such reasonings—they have occurred in e minds of every one of us. Suppose I am confronted by a crisis— my health, my family, my finances, my circumstances. The quiet oice of my reborn spirit whispers: "God and His Word are trustwor- y. Rely on them." But my mind has been programmed to go to the orld for help on so many past occasions—the voice of just one atural mind around me cries louder than the voice of His Spirit

95

within. So I am storm-tossed, torn between the words of my spirit and the incessant cries of the rational knowledge around me.

In chapter 4, James gives us a portion of the answer to this plight. While we shall return here later on in the book, note the steps as he outlines them: We must humble ourselves before God, resist the devil, draw near unto God, cleanse our hands and purify our hearts before our double-mindedness will be dealt with.

What is the central plight of the carnal mind? It is forever waging war with unbelief. Doubt and double-mindedness are the central qualities of the carnal man. Untold years of experiences have programmed the mind of carnal man to trust almost implicitly the rational input of the five basic senses. At the same time his spirit has been made alive and the voice of the Holy Spirit speaks to his spirit, "Trust His Word." Again and again the soft whispers of his own spirit, hearing the voice of the Holy Spirit, offers new points of hope, "Come up higher into the ways of God. Trust Him and His Word." But the mind, still set on the flesh and the reality of a thousand past experiences, finds rational knowledge so much more trustworthy than the unknown biddings of the spirit.

So the carnal mind remains immature, always rejecting things of the Word. By definition, carnal man is vulnerable, easily led astray by every worldly argument. His emotions and desires are ever so fleshly. His mind is set on the flesh, and consequently on death.

In a word, carnal man has decided to follow Christ, but his eternal battle is the war he wages with unbelief.

The Tragic Dualism of Most Christians

Having taught this series on numerous occasions in the past, it is about this point that the early feedback begins: "Would you stop picking on me? You are revealing the innermost struggles of my heart! Every illustration could be drawn from my own life!"

Please let me reassure you: All newborn Christians begin right here. Every one of us comes to the Lord with a natural mind; this immediately becomes a carnal mind when our spirits are made alive in Jesus Christ. The tragedy is this: No Christian goes on to a Renewed Mind without much deep, careful searching of the Word or sound sustained teaching of the Word. Putting it differently, I am absolutely convinced that none of us can ever achieve the Renewed Mind on an accidental basis.

At this point let's return to some ground that we traversed much earlier. Most Christians are caught in a tragic dualism that is almost beyond their understanding. Being reborn Christians, the natural mind has suddenly become the carnal mind. All of this would not be so bad if it were only last week that we came to know Christ as Savior; however, if months have stretched into years and our thinking is basically unchanged then there is no task before us of greater importance than to pursue a Renewed Mind.

Chart 7 (on page 115) graphically depicts that at the point at which a man is redeemed the line for his reborn spirit goes straight up. He is either dead or he is alive. But the line portraying that of the mind is always a gradual line, a step-by-step learning of God's ways and moving toward a Renewed Mind. Unfortunately for some Christians—carnal believers—this line remains nearly horizontal near the bottom of the chart.

Back to the dualism of the carnal man. His spirit has been reborn and is alive, and he has before him the full potential of created man: the capacity for knowing and fellowshipping with the almighty God, his Creator; the capability of hearing the voice of his heavenly Father on a regular basis and receiving revelation knowledge as the normal order of the day. The problem is simply this: his mind is unrenewed. Years and years of programming the mind with rational knowledge obtained through the senses have created such a dependency on the wisdom of this age that until he makes a conscious decision to begin to walk by faith in the Word of God, there is little hope that carnal man will achieve his God-given potential.

As carnal man is in prayer before God, he hears the wooing of the Holy Spirit speaking to him. Thrilled by that, he begins to reach out for revelation results, but tragically he seeks them by rational means. Let me say it again with such emphasis that it reverberates through your whole being: The problem of carnal man is that he hears the voice of the Spirit and seeks revelation results, but he goes after them by rational means.

Why should we be surprised to discover that all across this land millions of professed Christians gather together on Sunday to worship the Lord, sing the great hymns of the church, worship Him with the great Scripture choruses and thrill to the things of the Spirit, only to go forth on Monday and handle every perplexity of life through the old tools of rational knowledge? The teacher is still dependent upon his old humanistic wisdom and the businessman is dependent on his own cleverness and skills—all with virtually no understanding of the impact a Renewed Mind could make on the daily walk of the Christian.

The walk by faith is the walk by the Word of God. Trust, by very definition, is dependent upon the integrity of our heavenly Father and the dependability of His promises. And yet, even for the average Christian, the normal course of events are fully predictable.

For example, a child is discovered to be mortally ill. The local doctor is approached and he refers the family to a specialist who sends them off to the best hospital in the land. Every known remedy is exhausted. Finally it is determined that there is absolutely no hope left for the child. Then comes the urgent request: "Quick! Come pray for my child." Only after we have exhausted the resources of the world, we turn to the Lord with our plight. I would not disparage the wonderful skills of the physicians and their staff, but let us ask ourselves one simple question: Why do we not turn to God first, seeking His wisdom, His will and His healing power? Because we can see doctors, hear doctors and have been taught to put our trust in them, it is just in the natural course of events that we live our lives dependent on the rational knowledge of doctors.

If all of this seems to be an overemphasis, let me ask you to perform a very simple piece of research. Ask the next twenty Christians you meet this simple question: "Do you find it easier, safer, more trustworthy, to trust what you can see and hear and read around you than the voice of the Spirit within you?" We have had drilled into us so many times to always trust the reasonable, the sensible, that we find that placing full confidence in revealed knowledge stretches our faith to the very limits.

Let me illustrate. Satan's most basic trick is to get each of us to trust our own reason, our own strength, our own effort in every situation—over and above our faith in God. As an example, in most of the mainline denominational churches around the world today, salvation is presented as a matter of our own righteous living—our own good works. Likewise there are many Christians who are taught the need for living a holy, sanctified life, but the avenue presented is frequently one of self-effort and trying harder, ignoring the grace of God. Further, I have heard numerous pastors, who believe in the baptism of the Holy Spirit, present this as an event for which one must wait for months or years following salvation—until one's life is greatly cleaned up and improved, and one is "good enough" to merit the Spirit's presence. And I have heard sincere Christians speak in wistful tones hoping that someday they could come to the point that God's miraculous power would flow through their lives, producing healings, miracles and victorious living every day.

The Bible, however, does not so teach. The Word of God is consistent. Regarding salvation: "By grace you have been saved through faith;...it is the gift of God" (Ephesians 2:8). Regarding sanctification: "Christ Jesus...became to us wisdom from God, and righteousness and sanctification" (1 Corinthians 1:30). Regarding the baptism of the Holy Spirit: "How much more shall your heavenly Father give the Holy Spirit to those who ask Him?" (Luke 11:13). Regarding victorious living: "He who believes in Me, the works that I do shall he do also; and greater works than these shall he do; because I go to the Father." (John 14:12).

My point is simple: To the extent that the enemy of our souls can keep us focused on earning or deserving every gift we receive from God by our own efforts, just to that extent he will keep us focused upon the importance of our own rational knowing, upon our own reasoning, upon being "reasonable" in spiritual matters. All of that simply voids the life of faith, trust in God's promises, knowing by revealed knowledge and being led by His Spirit.

And so the battle within the mind of carnal man seems to be exacerbated with each new crisis. The voice of man's spirit, hearing the voice of the Holy Spirit, holds forth the wonderful possibilities of revelation results. Cast against this is the voice of the mind—the product of thirty, forty or fifty years' experience—offering rational solutions to the crisis. Walking by the senses, carnal man feels the pull of the flesh. Double-minded and vacillating, he is ever seeking revelation results by rational means.

The Problem Illustrated

My heart aches for newborn Christians. The fantastic possibilities of living by faith are dashed so soon. If a newborn believer does not get solid teaching very early on, he soon settles into a routine of the familiar and the comfortable, living by the rational knowledge of past experience. Soon a dozen Christian voices confirm his way of living, saying: "This is the Christian life."

Having been in education many years, I have often wondered how much more we could accomplish in the lives of the incoming freshmen if we could keep them from the cynicism of the upper classmen. And I feel the same way about newborn Christians— only one could keep them from the "mature" Christians and the cynicism born of living with rational knowledge. Sadly, on rare occasions when there does come a teacher who presents the biblical ways of living a transformed, victorious Christian life—who teaches that one can get revelation results by revelation means—these "mature" Christians cry: "No, no, we tried that once and it doesn't work."

There is a classic illustration of this dualism in Matthew 14:

> *But the boat was already many stadia away from the land, battered by the waves; for the wind was contrary. And in the fourth watch of the night He came to them, walking upon the sea. And when the disciples saw Him walking on the sea, they were frightened, saying, "It is a ghost!" And they cried out for fear. But immediately Jesus spoke to them, saying, "Take courage, it is I; do not be afraid." And Peter answered Him and said, "Lord, if it is You, command me to come to You on the water." And He said, "Come!" And Peter got out of the boat, and walked on the water and came toward Jesus. But seeing the wind, he became afraid, and beginning to sink, he cried out, saying, "Lord, save me!" And immediately Jesus stretched out His hand and took hold of him, and said to him, "O you of little faith, why did you doubt?" And when they got into the boat, the wind stopped. (Matthew 14:24-32)*

Nearly every commentator on this passage focuses on the fact that Peter failed and nearly drowned. Let me call you to a higher view. I would emphasize to you that Peter did walk on the water and he did move toward Jesus. The voice of the Master came to the disciples across the turbulent waters. Peter's faith reached out: "Lord, let me come to You." Jesus responded with a single word: "Come!" There is such a wealth of revealed truth in that single word. Rational knowledge, seeing the storm raging about the boat, would never have dreamed of venturing forth. But Jesus spoke to Peter the word of God's higher kingdom: "Come!" I believe that Peter heard the voice of God in his spirit and, with his eyes fixed on Jesus, he stepped over the edge of that boat and walked on the water to our Lord.

While not denying that he failed a few seconds later, fix your attention for a moment on Peter walking on the water. The impact of this account is straightforward: It is possible to hear the voice of God speaking to our spirits in revealed truth, to fix our gaze upon Him, to order our walk by revelation knowledge and to live in victory over the storm. Like Peter we may fail. However, whether we fail five percent of the time or ninety-five percent of the time does not take away from the central fact: We can walk above the storms at Jesus' command. Once we have admitted that possibility to ourselves, then all that remains is for our spirits to improve the percentages by following revealed truth.

It is instructive for us to see why Peter failed in this instance. The answers are all here in the Word. First, he took his eyes off Jesus. Second, he saw the wind. Third, he became afraid. The result was inevitable—he began to sink. Jesus' response to Peter as He reaches out to pluck him out of the water was that term He used so often of the disciples: "O you little faith!"

It is essential that you grasp the significance of this passage. In his spirit, Peter heard the voice of Jesus speaking forth the eternal revealed truth of God: "Come!" The natural eyes of Peter were focused on the raging storm around him, but for one moment his mind paid no attention to what his senses were telling him. For one brief, glorious moment he fixed his full attention on the command of Jesus! You may choose to focus on the fact that Peter failed. I choose to focus on the eternal possibility: If I can keep my eyes fixed upon my Lord one hundred percent of the time, I can live the kingdom life one hundred percent of the time, following His revealed Word and revealed means. Hallelujah!

In Matthew 16 there is a similar but sadder story:

> *And the Pharisees and Sadducees came up, and testing Him asked Him to show them a sign from heaven. But He answered and said to them, "When it is evening, you say, It will be fair weather, for the sky is red.' and in the morning, `There will be a storm today, for the sky is red and threatening.' Do you know how to discern the appearance of the sky, but cannot discern the signs of the times? An evil and adulterous generation seeks after a sign; and a sign will not be given it, except the sign of Jonah." And He left them, and went away.* (Matthew 16:1-4)

The Jewish religious leaders had already made up their mind about Jesus. The eyes of their spirits were closed to all revealed truth about Him and from Him. They had no intention of accepting Him as their Messiah. And so they turned to Him for a sign in the realm of sense knowledge so that they might trick Him and trap Him. God will not honor the dependency upon sense knowledge of the rebellious heart. On the other hand, if the heart is tender and open, He will reveal Himself through His Word to our spirits, and with Peter we shall be able to walk above the storms.

On another occasion (Matthew 22:23-32), the Sadducees come to Him with the fabricated story of seven brothers who had all in turn been married to the same woman after the one before him had died. Their question was: Whose wife would she be when all seven got to heaven? Once again Jesus rejects a sense knowledge attempt to understand the kingdom of God. In verse 29 He says: "You are mistaken, not understanding the Scriptures, or the power of God." Sense knowledge fails in its attempt to comprehend the kingdom of God.

On still another occasion (Mark 6:49-52), after feeding the five thousand, Jesus comes walking to the disciples on the Galilee in the midst of a raging storm. As He gets into the boat with them the winds

102

stop and "they were greatly astonished." Mark's comment on this passage is that they were greatly astonished because "they had not gained any insight from the incident of the loaves, but rather their heart was hardened" (verse 52). In other words, they missed the fact that Jesus was in the business of the supernatural every moment of His life. When your mind is fixed on rational knowledge all the time, observing one miracle won't help you understand the next one. The carnal mind simply is not set on the Spirit—it is set on the flesh.

In Mark 7 we are told of the Pharisees' criticism of Jesus and His disciples for not following their ceremonial practice of washing before they ate. Jesus' response to them gives us an important understanding in relation to the carnal mind:

> *And the Pharisees and the scribes asked Him, "Why do Your disciples not walk according to the tradition of the elders, but eat their bread with impure hands?" And He said to them, "Rightly did Isaiah prophesy of you hypocrites, as it is written, `This people honors Me with their lips, but their heart is far away from Me. But in vain do they worship Me, teaching as doctrines the precepts of men.' Neglecting the commandment of God, you hold to the tradition of men." He was also saying to them, "You nicely set aside the commandment of God in order to keep your tradition." (Mark 7:5-9)*

Tradition is the accumulated wisdom of the sense knowledge of this age. Jesus' response to the Jewish leaders was essentially this: "Because your heart is closed and far from Me, you are not attuned to revelation knowledge. Therefore you readily accept the doctrine and precepts of men that are generated in the realm of rational knowledge. Neglecting the commandments of God, you replace them with the wisdom of this age."

Most Christians today would rise up in holy indignation if accused of substituting their own traditions for the Word of God. Yet is this really not the end result when we live by the knowing of our senses, rather than by the revealed Word of God?

Here is another illustration, again from the life of Peter. Frequently someone says to me, "I think I have made a start toward the Renewed Mind, only to find that I fall flat on my face again. Is there any hope for me?" Note the following passage:

> *Now when Jesus came into the district of Caesarea Philippi, He began asking His disciples, saying, "Who do people say that the Son of Man is?" And they said, "Some say John the Baptist; some, Elijah; and others, Jeremiah, or one of the prophets." He said to them, "But who do you say that I am?" And Simon Peter answered and said, "Thou art the Christ, the Son of the living God." And Jesus answered and said to him, "Blessed are you, Simon Barjona, because flesh and blood did not reveal this to you, but My Father who is in heaven."* (Matthew 16:13-17)

> *From that time Jesus Christ began to show His disciples that He must go to Jerusalem, and suffer many things from the elders and chief priests and scribes, and be killed, and be raised up on the third day. And Peter took Him aside and began to rebuke Him, saying, "God forbid it, Lord! This shall never happen to You." But He turned and said to Peter, "Get behind Me, Satan! You are a stumbling block to Me; for you are not setting your mind on God's interests, but man's."* (Matthew 16:21-23)

In this passage Jesus is querying the disciples about the conventional wisdom concerning Him in that day. As they offer varying answers, Jesus asks, "But who do you say that I am?" Peter responds, "Thou art the Christ, the Son of the living God." Jesus' evaluation was, "Flesh and blood did not reveal this to you, but My Father who is in heaven." You can get no clearer illustration of revelation knowledge than that. Jesus is saying to Peter: "You could not possibly know this of yourself, Peter, but My heavenly Father has revealed this to your spirit."

They had barely started the journey to Jerusalem, when Jesus explained to them that He was on His way to His own death and resurrection. Peter took Him aside and rebuked Him, "God forbid it, Lord!" Jesus answers, "Get behind Me, Satan!...you are not setting your mind on God's interests but man's." Now Jesus is explaining to Peter that he has abandoned revelation knowledge and has made his determination solely on the basis of rational, fleshly knowledge. Moreover, Peter has allowed Satan to speak through him. This passage is a classical textbook case illustrating both revealed knowledge and rational knowledge in the life of one individual in a matter of moments.

But I like this passage for one more reason: If Peter could ultimately rise above such a carnal mind and become the great spokesman for Christ that we see in Acts, perhaps there is still hope for each of us in the pursuit of the Renewed Mind.

Conclusion

We began this venture with a brief glimpse of Adam in the garden: created man in perfect fellowship with the Father, taught by Him, with virtually limitless dominion over God's creation. However, because of his rebellion against God in the garden, created man would soon become natural man, caught in the awful clutches of sin, terror and anger toward God. There man would have stayed had it not been for the gracious and merciful gift of our Father God at Calvary. Because Jesus came, the tragic results of the Fall have been reversed, and the potential of total restoration to created man is a real possibility.

In this chapter we have focused on the nature of the man who has turned to Calvary to accept the redemption for his soul that Jesus offers. On one level the outcome for such a man is glorious: his spirit is made alive, he has every hope of eternal life, and he is a new creation in Christ Jesus. He certainly has within him the seeds of all of the possibilities of the first created man—the possibility of close fellowship with the heavenly Father, of being taught through His spirit and of living in dominion over the world around him.

At the level of his mind, the picture of carnal man is far more dismal. While the mind now has access to man's spirit, and his spirit access to the Holy Spirit and the voice of the Father, the reality is that man's mind has been so programmed in its dependency on the rational knowledge of the flesh, that the warfare between the flesh and spirit is a raging inferno within his mind.

In actuality, reborn man with a carnal mind walks, talks, thinks and reacts very much as natural man. He is immature, fleshly, worldly. Though he could, he does not grasp spiritual truths. In fact, he is as vulnerable as natural man to the attacks of the enemy, and now he has become a special target of Satan for he has become a potential threat to the evil kingdom of this world.

And so we have the plight of the carnal mind: Carnal man is unstable, double-minded, torn between the whispering of his spirit and the Holy Spirit on the one hand and the accumulated wisdom of his past experiences on the other. Immature, he rejects the Word of God. He is easily led astray into worldly arguments; his emotions are fleshly, characterized by jealousy and strife. His mind is set on the flesh, which Paul tells us leads unto death. He is ruled by the wisdom of this age.

The tragic reality is that this dualistic tearing between things of the spirit and things of the flesh is so subtle that the average Christian is willing to settle down and live with it for the rest of his life. Simply unaware of the possibilities of his spirit soaring with almighty God, he is willing to live a day-by-day battle, groveling in the flesh with the circumstances about him. At this point, his reason and rational knowledge seem so much safer than that of revelation knowledge. Such a portrait of the hopelessness of carnal man— apart from the power of the Holy Spirit and a Renewed Mind—ought to drive every Christian running to his heavenly Father and to the Word of God, crying out, "Lord, teach me Thy ways."

* * * * * * * * * *

Once again, a word with you, my reader friend. If I could have engaged you in conversation before you ever picked up this book you probably would have poured out your heart to me of how you long to grow spiritually, how you long to know the will of God more perfectly, how you long to serve Him more completely, how you long to be led by the Spirit of God. And had I responded to you that all you desire is really a matter of your mind, you probably would have cried out, "Heresy! Heretic!"

There is always the possible danger of falling in with those Gnostic types who assume that what one knows will bring about his salvation. However, if you are alert to what we have been saying, you know that our present teaching is poles apart from Gnosticism. It is not a matter of knowing great secrets of mystery religions for which I am appealing, for that is rational knowledge carried to the nth degree. Rather, I simply want you to understand that the effectiveness of your Christian life, the possibility of your being a victorious member of God's end-time army, is more a matter of the orientation of your mind than you can imagine. If you have accepted Jesus Christ as your personal Savior, how I rejoice with you. My appeal to you is simply to bring yourself to the point where your spirit has its rightful place of authority in your entire being once again and your mind comes to reverence the things of the Spirit more than the things of the world around it, even as God first intended. If you will do this, the things of the flesh will simply fall into place in due time. My prayer is that you will continue with me on this venture and not grow weary in well-doing.

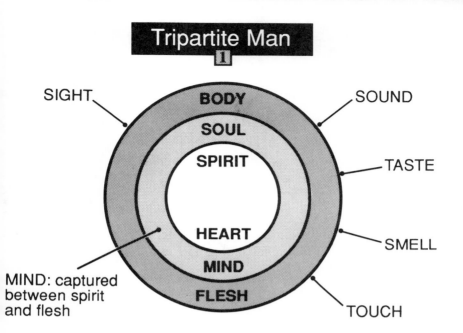

Tripartite Man
1

SIGHT

BODY

SOUL

SPIRIT

HEART

MIND

FLESH

SOUND

TASTE

SMELL

TOUCH

MIND: captured
between spirit
and flesh

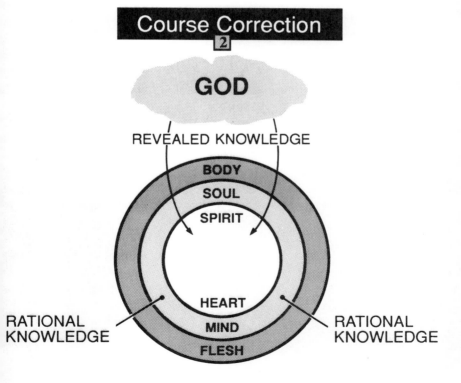

Course Correction
2

GOD

REVEALED KNOWLEDGE

BODY

SOUL

SPIRIT

HEART

MIND

FLESH

RATIONAL
KNOWLEDGE

RATIONAL
KNOWLEDGE

Knowledge: By Source
3

REVEALED	RATIONAL
Of the Spirit	Of the Flesh
From God	Open toSatanic Influences
Spiritual	Fleshly-Soulish
Glorifies God	Questions, Blames God
Accepted by Faith	Demands Rational Explanation
Agrees with Word	Frequently Contests Word

Source & Nature of Wisdom/Knowing
4

KNOWLEDGE	WISDOM
REVEALED	**ABOVE**
Truth Sets Free Through Word From God	Pure Peaceable Gentle Merciful Unwavering Without Hypocrisy
RATIONAL	**BELOW**
Deceptive Error Blinds Partial Truths From Devil	Earthly Natural Demonic

John 8:31-47   *James 3:13-17*

111

The Fall
5

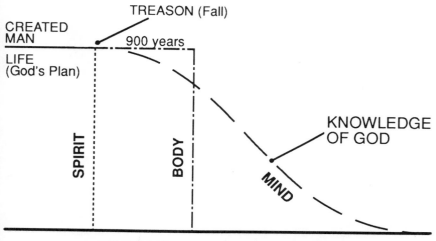

CREATED MAN

TREASON (Fall)

900 years

LIFE (God's Plan)

KNOWLEDGE OF GOD

SPIRIT

BODY

MIND

DEATH (Satan's Goal) *John 10:10*

Fallen Man
6

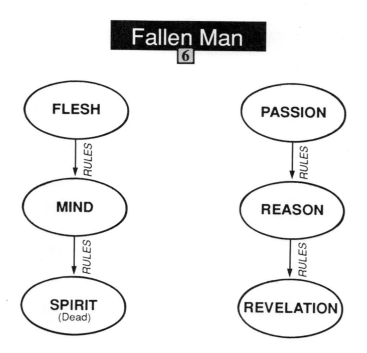

FLESH

RULES

MIND

RULES

SPIRIT
(Dead)

PASSION

RULES

REASON

RULES

REVELATION

113

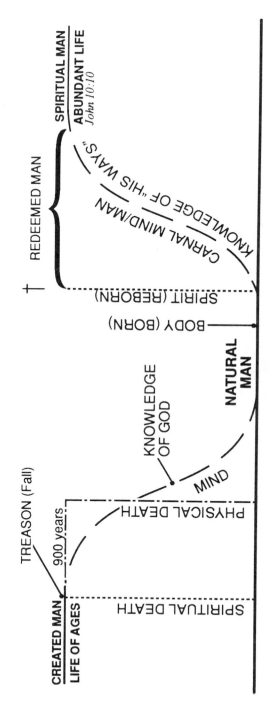

Redemption 7

CREATED MAN
LIFE OF AGES

TREASON (Fall)

900 years

SPIRITUAL DEATH

PHYSICAL DEATH

MIND

KNOWLEDGE OF GOD

NATURAL MAN

BODY (BORN)

SPIRIT (REBORN)

REDEEMED MAN

CARNAL MIND/MAN
KNOWLEDGE OF "HIS WAYS"

SPIRITUAL MAN
ABUNDANT LIFE
John 10:10

DEATH - ETERNAL DEATH - SATAN'S AGENDA *John 10:10*

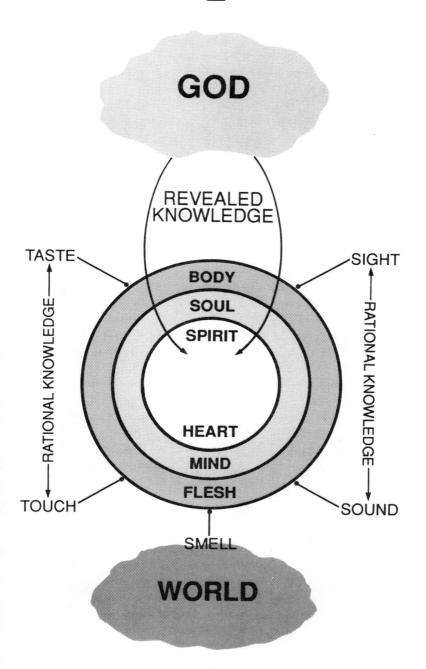

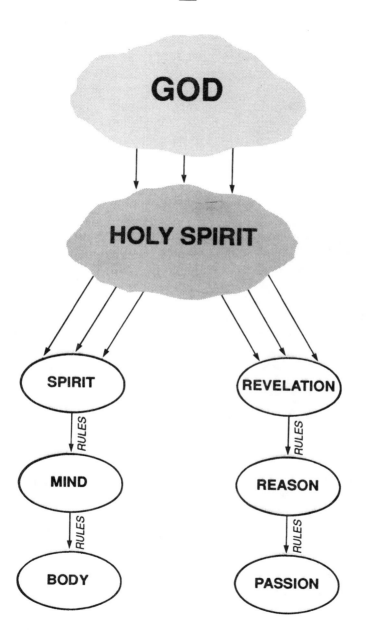

Eight Steps To A Renewed Mind

10

The Renewing Of The Mind

11

8.	Reality of the Miraculous
7.	Accept Revelation
6.	Feed on Word
5.	Filled with Holy Spirit
4.	Set Mind on Spirit (Determination)
3.	Humility of Mind
2.	Sacrifice Body
1.	Reborn Spirit

SEQUENCE CRUCIAL!

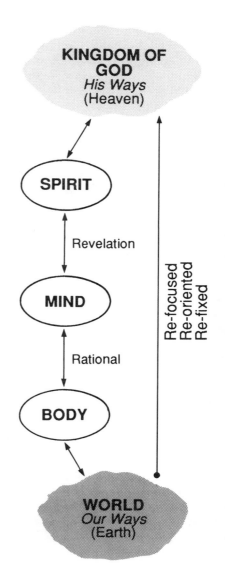

KINGDOM OF GOD
His Ways
(Heaven)

SPIRIT

Revelation

MIND

Rational

BODY

WORLD
Our Ways
(Earth)

Re-focused
Re-oriented
Re-fixed

121

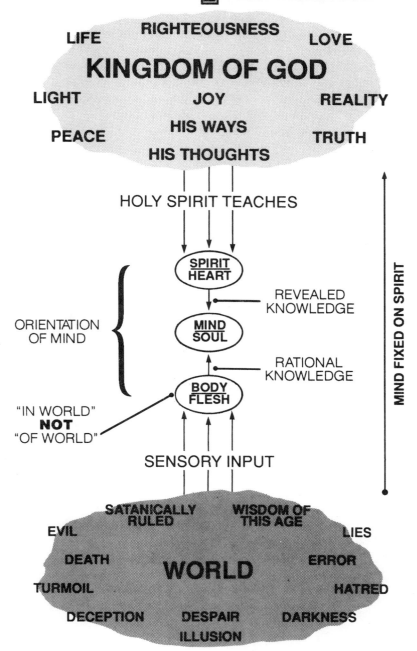

CHAPTER FOUR

THE EIGHT MARKS OF
THE RENEWED MIND

At this point we come to a major juncture in our study. All of our Scripture studies and discussions thus far have focused on the plight of man in the world today. Without exaggeration we can say that every trace of the evil we see about us is the direct result of man's loss of the knowledge of the glory of the Lord. The end result is that his mind has been totally captivated by the enemy of his soul. But if we have focused thus far on the perilous plight of the mind of man, what a joy to turn our attention to the profound possibilities ahead.

If at this point, my reader friend, you are a born-again Christian with an ongoing personal relationship with Jesus Christ, then the first two chapters which we have studied together are primarily academic. We sketched first for you created man, framed in the very image of his heavenly Father. His spirit was alive, in constant fellowship with the Father, and through his spirit he was the continuous recipient of revelation knowledge. His created mind was ruled by revealed knowledge. He was taught of God and Spirit-led, and the ways of God were his ways. I call this picture of man academic, for you and I share in the fallen nature of rebellious Adam and the possibility of knowing the Father as he did is beyond our fondest hopes in the natural. Yet we have sketched the picture of created man here because of the hope that is ours through Christ's redemption and restoration on Calvary.

Then there was natural man. Spiritually dead, he is totally alienated from the Father and has no hope of grasping the things of God. With no tools for understanding the principles of God's kingdom, the mind of natural man is eternally doomed to being captive to the rational world around him. Again I say to you that this picture is also academic. As a new creature in Christ Jesus, your spirit has been made alive, and the things of the kingdom of God and all eternity are potentially open before you.

No, it is the plight of the carnal mind that tears at our heart strings. There is nothing academic about this picture. Sad to say, this is the condition of millions of Christians. If I may trust my own limited experience, I would say that this is the condition of a significant majority of all believers.

Carnal man has been made alive in his spirit with all the possibilities of spiritual man. He longs to see the results of living in the kingdom of revealed knowledge, but he pursues those results through the tools of the rational mind. The most obvious thing about carnal man is that he seems always to be waging war with unbelief. While he dreams of victorious living with Jesus, in his mind he "knows" he cannot accomplish it. While natural man *cannot* grasp the things of God, the carnal mind *does not* perceive them, for his mind is the undiscerning victim of many years of rational programming. The end result is that no matter how much the spirit of the carnal man leads him to the things of God, he still walks, talks, thinks and acts like a natural man. As Paul would describe him, Carnal man is immature, fleshly, worldly and blinded to the deep truths of God's kingdom. Being double-minded and unstable, he is readily led astray by vain and worldly arguments. The wisdom of this age is appealing and the fleshly emotions of jealousy and strife lurk beneath the surface of his consciousness.

Most poignant of all: Carnal man is at least as vulnerable as natural man to the wisdom of this age, but he bears the additional problem of now being a direct target of Satan.

126

At this point you may feel yourself drowning in a sea of hopelessness, recognizing that the characteristics of the carnal mind describe your spiritual condition perfectly. Not to despair! If we are honest, every Christian will acknowledge he either has a carnal mind now or began his Christian walk with one.

Let me make three basic observations at this point. First, the older you were when you came to know Jesus Christ as Savior, the more of this world's rational programming you will have to unlearn before you can get on with the business of a Renewed Mind.

Second, the longer it has been since you were born again, the greater the likelihood that you have been steeped in tradition and "religious teaching," and thus you also will have a great deal of bad teaching to unlearn. And, having tried to walk in a victorious Christian life and failed, you may have many discouraging experiences to overcome.

Third, the more you have been steeped in the academic traditions of man and the more you are impressed with the cleverness of your own mind, the greater the degree of brokenness that will be required of you as you press on toward a genuinely Renewed Mind. From past experience I believe the person who can make the most rapid progress toward a Renewed Mind is the person who is relatively young, who has recently come to know Christ as Savior and who has a basic humility toward his Lord.

Once again, we stand at the major turning point in this study. Against this background portrait of man alienated from the knowledge of the glory of the Lord and from the knowing of His ways, we move on to the thrilling possibility before us of reclaiming the revealed knowledge of God which Adam lost. Leaving our pictures of the created mind, the natural mind and the carnal mind, we turn our attention to the picture of Paul's third man: the spiritual man. In fact, while this chapter is titled "Marks of the Renewed Mind," an equally acceptable title might well be "Characteristics of the Spiritual Man."

The Profound Possibility: A Renewed Mind

In Paul's masterful theology that we call the epistle to the Romans, he gives us a penetrating understanding of the mind that surpasses anything else in the Word of God or in other recorded literature. In Romans 1 Paul traces the downfall of rebellious man. As he rejects all knowledge of God from his thinking, God gives him over to a depraved or reprobate mind. Thus, the natural mind at its nadir. In Romans 7, Paul portrays for us so graphically the carnal mind's struggle between the law of God at work in the inner man and the pulling of the flesh. With this war raging within, Paul cries out "Who will set me free from the body of this death?" In chapter 8 Paul draws the further contrast of walking after the flesh or after the Spirit, concluding that the mind set on the flesh is death, but the mind set on the Spirit is life and peace. In Romans 12 Paul offers the believer this thrilling option of total transformation by the renewing of the mind.

Few passages in the Bible are as crucial to your Christian walk as the opening verses of Romans 12. I urge you to take a few minutes right now and read those opening verses over and over again. For your convenience I offer you Romans 12:1-3 in four different translations:

> *I beseech you therefore, brethren, by the mercies of God, that ye present your bodies a living sacrifice, holy, acceptable unto God, which is your reasonable service. And be not conformed to this world: but be ye transformed by the renewing of your mind, that ye may prove what is that good, and acceptable, and perfect, will of God. For I say, through the grace given unto me, to every man that is among you, not to think of himself more highly than he ought to think; but to think soberly, according as God hath dealt to every man the measure of faith.* (King James Version)

> *I urge you therefore, brethren, by the mercies of God, to present your bodies a living and holy sacrifice, acceptable to God, which is your spiritual service of worship. And do not be conformed to this world, but be transformed by the renewing of your mind, that you may prove what the will of God is, that which is good and acceptable and perfect. For through the grace given to*

128

me I say to every man among you not to think more highly of himself than he ought to think; but to think so as to have sound judgment, as God has allotted to each a measure of faith. (New American Standard Bible)

Therefore, I urge you, brothers, in view of God's mercy, to offer your bodies as living sacrifices, holy and pleasing to God—this is your spiritual act of worship. Do not conform any longer to the pattern of this world, but be transformed by the renewing of your mind. Then you will be able to test and approve what God's will is— his good, pleasing and perfect will. For by the grace given me I say to every one of you: Do not think of yourself more highly than you ought, but rather think of yourself with sober judgment, in accordance with the measure of faith God has given you. (New International Version)

With eyes wide open to the mercies of God, I beg you, my brothers, as an act of intelligent worship, to give Him your bodies, as a living sacrifice, consecrated to Him and acceptable by Him. Don't let the world around you squeeze you into its own mold, but let God re-mold your minds from within, so that you may prove in practice that the Plan of God for you is good, meets all His demands and moves toward the goal of true maturity. As your spiritual teacher I give this piece of advice to each one of you. Don't cherish exaggerated ideas of yourself or your importance, but try to have a sane estimate of your capabilities by the light of the faith that God has given to you all. (J.B. Phillips)

First, note with me that Paul is clearly addressing believers here, s in 11:25 and again in 12:1 he speaks to them as "brethren." I mphasize this for you particularly at this point for there is the false aching abroad that with the rebirth of one's spirit there comes the utomatic renewing of the mind. This is clearly not the case in Paul's ninking, for he writes to the brethren these powerful words.

129

Tucked away in this passage of Scripture like a jewel hidden in th
bedrock of the earth is this beautiful phrase: "the renewing of you
mind." If you have been totally honest with yourself about the awfu
anguish of your own carnal mind, then these words are mor
precious to your spirit than the buoy that is tossed to a drownin
man: "the renewing of your mind."

Recognize with me a very important fact. In all of the evangelica
church's teaching of the last several generations, the basic theolog
could be summed up with one phrase: "Ye must be born again
Praise God for this teaching, for had it not been, we would not eve
be here. However, there has been a strange lack of emphasis on th
deep truths of the Word of God. Untold numbers of shepherds wh
were not taught have left sheep untaught as well. Like babe
exposed to the elements, many simply died as spiritual newborn
We wondered why vast numbers of other newborn Christian
stagnated in their Christian life and made no visible progress towar
maturity. No matter how many promises of God are in the Wor
spiritual lethargy, if not defeat, was the order of the day.

Thrilling enough, even without sound teaching, here and ther
an occasional humble-minded new Christian closeted himself awa
with the Word of God and simply accepted the truths he found ther
Unfortunately, as he began to live in true spiritual victory, he wa
systematically shunned by his spiritual brothers and sisters. Som
explained that this individual had spent more time in prayer, wa
more deeply consecrated, etc. The comedy team of the Smothe
Brothers had the ongoing argument "Mom always liked you bes"
and there were Christians who suggested that perhaps God di
have favorites and thus this brother was so blessed! I remember
class of young people I taught in a Spirit-filled church. As they bega
to get hold of the truths of God and move toward a Renewed Min
they saw many miracles in their lives. One dear saint stopped me o
a Sunday evening to complain: "It's not fair. I have been serving th
Lord for over forty years and I have never seen one miracle in m
life."

Out of this heartfelt complaint comes the central point I want
make with you here: The profound possibility of a Renewed Min
for the believer is just that—a possibility. You will never come to t
position of Paul's spiritual man with a truly Renewed Mind accide

lly. There is an enormous price to pay: the sacrifice of the flesh, the sacrifice of our own willfulness and—perhaps most critical of all— the sacrifice of our own cherished ego. Let me say it again—you will never wake up one morning to discover, "Ah-ha! I suddenly have a Renewed Mind."

Let me offer you one more crucial insight. The single greatest deterrent to your coming to a Renewed Mind will be the day-by-day peer pressure of those around you. As Paul opens verse two: "Do not be conformed to this world (this age)." As J.B. Phillips puts it: "Don't let the world around you squeeze you into its own mold." In other words: Don't continue to think as the world thinks and don't accept the world's unquestioned assumptions. Yet the fact is that you and I have been so imbued with this world's assumptions, many of which we have picked up almost by osmosis, that the very best intentioned of us find that our ways fall far short of God's ways.

At the risk of alienating you midway through this book, let me say firmly: If you cannot come to grips with what others think of you and what you believe and rise above this to the truths of God, you are not likely to go far down the road to a Renewed Mind.

I believe one of the greatest stumbling blocks on the road to Christian maturity today is a man-fearing spirit. I find it highly significant that just before Paul said, "Be ye transformed by the renewing of your mind," he had said, "Do not be conformed to this age." As the Holy Spirit speaks to your heart as you read this book, may He impress upon you the urgency of realizing that many people will think you have taken leave of your senses as you move toward the mind of Christ.

But whatever the hurdles, whatever the enormous cost to us, whatever hindrances Satan would put in our paths, whatever the peer pressure against us, there is before us the glorious possibility of a Renewed Mind. We have the potential for having a mind that is in fellowship with the Father, a mind that can hear His voice, a mind that can transform our entire lives!

The central question of this chapter is very simple: How do you recognize the essential characteristics of a Renewed Mind?

The First Mark of the Renewed Mind: Knowing the Will of God

In Romans 12:2 Paul emphasizes: "Do not be conformed to thi world, but be transformed by the renewing of your mind, that yo may prove what the will of God is," and there in simple English yo have the apostle Paul's understanding of the central outcome of th Renewed Mind. Anything short of a truly Renewed Mind will neve discern the absolute will of God.

Everywhere I speak today people are crying out, "How can I kno God's will for my life?" Usually there is the further question: "Ho can I know if it is the voice of God, the voice of Satan or the voice (my own fleshly desires?" What a tremendous lot of nonsense is bein offered to Christian people these days on the subject of knowing th will of God. Much, if not most, of it deals in the realm of "sens knowledge" rather than revealed knowledge from God. Just a Gideon spread fleeces out on the stone threshing floor, people ar advised to watch how God opens and closes doors around them. L me not demean the fact that God does open and close doors, bu these matters are still in the realm of sense knowledge and leave u open to great deceit from the enemy.

By now the simple truth must have leaped out at you: No matte how many times we consecrate ourselves at the altar, no matter ho many times we plead before our heavenly Father for guidanc *knowing the will of God is the result of a Renewed Mind.* Harsl Perhaps, but God's Word allows no other interpretation.

I would emphasize again and again in this study that while w come to know Jesus Christ as our Savior in an instant and are mad alive in Him in that moment, the process of the Renewed Mind is gradual one as we unlearn the old sense knowledge, rational know edge, and learn to know His voice and hear revealed knowledge fro Him. This is beautifully borne out in the closing words of verse "That you may prove what the will of God is, that which is good an acceptable and perfect." When a child speaks his first babblin words, we are thrilled. But those words pale in comparison to th complicated truths he later grasps as a young man. Just so, our fir halting understanding of the ways of God must thrill the Father eart, and He calls it good. But as we move toward a Renewed Mind nd become saturated in the Word, there remains before us an nderstanding of His will that is first acceptable and finally perfect.

Follow with me now to what I believe is the next obvious truth. 'he most obvious outcome of having a Renewed Mind is the ability) discern the will of God. Since the will of God is revealed in His Vord, then even any deep understanding of the Word of God equires a Renewed Mind.

What I am suggesting is that concomitant with the developing Re-ewed Mind is our beginning to walk in the light of His Word. This ; always in contradistinction to the cleverness of our own will and ninking, as the apostle Paul points out in the following two pas-ages:

> *For Christ did not send me to baptize, but to preach the gospel, not in cleverness of speech, that the cross of Christ should not be made void. For the word of the cross is to those who are perishing foolishness, but to us who are being saved it is the power of God. For it is written, "I will destroy the wisdom of the wise, and the cleverness of the clever I will set aside." Where is the wise man? Where is the scribe? Where is the debater of this age? Has not God made foolish the wisdom of the world?* (1 Corinthians 1:17-20)

> *And when I came to you, brethren, I did not come with superiority of speech or of wisdom, proclaiming to you the testimony of God. For I determined to know nothing among you except Jesus Christ, and Him crucified. And I was with you in weakness and in fear and in much trembling. And my message and my preaching were not in persuasive words of wisdom, but in demonstration of the Spirit and of power, that your faith should not rest on the wisdom of men, but on the power of God. Yet we do speak wisdom among those who are mature; a wisdom, however, not of this age, nor of the rulers of this age, who are passing away; but we speak God's wisdom in a mystery, the hidden wisdom, which*

God predestined before the ages to our glory; the wisdom which none of the rulers of this age has understood; for if they had understood it, they would not have crucified the Lord of glory. (1 Corinthians 2:1-8)

The mystery of Calvary comes to us only as revealed knowledge and this is obviously foolishness to those who are perishing, which Paul means the natural man. But the first step of the Renewed Mind is to discern the will of God and to walk in the light of the Word as it is presented. Further, note that the wisdom which Paul presents is not the wisdom of this age nor of the rulers of this age, for such rational knowledge is passing away. But Paul's wisdom is from above, God-given, revealed. To recapitulate, the first product of the Renewed Mind according to Romans 12:2 is the discerning of the will of God. And this leads the newborn Christian into a walk in the light of His Word where he will find the central truth revealed to him. The salvation which he has now experienced is God's gift to him through Jesus Christ and His death on the cross. There will be other and more profound truths to know, but to begin to grasp the unveiling of His will must be the exciting first characteristic of the Renewed Mind.

Let me illustrate from the words of Christ:

Jesus therefore answered and was saying to them, "Truly, truly, I say to you, the Son can do nothing of Himself, unless it is something He sees the Father doing; for whatever the Father does, these things the Son also does in like manner. For the Father loves the Son, and shows Him all things that He Himself is doing; and greater works than these will He show Him, that you may marvel. (John 5:19-20)

Jesus therefore said, "When you lift up the Son of Man, then you will know that I am He, and I do nothing on My own initiative, but I speak these things as the Father taught Me. And He who sent Me is with Me; He has not left Me alone, for I always do the things that are

134

pleasing to Him." (John 8:28-29)

Note if you will how closely Jesus identified with the words of Paul to the Romans. Let me paraphrase: "I do nothing of myself; I do only the things that I see my heavenly Father doing. I do nothing on my own initiative, but I speak the things that my Father taught Me. I always do the things that are pleasing to Him." To make such a statement, Jesus had to know the mind of the Father intimately. Paul would return to his theme of knowing the will of the Father again and again:

> *So then do not be foolish, but understand what the will of the Lord is.* (Ephesians 5:17)

> *For this reason also, since the day we heard of it, we have not ceased to pray for you and to ask that you may be filled with the knowledge of His will in all spiritual wisdom and understanding.* (Colossians 1:9)

> *Now flee from youthful lusts, and pursue righteousness, faith, love and peace, with those who call on the Lord from a pure heart. But refuse foolish and ignorant speculations, knowing that they produce quarrels. And the Lord's bond-servant must not be quarrelsome, but be kind to all, able to teach, patient when wronged, with gentleness correcting those who are in opposition, if perhaps God may grant them repentance leading to the knowledge of the truth, and they may come to their senses and escape from the snare to the devil, having been held captive by him to do his will.* (2 Timothy 2:22-26)

For the Colossians, Paul prayed that they would be filled up with the knowledge of His will, and for the Ephesians, a simple admonition to understand what the will of the Lord is. To Timothy he speaks of repentance which leads to the knowledge of the truth.

In brief, the first quality of the spiritual man is that he knows the will of his heavenly Father. As Paul put it: "Be transformed by the

135

renewing of your mind, that you may prove what the will of God is." Paul's word "prove" means literally to put it to the test or to discern. And there you have it. Spiritual man discerns the will of his heavenly Father.

The Second Mark of the Renewed Mind: Being Led by His Spirit

In Romans 8 Paul writes:

> *So then, brethren, we are under obligation, not to the flesh, to live according to the flesh—for if you are living according to the flesh, you must die; but if by the Spirit you are putting to death the deeds of the body, you will live. For all who are being led by the Spirit of God, these are sons of God.* (Romans 8:12-14)

Once again Paul is drawing a very clear contrast as he did in verse 6 of the mind set on the flesh, which is death, or the mind set on the Spirit, which is life. Only in this instance he extends his reasoning. If you are living according to the Spirit, putting to death the deeds of the flesh, then you are led by the Spirit of God and are a son of God. I find this a particularly precious promise for two reasons. Not only does the voice of His Spirit speaking in my heart confirm my sonship to me regularly, but, conversely, if I am truly a son of God, having been born through the blood of Jesus Christ, then I have every right to expect to be led by His Spirit. But most importantly, from the perspective of this study, the second quality of the spiritual man is that he is led by the Spirit of God.

I see the eight qualities we are outlining in this chapter as progressive. For example, I believe it is fully possible to hear the voice of the Spirit revealing the will of the Father without yielding to the leading of His Spirit and following His directives. So while the Renewed Mind may begin by discerning the will of the Father, it is yet another step to the yieldedness resulting in the leading of the Holy Spirit.

In the Good Shepherd passage recorded in John 10, Jesus leads us to a similar understanding. Here Jesus says: "My sheep know Me and hear My voice" (see John 10:14,27). He also states: "The voice

136

of a stranger they will not know, but they will know My voice and follow me" (see John 10:4-5).

There is nothing here that should surprise us. The first and most obvious characteristic of created man was the fact that the very Father God, the Creator of the universe, chose to come down and spend His evenings walking with Adam in the beauty of the garden. Only because of man's awful rebelliousness and sin was this precious fellowship broken. Once again, through Calvary man's spirit is made alive in Christ and the potential for divine fellowship is restored.

Now we can readily understand Paul's comments that a key characteristic of being a son of God is to be led by the Spirit of God. Likewise, Jesus said that His sheep would hear and know His voice. However, there is a problem with all this. The heavenly Father may speak, His Spirit to our spirit, and our mind may hear the voice of our spirit speaking; but many years of trusting only the input from the rational mind through the senses has taught the mind to be highly suspicious of any other voice. This reschooling of the ear of the mind is one of the central tasks of moving into a Renewed Mind. How precious to know that one of the nine gifts of the Holy Spirit outlined in 1 Corinthians 12 is the gift of discernment—His gift of divine protection for His children.

Let me offer a strong word of caution at this point. Nearly everywhere I go today I am confronted with one particular question: "Do you have a word from the Lord for me?" Christian people are absolutely starved to hear a word from the Lord, but unfortunately no one is teaching them that they can hear the voice of His Spirit for themselves. Further, to hear the voice of God there is an enormous price to be paid in terms of time spent and the humbling of one's spirit before the Father.

It is my observation that Christian people are simply not willing to pay the price to hear the voice of the Lord today, and so they are exceedingly vulnerable. Not surprisingly, hireling shepherds are quick to step into this void. Again and again I hear accounts of mass prophecy sessions and professed words from the Lord which are at best self-serving to the prophet. Hear me clearly—there is a beautiful place for the confirming prophetic word of the Lord. Once you have been before the Lord and know His voice and know what He

is saying to you, He has confirmed it to you through His Word and
His leading is clear, then the soft word of confirmation coming
through a dear Christian brother or sister can be pleasant indeed.
My deep concern, however, is for the vast numbers of Christian
people who at best are led astray by the good intentions of self
appointed prophets, and at worst flagrantly deceived by false shep
herds. My Christian friends, there is but one answer to this problem
and that is to learn to know the voice of the Lord for yourself.

Briefly, I am aware that these first two characteristics of the Re
newed Mind are parallel, very closely related. However, I am fully
convinced that they are distinct, mandatory, and they form the foun
dation for a Renewed Mind. The ability to discern the will of the
Father and the ability to know His voice and obey His Holy Spirit—
these are the cornerstones of a spiritually rebuilt house.

The Third Mark of the Renewed Mind: Focusing on the Things of the Spirit

If I may take you back for a moment to chapter one and our
glimpse of created man, we saw there that one of the primary
qualities of the mind of created man was that it was oriented to
spiritual things. In other words, the mind of Adam was more clearly
focused on the things of his spirit and God's Spirit than on things
about him.

I have cited repeatedly the opening verses of Romans 8, but let's
return there now for a more in-depth view of this crucial passage.

> *There is therefore now no condemnation for those who
> are in Christ Jesus. For the law of the Spirit of life in
> Christ Jesus has set you free from the law of sin and of
> death. For what the Law could not do, weak as it was
> through the flesh, God did: sending His own Son in the
> likeness of sinful flesh and as an offering for sin, He
> condemned sin in the flesh, in order that the require-
> ment of the Law might be fulfilled in us, who do not
> walk according to the flesh, but according to the Spirit.
> For those who are according to the flesh set their minds
> on the things of the flesh, but those who are according*

138

to the Spirit, the things of the Spirit. For the mind set on the flesh is death, but the mind set on the Spirit is life and peace, because the mind set on the flesh is hostile toward God; for it does not subject itself to the law of God, for it is not even able to do so. (Romans 8:1-7)

It should be apparent by now that the set of the mind, the direction in which it is focused, is going to determine your nature as an individual. As we go along we will observe that the set of the mind, like the set of the sail on a ship, determines the course you will take—what you believe, what choices you make and how you make them, your behavior and your entire life.

Now look again at the opening verses of Romans 8 and keep your focus on the place of the mind verse by verse. In the first three verses, one profound truth leaps out: Until Christ came, the soul and mind of man was bound by the law of sin and death in his very being. But Christ came, and the Spirit of life in Christ Jesus has loosed the mind from the law of sin and death. The law could never have accomplished this, but Christ through His atoning death condemns sin in the flesh.

Now this point is exceedingly important and you must grasp it if you are to go on to a Renewed Mind. In teaching this series I frequently hear someone say, "I do want to go on to a Renewed Mind, but the power of the flesh is so strong." That is Satan talking to you, for the Word clearly states that Jesus condemned sin in the flesh and broke its hold over your mind. Now verse 4 tells us that the requirements of the law upon our lives can be fulfilled not by the external effort of the flesh, but by the transformation of the heart.

The next three verses may be the most important you have ever read in the Word of God. Their impact on your Christian life is potentially so powerful that I cannot overstate it. We have already seen that through Calvary your mind has been set free from the chains of sin that bound it to the flesh. But God in His infinite wisdom still gives us the freedom of choice. It is precisely at this point that you will determine the nature and maturity of your spiritual life. If you choose to set your mind on the flesh (even when it has been set free), only spiritual death is before you. But if you choose to set your mind on spiritual things—the things of your spirit and the things of the Holy Spirit—life and peace are your destiny.

A mind set on the *Spirit* is of necessity a mind set on the *spirit*, for it is through the reborn human spirit that the Holy Spirit reveals the things of God. And though your spirit has been made alive in Christ, the very act of setting your mind on your flesh is hostility toward God, since the mind set on the flesh is not subject to the things of God and cannot subject itself to the things of God.

Paul wrote to the Colossians in an equally beautiful and powerful passage:

> *If then you have been raised up with Christ, keep seeking the things above, where Christ is, seated at the right hand of God. Set your mind on the things above, not on the things that are on earth. For you have died and your life is hidden with Christ in God. When Christ, who is our life, is revealed, then you also will be revealed with Him in glory. Therefore consider the members of your earthly body as dead to immorality, impurity, passion, evil desire, and greed, which amounts to idolatry. For it is on account of these things that the wrath of God will come, and in them you also once walked, when you were living in them. But now you also, put them all aside: anger, wrath, malice, slander, and abusive speech from your mouth. Do not lie to one another, since you laid aside the old self with its evil practices, and have put on the new self who is being renewed to a true knowledge according to the image of the One who created him, —a renewal in which there is no distinction between Greek and Jew, circumcised and uncircumcised, barbarian, Scythian, slave and freeman, but Christ is all, and in all.*
> (Colossians 3:1-11)

Here Paul continues his emphasis on choice as he began it in the book of Romans. If you have been made alive with Christ, then it is your responsibility to continually keep seeking the things that are above. The things that are above are the things of the Spirit, for

God's kingdom is a spiritual kingdom. Note that powerful verse 2: "Set your mind [be intent on] the things above, not on the things that are on earth."

Then Paul goes on—the same point as in Romans: When we accepted Christ we died unto self and our life is now hidden with Him. Because of His death, the hold of sin in our flesh is broken. Therefore, the members of our earthly body are dead to immorality, impurity, passion, evil desire, greed, etc. Yet there is still a higher way: Anger, wrath, malice and slander are to be put away; all lying is to be done away with.

Verse 10 is the goal of this entire book. Once you have put on the new man (self), you are from that point on being renewed to true knowledge according to the very image of your Creator.

Now here is the very heart of this third characteristic of the Renewed Mind: The mind, which for so very long has been set on things of the flesh, is now set on the spirit. In other words, the mind is reoriented.

Chart 9 (on page 119) illustrates the nature of spiritual man. Let me remind you from earlier chapters: God meant for man's spirit to rule his mind and together the spirit and mind should rule his body. However, in man's rebellious condition following the Fall, that order was soon completely reversed. When the demands of the flesh fully rule the entire being, we have a simple picture of a *barbaric* man. When the mind of man gains some semblance of authority, we might easily have what is called *civilized* man. Now, when the mind of man is set on spiritual things then, in our idealized model, the Spirit-controlled spirit of man rules the mind of man and these together rule the body. Likewise, we have just seen in the Colossian passage that the passions of man are brought back to proper position, with reason ruling them, but both ruled by revelation knowledge from God.

When this third characteristic of the Renewed Mind has been firmly accomplished and the mind of man is truly set on the spirit, then there are three observations I would like to make for you. First, his "knowing" is immediately changed. The knowing which came from the sense knowledge is still there, but there is at once a higher "knowing" from the things of the Spirit. I hasten to point out that this is an idealized model and that this sudden switch of attention from fleshly things to spiritual things is highly unlikely. Actually, you will find yourself choosing over and over again to refix your mind on spiritual things. But in order to understand it, let me say again that the "knowing" of the mind is changed and reoriented.

A second observation: Man has a new definition of reality. In the old definition, he said something like this: "I know I have prayed and I believe the promises of God, but in reality my tummy still hurts." In the new reality, man so lives in the things of God and in fellowship with his heavenly Father that the things of God's kingdom form a reality far more obvious to the perception of his mind than the things about him.

And this brings us to the third point: Under the new reality faith begins to grow. And let me say it clearly: This is the only way that faith can grow! If ultimate reality to your mind consists of the things of the senses, then faith never has a chance to be born within you.

I know a multitude of Christians who talk faith, preach faith and would avow on a stack of Bibles that they are strong people of faith; yet they really have no shred of understanding of it. The reason is simple: Reality for them is not the kingdom of God, but the world around them. I know of one man who talks about small-faith people and big-faith people. What he really wants to say is, there are some people who talk a lot about faith, but in fact produce almost no fruit. But if you will understand faith as growing in the hothouse of spiritual reality, then you will begin to understand what I am talking about. As spiritual things—the things of your spirit and God's Spirit—begin to frame the reality for your mind, then your faith will automatically begin to grow.

Let me point you once again to Paul's crucial words to the Corinthians:

> *Now we have received, not the spirit of the world, but the Spirit who is from God, that we might know the things freely given to us by God, which things we also speak, not in words taught by human wisdom, but in those taught by the Spirit, combining spiritual thoughts with spiritual words. But a natural man does not accept the things of the Spirit of God; for they are foolishness to him, and he cannot understand them,*

because they are spiritually appraised. But he who is spiritual appraises all things, yet he himself is appraised by no man. (1 Corinthians 2:12-15)

Follow closely. We have not received the spirit of this world, but the Holy Spirit from God so that we might know the things which are freely given to us of God. Now the reason the natural man cannot accept the things of the Spirit of God is that his mind is still chained to the things of the flesh. But, as Paul has pointed out to us, the mind is now free from the things of the flesh in Christ Jesus. Therefore, the mind set on the Spirit can begin to grasp the things of the kingdom of God, for these things revealed by the Spirit begin to form the new reality for the mind.

Jesus taught us that a man's words reveal what is in his heart. Therefore, one way to measure this third mark of the Renewed Mind (the mind set on the things of the Spirit) is to listen to a man's words. Is his mind fixed on the things of this world or on the things of the kingdom of God? I have a good friend that claims the best way to judge the spiritual condition of any church is to attend one of their carry-in suppers and listen for a couple of hours to the conversation of the people there. I have thought much about this and have concluded that he is exactly right. I have attended such suppers where the conversation focused on farm equipment, soybean production, the real estate market, the best of current investments or even the fortunes of professional athletes. But I have attended other such functions, albeit much more rarely, where conversations focused on answered prayers, miracles in people's lives, the goodness of the Lord, and just sheer praise and adoration of God.

The Fourth Mark of the Renewed Mind: Fellowshipping With the Reborn Spirit

Come back with me one more time to the words of Romans 8:

The mind set on the flesh is death, but the mind set on the Spirit is life and peace, because the mind set on the flesh is hostile toward God; for it does not subject itself

to the law of God, for it is not even able to do so.
(Romans 8:6-7)

I can hear your caution: "Wait! This is redundant; this fourth mark of the Renewed Mind is exactly the same as the third." And first glance would suggest that the mind set on the spirit and the mind brought into fellowship with the spirit are different ways of stating the same truth.

In the powerful Scripture passage we cited above, Paul reminds us that the mind in its natural state—either the natural mind or the carnal mind—is hostile toward God. We discovered this fact early on in our studies as we noted that man, as he is estranged from God, quickly becomes a hater of God. Without rebuilding that entire line of reasoning, let me refer you to chapter two once again. Briefly, cut off from all knowledge of God's glory and goodness, man sees all about him a world under the control of the enemy. Not knowing the source of this awful evil, he blames and hates God for all that he sees around him.

This scene is recreated in our world millions of times every day: The hammer slips off of the nail and hits the carpenter's thumb. He utters a string of oaths blaspheming the name of God, somehow assuming that God is the source of his problem. And before we become too smug as Christians about that line of reasoning, notice how many times a dread disease strikes a loved one and we say, "God must have put it on him for a reason."

The mind set on the flesh is death—the mind set on the flesh is hostile toward God. Now here is the crux of the matter: The old enmity between the mind and the spirit must be overcome, and they must be brought into harmony with each other. In the previous point, we focused on the fact that the mind must be set on the Spirit rather than on the flesh. The attention of the mind is reoriented from the "reality" of fleshly things to the "reality" of spiritual things—the things of the human spirit and the things of God's Spirit. Though the mind may be refocused on the spiritual things, however, it doesn't necessarily like it. The natural mind has been steeped in suspicion for years about spiritual things, and as Paul would summarize it, outright hostility is the better description. Now suddenly the mind and the Spirit-controlled spirit have to work together and the old

144

enmity is still there.

There is an old story about a little 3-year-old boy who was brought by his parents to church on a Sunday evening. The service was long and the little boy grew restless. He stood up and began walking around on the pew. His daddy said, "Sit down, Johnny." Johnny's natural response was just to smile at his daddy and go on walking around. After the third warning, his daddy picked him up, swung his legs out and set him down on the seat with such force that he nearly stuck. A couple of minutes later with that same little smile, Johnny looked at his daddy and said, "I am still standing up inside."

And therein is the truth of this fourth mark of the Renewed Mind. By conscious, deliberate choice you determine that you will set your mind on the spirit, but the mind is frequently dragged kicking and screaming into the presence of spiritual things and an armed truce is about the best that can be mustered.

If the picture of spiritual man as diagramed in Chart 9 is ever to become a living reality, then the mind must move from forced submission to the things of the Spirit to a genuine love for the things of God. Put differently, the mind must become teachable—both by our own spirits and by the Holy Spirit as He shows us the truths and ways of God.

As we noted in the previous point, this reorientation of the mind may begin with a determined decision to be set on spiritual things. But this process will never be complete until the mind, quite literally, falls in love with the Spirit-controlled spirit. No mind may ever be called truly renewed until the instinctive, natural hostility of the carnal mind toward heavenly things is transformed into a genuine love for and fellowship with the recreated spirit. Once this has been fully accomplished, then the spirit and the mind working together can begin to govern the body and the flesh and bring it into subjection to the Word of God.

One further observation on Romans 8:7. As long as the carnal mind is set on the flesh it is not only hostile toward God, but it cannot submit itself to the law and the will of God for it is not able to do so. As we will discover a bit later, the mind of man governs the entire behavior of man. Let us translate verse 7 rather loosely: The mind cannot at one time be set on the flesh and still be submitted to the will and law of God. Jesus put it simply: You cannot serve God and mammon.

Paul wrote a passage to the people of Galatia that sums these thoughts very well:

> But I say, walk by the Spirit, and you will not carry out the desire of the flesh. For the flesh sets its desire against the Spirit, and the Spirit against the flesh; for these are in opposition to one another, so that you may not do the things that you please. But if you are led by the Spirit, you are not under the Law. Now the deeds of the flesh are evident, which are: immorality, impurity, sensuality, idolatry, sorcery, enmities, strife, jealousy, outbursts of anger, disputes, dissensions, factions, envyings, drunkenness, carousings, and things like these, of which I forewarn you just as I have forewarned you that those who practice such things shall not inherit the kingdom of God. (Galatians 5:16-21)

The King James Version says that "the flesh lusteth against the Spirit," or as the NASB puts it, "The flesh sets its desire against the Spirit." Any sensitive Christian recognizes this opposition of which Paul speaks. But he gives the immediate solution: If you are led by the Spirit, then you are not under the control of the flesh (law). When the flesh remains in control, the end results which Paul catalogs here are no pretty picture: immorality, impurity, sensuality, idolatry, sorcery, enmities, strife, jealousy, outbursts of anger, and on it goes. It is urgent that you note, of course, that unless one gets victory over these things he shall not inherit the kingdom of God.

And now a moment of review. The third mark of the Renewed Mind suggests that the mind is reoriented from the things of the flesh to the things of the Spirit. By a certain willful determination, the mind is set on the things of the Spirit. The fourth mark of the Renewed Mind says very simply: The mind comes to like this new arrangement. The things of the Spirit and the kingdom of God that once seemed so foreign now bring great joy and peace. You may have noticed by now that created man is coming back together in the order in which God made him. His spirit is now in control over his mind and together they rule the flesh. This fourth point also suggests that there is a basic internal cohesiveness, love and fellow-ship among the parts of man.

I am a trained psychologist, and I believe if my colleagues around the world could get hold of the truth that I have just explained to you, the lives of untold millions of people could be transformed. As any psychologist can tell you, at the heart of the emotional problems of man everywhere is an ego-defense system that has gone awry. Whether it is depression, anger, jealousy, envy, pride or denial, the human mind is lashing out to defend its own self-image against the perceptions that those around it may hold. The psychologist may spend hundreds of hours of therapy rearranging the symptoms, but the cure is beyond his grasp. Only as the mind of man is brought into fellowship with his reborn spirit and in turn the whole being is brought into submission and fellowship with his Creator can man ever discover the peace for which he seeks. This subject deserves extensive treatment in another book, but suffice it to say that I believe the Lord has revealed to me that apart from a truly Renewed Mind, all of the accumulated therapy known to man will simply put a Band-aid on the human condition.

* * * * * * * * * *

This is a good point to stop momentarily and consider a problem that the church has struggled with for several generations. The issue is this: What does it mean when we say that someone is very spiritual? This was a prime topic of conversation when I was a boy. Again and again some young person was singled out for the descrip-tion: "He (or she) is very spiritual!" As with the Pharisees of old, the criteria seemed always to be external: If the person attended church three times a week, did not smoke or drink alcohol, did not dance or go to movies, used very religious language and dressed in the prescribed manner, he or she was said to be spiritual. I hope our discussion to this point has helped you to see the fallacy of all this.

Let me offer you a scriptural definition: A person is truly spiritual when his spirit governs his mind and together spirit and mind govern his flesh. To be spiritual is to be Spirit-led and Spirit-controlled, with the mind loving every minute of it. Put another way, the natural man can never be spiritual because his spirit is totally

dead to the things of God. The carnal mind is not spiritual either—
though his spirit is alive, it does not control his mind or his flesh. By
now it should be clear why I have offered you alternate titles for this
chapter: "The Marks of the Renewed Mind" or "The Basic Characteristics of Spiritual Man." The premise is simple: To have a fully
Renewed Mind is to be a spiritual man.

The Fifth Mark of the Renewed Mind:
Being Saturated With the Word of Christ

Paul's precious words to the Colossians include these:

> *Let the word of Christ richly dwell within you, with all*
> *wisdom teaching and admonishing one another with*
> *psalms and hymns and spiritual songs, singing with*
> *thankfulness in your hearts to God. And whatever you*
> *do in word or deed, do all in the name of the Lord Jesus,*
> *giving thanks through Him to God the Father.* (Colos-
> sians 3:16-17)

Let the Word of Christ dwell in you richly! And out of the Word
flows wisdom, helpful teachings and admonitions to one another,
psalms, hymns and spiritual songs whereby we sing with great
thankfulness in our hearts to God, worshiping the Lord, praising
Him!

That hardly sounds like a mind that is hostile toward God, does
it? And here is precisely the point: The old mind, the hostile mind,
has garnered all of its "knowing" from a world under the dominion
of Satan. He has not only made every attempt to destroy the
knowledge of God, but if there is some lingering understanding of
a Creator he will again and again insinuate that God is evil and has
evil motives, even as he did to Eve.

Now the mind has been reoriented to the things of the Spirit. In
fact, the fellowship between the spirit and the mind is genuine and
there is a new love for the truths from God. Suddenly this redirected
mind is absolutely starved for revealed knowledge—knowledge
that is truth. What an opportunity for the mind to be filled with the
Word of Christ and for that Word to dwell richly as the focal point

of every thought.

Pause with me a moment for an urgent observation. Every child of God recalls fondly that moment in which Christ Jesus came to indwell his heart and gave him new life. This was almost certainly followed by a period of intense hunger for the Word of God and a time of rapidly devouring the Word. But there came a point—maybe a few days, a few weeks or a couple of months later—when there was less zeal for the Word of God. At best, the daily time spent in the Word was pure drudgery; at worst, these appointments were abandoned completely. What is the explanation for this? The answer lies in this ongoing struggle which we have just described: A hostile mind is at enmity with a reborn spirit. And the mind set upon the flesh has more important and better things to do than to waste time studying the Word of God and praying. That is the reason why this fifth mark of the Renewed Mind—the Word of Christ dwelling in us richly—can never truly come to pass until the mind has been set on the spirit and has come to love spiritual things with such an ardor that the things of the flesh pale by comparison.

But back to our fifth point. One of the simplest ways to recognize a person with a Renewed Mind is that the Word floods his spirit and his mind. Poke such a person anywhere and the Word oozes out. Give such a brother a Holy Spirit hug and you squeeze three Scripture verses into your ear in the process. Praise God! He is saturated in the Word of Christ.

The apostle Paul put it a bit differently in his words to the Philippians:

> *Rejoice in the Lord always; again I will say, rejoice! Let your forbearing spirit be known to all men. The Lord is near. Be anxious for nothing, but in everything by prayer and supplication with thanksgiving let your requests be made known to God. And the peace of God, which surpasses all comprehension, shall guard your hearts and your minds in Christ Jesus. Finally, brethren, whatever is true, whatever is honorable, whatever is right, whatever is pure, whatever is lovely, whatever is of good repute, if there is any excellence and if anything worthy of praise, let your mind dwell on these*

things. (Philippians 4:4-8)

Let your mind dwell on these things. Herein is the best explanation I know. The mind which for years has been dwelling on the things of the flesh—on every evil, godless thing around it—suddenly needs to be occupied in a better fashion. As the mind becomes saturated in the Word of God and the Word of Christ dwells richly within, then, as Paul would state it, whatever is true, honorable, right or pure, let your mind dwell on these things.

I believe we would do no damage to this fifth point if we stated it thus: The mind which is truly renewed is far more occupied with the things of the kingdom of God than with the things of this earth.

Without stating it directly, the writer to the Hebrews describes perfectly this Renewed Mind in two critical passages:

> *For this is the covenant that I will make with the house of Israel after those days, says the Lord: I will put My laws into their minds, and I will write them upon their hearts. And I will be their God, and they shall be My people. And they shall not teach every one His fellow-citizen, and every one his brother, saying, "Know the Lord," for all shall know Me, from the least to the greatest of them. For I will be merciful to their iniquities, and I will remember their sins no more.* (Hebrews 8:10-12)

> *This is the covenant that I will make with them after those days, says the Lord: I will put My laws upon their heart, and upon their mind I will write them.* (Hebrews 10:16)

Follow this author's reasoning. The mind is now occupied with the laws and ways of God, for they are written upon his very heart. No longer will each one admonish his brother, "Know the Lord!," for all shall know Him.

Observe! Satan's central goal in the Garden of Eden was to destroy the knowledge of the glory of the Lord. But as the mind is renewed the Word is restored to the hearts and minds of men, that

150

knowledge of the Lord returns and Satan is defeated. Consequently, spiritual man looks more and more like created man.

There is a beautiful out-working of all this recorded in Acts. Paul had been ministering at Ephesus and God had honored his labors with great results. Then come these two precious verses:

> *And many of those who practiced magic brought their books together and began burning them in the sight of all; and they counted up the price of them and found it fifty thousand pieces of silver. So the word of the Lord was growing mightily and prevailing.* (Acts 19:19-20)

As the natural mind—which was hostile against God, practicing things of the occult—suddenly becomes reoriented to the things of God, the books and the artifacts that represented the old life are brought together and burned. But the outcome is thrilling: "So the word of the Lord was growing mightily and prevailing."

Once again, the fifth mark of the Renewed Mind: The Word of Christ dwells in us richly. In one sense this is one of the easiest marks to observe in a fellow Christian. Jesus said that out of the abundance of the heart the mouth speaks and how true it is. If a man eats, sleeps and dreams baseball, he is going to talk baseball. If a man eats, sleeps and dreams building his business, he is going to talk his business. And if a man eats, sleeps and dreams the Word of God, he is going to talk the Word of God.

We have already pointed out that only after the mind has been reoriented to the things of the Spirit and has fallen in love with the ways of God can the Word really take root in the heart of man.

I know several men who spend a considerable amount of time in prayer and might be called men of prayer. Yet in their lives one observes very few spiritual victories and, to be honest, their every word reveals that they are basically sense-ruled men still. How shall we understand this? I believe the answer is precisely this: The mind must be Word-taught in order to pray effectively. It was James who taught us that it is possible to pray not according to the will of God but after our own fleshly desires; and because we pray amiss our prayers are not answered. The mind that is deeply instructed in the Word of God and the ways of God can pray far more effectively. And

151

while the Father may answer the simplest prayers of a small child or a newborn Christian, that is no excuse for the misguided prayers of those who ought to be steeped in the Word of God. Near the end of his life, Dwight L. Moody was quoted as saying: "If I could live my life over again there is but one thing I would change, and that is that I would spend much more time in the Word and less in prayer." You understand, of course, that neither Moody nor I are suggesting that we spend too much time in prayer. Rather that informed prayer—Word-saturated and Word-taught prayer—will accomplish much.

The Sixth Mark of the Renewed Mind: Walking Worthy of the Lord

Paul wrote this matter to the Colossian people:

> *For this reason also, since the day we heard of it, we have not ceased to pray for you and to ask that you may be filled with the knowledge of His will in all spiritual wisdom and understanding, so that you may walk in a manner worthy of the Lord, to please Him in all respects, bearing fruit in every good work and increasing in the knowledge of God.* (Colossians 1:9-10)

Follow closely Paul's reasoning: Once you are filled up with the knowledge of His will (our first mark of the Renewed Mind) and you have wisdom and understanding which is spiritual—governed by revealed knowledge in the Word of God and not by the flesh—the result is that you are enabled to walk in a manner worthy of the Lord. Putting it bluntly, if a Renewed Mind does not clean up your act outwardly, it is not the genuine thing. Paul goes on to emphasize this in Colossians:

> *For even though I am absent in body, nevertheless I am with you in spirit, rejoicing to see your good discipline and the stability of your faith in Christ. As you therefore have received Christ Jesus the Lord, so walk in Him, having been firmly rooted and now being built up in Him and established in your faith, just as you were*

instructed, and overflowing with gratitude. See to it
that no one takes you captive through philosophy and
empty deception, according to the tradition of men,
according to the elementary principles of the world,
rather than according to Christ. For in Him all the
fulness of Deity dwells in bodily form. (Colossians 2:5-
9)

As you have received Christ Jesus, so walk in Him or so lead your
life. One of the most crucial results of a truly Renewed Mind is that
you are being firmly rooted in Christ Jesus. You are built up in Him,
as Paul says. You are established in your faith and not driven back
and forth by the winds and doctrines that you hear, nor by the
temptations which come across your path.

In a parallel passage, Paul writes to the Ephesians:

I, therefore, the prisoner of the Lord, entreat you to
walk in a manner worthy of the calling with which you
have been called. (Ephesians 4:1)

Walk worthy of your calling. Walk worthy of the Lord. However
one phrases it, if the mind is truly renewed, then the external life
ought to shape up to the Word of God which dwells within.

I say it again: A Renewed Mind must clean up its act. As the mind
is renewed and fixed upon the Holy Spirit, and the mind and the
Spirit-controlled spirit come into fellowship with one another, then
together they should bring the body of this flesh under control and
change its walk. The only reason the flesh got away with what it did
for so long was that the mind thought about the same things and
desired what the flesh was doing. The mind was set on the flesh, and
because it constantly thought of those things, the flesh had full
license to proceed.

No act of the flesh begins there. The mind first conceives of the
deed and then it is carried out. This is why Jesus warned us that
hating a brother in our heart was equivalent to murder. He further
said that to look upon a woman to lust after her was equivalent to the
act of adultery. Now there is a false teaching going around that
suggests that if you think about it you might as well do it. This is

nonsense. The consequences of the act of adultery are far more serious than the consequences of the thought. However, from the point of view of acquiring a Renewed Mind, the thought does lead to the act. Therefore, when the walk of a man does not line up with the Word of God, it is a sure indication that his mind is not in line with the Word of God and is not truly renewed. One of the clearest summaries of this matter is found in Paul's words to the Galatians:

> For you were called to freedom, brethren; only do not turn your freedom into an opportunity for the flesh, but through love serve one another. For the whole Law is fulfilled in one word, in the statement, "You shall love your neighbor as yourself." But if you bite and devour one another, take care lest you be consumed by one another. But I say, walk by the Spirit, and you will not carry out the desire of the flesh. (Galatians 5:13-16)

So many confuse freedom in the Spirit with the freedom to indulge the flesh, as Paul writes. But he says it so concisely: Walk by the Spirit and you will not carry out the desires of the flesh. In the words of this book, I would say it a little differently: Keep your minds set on the spirit, and let your walk be governed by the leadings of the Holy Spirit, and your behavior will come into line.

Yet again, Paul said in the same chapter: "But if you are led by the Spirit, you are not under the Law" (Galatians 5:18). If you are led by God's Holy Spirit, you are not under the Law. What does it mean? So long as the mind is set on the flesh, no matter how many laws we heap upon each other, the flesh will always find a way around each one and will live in rebellion against the will of God. However, if the mind is set on the spirit, and the Holy Spirit ruling our spirit governs our mind, then the Law is utterly unnecessary. Our spirit ruling our mind will govern our flesh.

Still later in the same chapter Paul writes:

> But the fruit of the Spirit is love, joy, peace, patience, kindness, goodness, faithfulness, gentleness, self-control; against such things there is no law. Now those who belong to Christ Jesus have crucified the flesh with its

passions and desires. If we live by the Spirit, let us also walk by the Spirit. (Galatians 5:22-25)

For years I read over this list of the fruit of the Spirit and thought what a nice idea, but how utterly impractical. There is just not that within me which could possibly ever bear such fruit. Then one day through the infilling of the Holy Spirit, the Lord began to nudge me toward a Renewed Mind. Suddenly, without much discernible effort on my part, I began to see little evidences of these fruit beginning to take root. I firmly believe that as the mind is fixed upon the Holy Spirit, the behavior will follow.

I have had the privilege of teaching young people for a number of years, and often they have come to me wailing: "I want so badly to live a clean life, but I keep slipping back." One church in which we worshiped had a Sunday evening service where it was common for the young people to spend a half hour around the altar in prayer and consecration at the close of the service. Following one such service I said to the young people, "You tell me you face many temptations. Were you tempted just now as you were in the presence of the Lord worshiping Him?" They were horrified! "Of course not," they said, "how could we think of those things when we were in the presence of the Lord?" My response to them that night was: "Here is your answer. When your mind is fixed on the things of the Spirit, then the things of the flesh do not tear at you."

Once again, Chart 9 (on page 119) diagrams spiritual man, which may be equated with the fully Renewed Mind. As the heavenly Father speaks through His Holy Spirit and reveals Himself, His will and His ways to the spirit, and as the mind is attuned to the spirit and ruled and governed by it, then the flesh will conform to the mandates of the spirit. In the words of Paul, we will walk in a manner worthy of the Lord, or we will walk worthy of our calling. His ways, His laws and the principles of His kingdom begin to saturate our spirit and in turn color the way in which our mind thinks. And with our mind fixed on His ways, then our ways begin to conform to His. Revelation knowledge begins to rule over rational knowledge, and our passions are brought into submission.

There is a related matter that would require literally another book were it fully developed. Psychologists have known for many years that our internal belief systems—our thinking—and our external behavior absolutely must agree. If they do not, we must bring one or the other into conformity. A simple illustration will suffice: For many years the Surgeon General's Office of the United States has been issuing more and more dire warnings on the impact of smoking upon our health. Numerous studies have been conducted on how the American people receive such reports and the degree of credibility they attach to such studies. Lumping many such studies together, I can tell you that out of heavy smokers only a small percentage (perhaps ten or fifteen percent) will indicate that they believe the Surgeon General's reports are accurate. However, nonsmokers will agree with the studies by a margin of well over ninety percent. The implications are very clear: If a man continues to perform an act which is certainly going to bring harm, then his mind cannot accept the truthfulness of what he is told. His thinking must be brought into conformity with his behavior. Remember, he had an option. He could have quit smoking and brought his behavior into conformity with his thinking.

When neither the thought nor the deed can be changed, then intense internal stress develops, producing a third alternative in the resolution of the struggle between thought and deed: guilt. By way of illustration imagine a young couple living in fornication. They handle this by rejecting all moral standards and saying: "Everyone does it today. There is obviously nothing wrong with it." Suppose these two young people come to know Jesus Christ as Savior and Lord. As their minds become fixed on the things of the Spirit, they immediately are aware that their fornication is unacceptable to their Savior. A number of options present themselves: They can move to separate apartments and discontinue their immorality; they can marry and ask God's blessing on their relationship; or they can continue their relationship as it is and generate intense guilt. In terms of this chapter, they will hear the words of Paul: "Walk in a manner worthy of the Lord." From that point on if their minds are set on the things of the Spirit, and they are each moving toward a Renewed Mind, they will clean up their behavior.

The Seventh Mark of the Renewed Mind: Speaking in Agreement With the Word of God

This seventh mark of the Renewed Mind—conforming the words of your mouth to agree with God's Word—is so urgent that I am hesitant to deal with it here in a few brief pages. In fact, I have another series of teachings devoted to this subject alone, in which I focus exclusively upon the power of the our words. There is widespread debate and confusion today over the subject of positive confession. Sheer space limitations prohibit my dealing in depth with this matter here, but you will find an extensive discussion of the matter in the above-mentioned teaching materials. Suffice it to say here that Satan often creates a counterfeit doctrine to one of the great truths of God in order to get people's eyes off the central truth and on the error of the false doctrine. This is a classic example of his technique. Men of every persuasion are talking about the power of positive thinking and much of this turns out to be little more than raw humanism. Even the New Age movement will try this technique. And many well-meaning teachers are quoting books that are straight from the pit of hell. However, if you let this satanic trick blind you to the urgency of the truth I am about to present, you will miss one of God's central teachings and have great difficulty in coming to a Renewed Mind.

One more time go back to Paul's marvelous three chapters at the opening of his first letter to the Corinthians:

> *Now we have received, not the spirit of the world, but the Spirit who is from God, that we might know the things freely given to us by God, which things we also speak, not in words taught by human wisdom, but in those taught by the Spirit, combining spiritual thought with spiritual words.* (1 Corinthians 2:12-13)

Follow carefully Paul's reasoning. Having discerned the difference between the spirit of this world and the Spirit who is from God, we then are free to know the things freely given to us by God! Now once we know these things, with the witness in our spirit that they truly are from God, we also speak the same. And the words that we use are not the words of human wisdom, not of sense knowledge, but words which are taught by the Holy Spirit.

Now Paul comes to an urgent truth. Having been taught the things of God by the Holy Spirit, we now combine spiritual thoughts with spiritual words. How can I say it strongly enough? You simply cannot separate thought and words. Spiritual thoughts must be expressed with spiritual words. You cannot have spiritual thoughts about the ways of God and speak the words which confirm all that you knew under sense knowledge.

Certainly Solomon had some grasp of all this when he wrote: "Death and life are in the power of the tongue" (Proverbs 18:21). I trust that one day you will fully discover that every word that comes forth from your mouth leads ultimately to either life or death.

James grasped the awful results of blessing and cursing coming forth from the same mouth when he wrote:

> *Let not many of you become teachers, my brethren, knowing that as such we shall incur a stricter judgment. For we all stumble in many ways. If anyone does not stumble in what he says, he is a perfect man, able to bridle the whole body as well. Now if we put the bits into the horses' mouths so that they may obey us, we direct their entire body as well. Behold, the ships also, though they are so great and are driven by strong winds, are still directed by a very small rudder, wherever the inclination of the pilot desires. So also the tongue is a small part of the body, and yet it boasts of great things. Behold, how great a forest is set aflame by such a small fire! And the tongue is a fire, the very world of iniquity; the tongue is set among our members as that which defiles the entire body, and sets on fire the course of our life, and is set on fire by hell. For every species of beasts and birds, of reptiles and creatures of the sea, is tamed, and has been tamed by the human race. But no one can tame the tongue; it is a restless evil and full of deadly poison. With it we bless our Lord and Father; and with it we curse men, who have been*

made in the likeness of God; from the same mouth
come both blessing and cursing. My brethren, these
things ought not to be this way. Does a fountain send
out from the same opening both fresh and bitter water?
Can a fig tree, my brethren, produce olives, or a vine
produce figs? Neither can salt water produce fresh.
(James 3:1-12)

In fact, James says it even stronger than I have: "If any man does not stumble in what he says [his words] he is a perfect man." Further, if anyone has the capacity for bridling or controlling every word that goes out of his mouth, he has the capacity of living a perfect life. Strong? I didn't write it, James did. He goes on: "From the same mouth come both blessing and cursing...these things ought not to be...." For how, James asks, can a single fountain send out both fresh and bitter water at the same time?

In many ways I believe that this seventh mark of the Renewed Mind is the most crucial test of a spiritual man. It may also be his most obvious outward characteristic. You and I may look at a man without really knowing whether or not he discerns the will of the Father, is led by the Spirit of God or has his mind set on the things of the Spirit. But we need only be with him a few seconds for the words of his mouth to reveal the extent of his Renewed Mind. If his every word is a negative confession, constantly confirming the input of his natural senses, that reveals his carnal nature. But if his every word confesses his confidence in the power of God, the power of His Word, the strength of His promises, His goodness and His utter dependability, that indicates his spiritual nature. If we hear a mixture of those two coming from his mouth, as is more likely the case, we must conclude that he is double-minded yet.

If all of this seems a bit overstated to you, hear the words of our Lord Jesus:

And whoever shall speak a word against the Son of
Man, it shall be forgiven him; but whoever shall speak
against the Holy Spirit, it shall not be forgiven him,
either in this age, or in the age to come. Either make
the tree good, and its fruit good; or make the tree rotten,

and its fruit rotten; for the tree is known by its fruits.
You brood of vipers, how can you, being evil, speak
what is good? For the mouth speaks out of that which
fills the heart. The good man out of his good treasure
brings forth what is good; and the evil man out of his
evil treasure brings forth what is evil. And I say to you,
that every careless word that men shall speak, they
shall render account for it in the day of judgment. For
by your words you shall be justified, and by your words
you shall be condemned. (Matthew 12:32-37)

Speaking of the fruit of a man's mouth, his words, Jesus says
either make the tree and its fruit good or make it rotten and evil
Then this very important truth: The mouth speaks out of that which
fills the heart. The good man out of a very good treasure brings forth
what is good, while the evil man has stored up evil treasures and
brings forth what is evil. Jesus is saying that the words of our mouth
are the best barometer of what is going on in our mind and our heart
Further, whatever has been stored up in our mind and our heart is
what will come out in our words. No matter how much we may claim
that our mind is set upon the things of the Spirit of God, and how
much we may claim to have a Renewed Mind—if the words of our
mouth constantly spew out rational knowledge, then we have
betrayed ourselves.

Then Jesus gave us what must be two of the most sobering verses
in the entire Word of God: "I say to you, that every careless word that
men shall speak, they shall render account for it in the day of
judgment. For by your words you shall be justified, and by your
words you shall be condemned." For those of you who have been
tempted to mock some of the beautiful teachings on positive confession as it relates to the Word of God, read those two verses again. I
rest my case.

Now a moment of review. The seventh mark of the Renewed
Mind simply says that the words of my mouth agree with His Word
Not that my words agree with my wishes, my whims or my desires
but that my words line up at all times with His Word. If He says
"Seek ye first the kingdom of God, and His righteousness; and all
these things shall be added unto you" (Matthew 6:33, KJV), then I

have absolutely no business confessing any lack whatsoever. If He says, "Truly I say to you, whoever says to this mountain, `Be taken up and cast into the sea,' and does not doubt in his heart, but believes that what he says is going to happen, it shall be granted him" (Mark 1:23), then I am to exercise the power of the Word that goes forth from my mouth. Truly death and life are in the power of the tongue.

Examine just one more scripture with me, this time from the pen of Paul:

> But what does it say? "The word is near you, in your mouth and in your heart"—that is, the word of faith which we are preaching, that if you confess with your mouth Jesus as Lord, and believe in your heart that God raised Him from the dead, you shall be saved; for with the heart man believes, resulting in righteousness, and with the mouth he confesses, resulting in salvation. (Romans 10:8-10)

Note first with me the tremendously close association Paul sees between the Word and the words of our mouth and heart, and note further that our very salvation depends upon the confession of this word. Paul says that with the mouth we confess, which results in our salvation. Jesus said: "Everyone therefore who confesses Me before men, I will also confess him before My Father who is in heaven" (Matthew 10:32). And there you have it, the Word of God combined with our words has an enormous impact on our lives and upon the world.

Finally, you may ask me: "If the words of my mouth are such a central test of whether or not I have a Renewed Mind, what do you mean by good and evil confessions?" Negative words are those which speak out of sense knowledge and confirm the world as natural man sees it, under satanic control and apart from any knowledge of the Lord. Such words may range from taking the Lord's name in vain, to foul stories, evil words or even gossip which destroys another. But more likely in the Christian life they are words of defeat, discouragement, of dire expectations, of expected and yet not arrived sickness, loss, fire, theft and so on. In John 10:10,

161

Jesus gave us Satan's agenda: to steal, kill and destroy. Any wor that brings Satan's agenda on the scene is evil. Any word that doub God's goodness or His power to intervene in the world is evil.

On the other hand, positive words are words of faith, words sat rated in the Word of God, expressing confidence in God's goodnes His power, His absolute holiness and integrity and His never failir provision. These include words of praise, adoration and blessing tl name of the Lord. In the same passage in John, Jesus gave us H own agenda: life, and that abundantly.

If you are still struggling with all this, then I invite you to tak every word that comes from your mouth for a few days and subm it to this simple test: Would that word, when carried to its fulle extent, come down on the side of death or life?

The Eighth Mark of the Renewed Mind: Possessing the Very Mind of Christ

Note with me two of the apostle Paul's most thrilling passage "Let this mind be in you, which was also in Christ Jesus" (Philippiar 2:5, KJV). "For who has known the mind of the Lord, that he shou instruct Him? But we have the mind of Christ" (1 Corinthians 2:16 Dare I even think it? Dare the words even cross my lips? Yet Pa said it, and even the remotest possibility of it stirs me beyond word That such a one as I might have the very mind of Christ! That suc a one as I—so caught up in humanism, so skeptical of His Wor with a mind that was anything but renewed—might have the ve mind of Christ!

But Paul said it: "Let this mind be in you which was also in Chri Jesus." And again: "We have the mind of Christ." Can you grasp tl scope of it? That Christ, the Son of the eternal God, who came earth and took upon Himself the form of man and yet was sinless every respect, might be the model for my Renewed Mind? Oh, tl awesomeness of it! The challenge has been fixed, and I for one mu press on to this eighth mark of a Renewed Mind.

Do you see the significance of it? I confess that I puzzled long ar hard here, but one day the Lord opened for me another verse fro Paul. As usual he was out ahead of the troops but in 1 Corinthiar

5:45 he says: "The first man, Adam, became a living soul. The last Adam became a life-giving spirit." And there it is! Jesus was the second Adam, the second man that God placed on this earth in a perfect, untainted condition. As in the first chapter we studied Adam as created man, so now we can look to our Lord Jesus Christ as the second created man, perfectly sinless, with all the limitless potential of that first created man.

Now aren't you excited? Paul says we have the mind of Christ, which means we have before us the fantastic possibility of recapturing the mind of that first created man in the garden before he trifled with obedience to the Father. Hallelujah! I must stop and praise the Father even as I pen these words, for few thoughts could more completely dazzle the mind of man.

Now all this makes me want to stop and do a lengthy, detailed study of what was involved in the mind of Christ. Space will permit us here only a glimpse or two, but join me for an exciting venture.

Not long ago I was reading Isaiah when a verse in chapter 11 leaped off the page:

> *Then a shoot will spring from the stem of Jesse, and a branch from his roots will bear fruit. And the Spirit of the Lord will rest on Him, the spirit of wisdom and understanding, the spirit of counsel and strength, the spirit of knowledge and the fear of the Lord. And He will delight in the fear of the Lord, and He will not judge by what His eyes see, nor make a decision by what His ears hear; but with righteousness He will judge the poor, and decide with fairness for the afflicted of the earth; and He will strike the earth with the rod of His mouth, and with the breath of His lips He will slay the wicked. Also righteousness will be the belt about His loins, and faithfulness the belt about His waist.* (Isaiah 11:1-5)

The Spirit of the Lord will rest on Him, from God He will have wisdom and understanding, the knowledge and the fear of the Lord will be upon Him. And then, there it was: His mind and His heart fully fixed upon the Lord in full fear of the Lord, He will not judge by what

163

His eyes see, nor make a decision by what His ears hear! An suddenly I saw the mind of Christ. Unswayed by the ration knowledge that was coming in through His eyes and His ears, H would judge in righteousness and in the fear of the Lord. M Christian friends, I believe this is the first quality of the mind c Christ: He is totally unswayed by what His eyes see and His ear hear.

Notice another occasion. When the boy Jesus was but twelv years old, He accompanied His parents to Jerusalem. There, su rounded by the greatest scholars alive in Mosaic law, He listene and in turn questioned them. Luke tells us that all who heard Hir were amazed at His understanding and His answers (2:47). And s here at an early age, we find the mind of Christ fixed upon things c the Spirit, saturated in God's Word and grasping the ways of th Lord.

As Jesus began His earthly ministry, the multitudes were a: tounded at His mind. Matthew informs us: "When Jesus had fi ished these words, the multitudes were amazed at His teaching, fo He was teaching them as one having authority, and not as the scribes" (Matthew 7:28-29). With His mind set upon the things c the Spirit and His Spirit in tune with His Father God, He spoke thos things which He heard from His Father and spoke with an authorit unheard of in any age thus far.

In John 8:26, Jesus says: "He who sent Me is true; and the thing which I heard from Him, these I speak to the world." In a paralle passage Jesus said: "All things that I have heard from My Father have made known to you" (John 15:15). Once again, attuned to th things of the Spirit, Jesus shared only those things that He hear from the Father. And that is the Renewed Mind—the mind con pletely fixed on the things which are above.

Just one more illustration. Mark records that the multitudes wer so amazed at the behavior of Jesus that they asked, "What is this? new teaching with authority! He commands even the unclea spirits, and they obey Him" (1:27). And there you have one mor dimension to the mind of Christ: With completely restored domir ion, even the evil spirits obey.

Once again, Paul summarized it best when he said that you "hav put on the new self who is being renewed to a true knowledg

164

according to the image of the One who created him" (Colossians 3:10).

The eighth mark of the Renewed Mind truly staggers us: We have the mind of Christ! When you see Him as the second Adam and realize that in Christ we have the created mind which God intended for man at the beginning, hope leaps within you. For we have seen in Christ that He does not judge by what His eyes see nor what His ears hear. His mind was so attuned to the things of the Spirit and so steeped in God's Word that He astounded the Jewish elders at the age of twelve. The multitudes were amazed at the authority with which He spoke, having words which were obviously direct from the Father. They were further astonished at the scope of His dominion, for the evil spirits obeyed Him. And Jesus Himself remarked to the disciples that all the words that He had heard from the Father He had faithfully shared with them.

Praise God! Dare you claim it with me?

Spiritual Man

These, then, are the eight marks of the Renewed Mind as I believe the Word of God outlines them, but I want to close this chapter as we began. I suggested to you then that an alternate title for the chapter might be "Characteristics of the Spiritual Man." What I am suggesting is that a man with a truly Renewed Mind meets the biblical definition of spiritual man. It is not within the scope of this study to press this point at length, but let me cite just a couple of passages of Scripture that will thrill your heart.

First, look with me at Paul's words to the Ephesians:

> *Blessed be the God and Father of our Lord Jesus Christ, who has blessed us with every spiritual blessing in the heavenly places in Christ, just as He chose us in Him before the foundation of the world, that we should be holy and blameless before Him.* (Ephesians 1:3-4)

What a glorious picture Paul paints here! God the Father has blessed us with every spiritual blessing in the heavenly places in Christ Jesus. But it is impossible for our spirits to be blessed without our minds being blessed, provided our minds are fixed upon the things of the Spirit. We have already noticed Jesus' precious promise that if we would seek first His kingdom and His righteousness, such things as housing, clothing and food would be added unto us in abundance. Now I propose to you that spiritual man is a man who relishes the things of God and revels in God's goodness, abundance and blessing. And yet spiritual man is the man who is blessed with every spiritual blessing out of the storehouses of God in the name of Christ Jesus.

If that also describes the Renewed Mind, count me in.

Finally, having quoted Paul endlessly throughout this book, let's have one quick glimpse of Paul's understanding of his own Renewed Mind. The passage is lengthy, but critical:

> And when I came to you, brethren, I did not come with superiority of speech or of wisdom, proclaiming to you the testimony of God. For I determined to know nothing among you except Jesus Christ, and Him crucified. And I was with you in weakness and in fear and in much trembling. And my message and my preaching were not in persuasive words of wisdom, but in demonstration of the Spirit and of power, that your faith should not rest on the wisdom of men, but on the power of God. Yet we do speak wisdom among those who are mature; a wisdom, however, not of this age, nor of the rulers of this age, who are passing away; but we speak God's wisdom in a mystery, the hidden wisdom, which God predestined before the ages to our glory; the wisdom which none of the rulers of this age has understood; for if they had understood it, they would not have crucified the Lord of glory; but just as it is written, "Things which eye has not seen and ear has not heard, and which have not entered the heart of man, all that God has prepared for those who love Him." For to us God revealed them through the Spirit; for the Spirit searches all things, even the depths of God. For who among men knows the thoughts of a man except the spirit of the man, which is in him? Even so

166

the thoughts of God no one knows except the Spirit of God. Now we have received, not the spirit of the world, but the Spirit who is from God, that we might know the things freely given to us by God, which things we also speak, not in words taught by human wisdom, but in those taught by the Spirit, combining spiritual thoughts with spiritual words. But a natural man does not accept the things of the Spirit of God; for they are foolishness to him, and he cannot understand them, because they are spiritually appraised. But he who is spiritual appraises all things, yet he himself is appraised by no man. For who has known the mind of the Lord, that he should instruct Him? But we have the mind of Christ. (1 Corinthians 2:1-16)

If I may paraphrase Paul, I believe he is saying this: I did not come to you in the cleverness of my own wisdom and understanding, but in my own weakness and trembling I came presenting to you the simple gospel of Jesus Christ. My message was not in the persuasiveness of human words, but under the anointing of the Holy Spirit, that your faith would not rest on my cleverness, but on the power of God. However, if you are mature to receive it, we have wisdom to offer you. Not the wisdom of the rationalism of this age, but the wisdom which is from above. All that I have, God has revealed to me through His Holy Spirit. And as we know the things of the Spirit, we hear the voice of the Father and have the knowledge of God. The natural mind will not understand what I am saying, but you who are spiritual will. Now that I know the leading of His Holy Spirit and the will of the Father, I make bold to say that I have the very mind of Christ!

Sadly, after that great testimonial Paul has to open chapter 3 addressing the Corinthian brethren by saying: "I, brethren, could not speak to you as spiritual men, but as to men of flesh."

Finally, what is spiritual man? He is a man whose spirit has been reborn through the presence of Jesus Christ in his life that submits his carnal nature to the transforming work of God. If such a man will follow through to the end, he will become spiritual man, man as God intended, man once again created in the image of God with all of the possibilities implied therein.

Conclusion

Without rehearsing here the eight marks of the Renewed Mind (pictured in Chart 8 on page 117), let me suggest that I believe they are in large part sequential. By this I mean that each quality or characteristic builds on those which have gone before. We might debate their relative position or importance, but each is critically important as they build to the complete picture of the spiritual man.

One may begin to discern the will of God in response to Paul's original plea for a Renewed Mind and soon hear the voice of the Lord and be led by His Spirit. Such early victories will only be turned into long-term gains as the mind that has been set on the flesh begins to be set on the spirit. Even this gain will only become permanent when the mind which has been hostile toward the spirit comes to love the things of God which are from above. By this time the mind which is in the process of being renewed becomes starved for the things of God and the Word must dwell richly in us. Almost concomitantly the flesh kicks up its heels and must be brought into submission through the rule of the spirit and the mind—our walk must be made worthy of the Lord. We barely have that battle under control when we notice that the words of our mouth are bringing us more defeat than victory, and we begin one of the most strenuous battles of all to bring our words into line with His Word. This process takes much longer than it sounds here, but if we are faithful, one day we just might say with our beloved Paul: "I have the mind of Christ."

168

CHAPTER FIVE

THE EIGHT STEPS TO A RENEWED MIND

As we begin this new chapter let me pause to answer a question that is raised fairly often. Just because I insist that we follow God's divine order for man—that his spirit must rule his mind, and together they must rule his body of flesh—does this mean I am denigrating the lower natures of man? Does this mean the spirit is all important, and that the mind and the body are to be neglected? Quite the contrary—I would argue that only as man comes to find his complete fulfillment in the order of God's intended creation can the various aspects of his being find complete fulfillment.

The body is still the temple of the Holy Spirit and has to be properly fed, exercised, rested, bathed and cared for. Occasionally an individual who is an exercise fanatic will suggest that my role for the body is demeaning. This is to be understood in a society where a number of our television advertisements suggest that as long as we have our health, we have everything. It was Jesus who said we should not fear the one who could destroy the body, but rather the One who has authority to destroy both the body and the soul in hell.

He quickly put it in perspective. The body is important, it is God-given and needs proper care, but I am simply arguing that the body of this flesh must not rule our minds or our spirits. Parenthetically, let me ask you, my Christian friend: How many hours a week do you spend exercising and caring for your body, and how many hours in feeding your spirit?

The more frequently asked question comes from the academic type. "Isn't all this business you are teaching really a warmed-over version of the old notion that if we are going to be Christians we need to turn our brains off?" I have four earned degrees and I have spent a lifetime in higher education, and I suggest to you that that question simply reflects terribly sloppy scholarship. I can only surmise that in most cases the questioner has been confronted face-to-face with the need for a Renewed Mind, has begun to evaluate the enormous cost to him if he goes that route and has decided that the better avenue is to attack the messenger. I too have been this route and I know something of the cost—the cost of facing the fact that much of a lifetime of scholarship has been conducted in a fashion diametrically opposed to the principles of God and will require enormous humility and relearning if one is ever to move toward a Renewed Mind.

In fact, I would go far beyond this entire line of reasoning. I believe that man is created in the image of God and that he is spirit. But I am further convinced that the finest tool God ever gave us as individual spirits is the incredibly beautiful and complex gift of the mind. I personally have spent forty years in studying the mind and its complexity in great depth, and I feel that I know little more than when I began. Oh, it is easy to talk about the mind in terms of storage and retrieval systems, of storage cells and synaptic connections, and we know much of the physiology of the mind. But as to how the mind wills, chooses, emotes and responds in a million different situations—we know very little of these.

It is my personal conviction that we have not even dreamed of the potential of the human mind if it were fully renewed and under the Lordship of Jesus Christ. One of my fondest visions is that some-where, somehow, we might assemble a couple hundred of the finest minds in the world selected from every discipline of knowledge known to man. My only requisite is that each of these minds must be 100 percent sold out to our Lord Jesus Christ and have gone through the process of a total renewing until each can hear the voice of the Spirit and in turn the will of the Father. Can you imagine what would happen if a half-dozen scholars in each of the thirty-five or forty disciplines now known to man could bring together the rational knowledge now available to the human mind and lay it at the foot of the cross, there to say: "Father, in your divine goodness, correct all this with revelation knowledge"? I am currently assembling some thoughts on each discipline, and I get absolutely thrilled even from my modest vantage point.

* * * * * * * * * *

But enough dreaming for now—back to the chapter at hand. We have just examined the eight crucial marks or characteristics of the Renewed Mind or, if you will, of spiritual man. The overwhelming question before us is, How does one get there? And so we move to the eight steps to a Renewed Mind.

As you might surmise, there is some slight overlap between the characteristics and the process, but that is to be expected. So let me add just one important forethought as we begin: I believe that as the Lord has revealed each step to my spirit, the sequence of their appearance in this chapter is critical. If this book becomes more to you than an academic study, as I pray it will, and you choose to pursue a Renewed Mind on your own, then let me strongly encourage you to take the steps sequentially. I will add my comments for the reasons as we move along. (see charts 10 and 11 on page 121)

The First Step Toward a Renewed Mind: Must Have a Reborn Spirit

I think it is instructive that many of the requisites for a Renewed Mind are found in the immediate context of Romans 12:2, where Paul issues his inexorable call. He begins this great chapter with: "I urge you therefore, brethren...." Paul is clearly addressing believers here.

In Jesus' great nighttime conversation with Nicodemus, "Jesus answered and said to him: 'Truly, truly I say to you, unless one is born again, he cannot see the kingdom of God'" (John 3:3). Certainly Jesus was saying to Nicodemus that unless a man is born again he cannot go to heaven. But from the point of view of this study, there is a deeper truth here: Except a man be born again, he cannot see into the kingdom of God nor can he grasp spiritual truths.

Without question the first step to a Renewed Mind requires that one's spirit be made alive in Christ. I do not mean to offer gratuitous comments by this repetition here, but let it be absolutely clear that there is no other first step on the road to the Renewed Mind.

God's first dire warning to Adam, the first man, was that the tree of knowledge of good and evil, the tree at the focal point of Eden, would open to man a world of "knowing" (evil) and expose not only Adam but all future generations to the awful destruction of sin. To Adam the warning was clear: The day in which you eat of it you shall surely die. And so in chapter two we traced the awful consequences of Adam's rebellion. The spirit within man died that day, fellowship with the Father was severed forever as far as he knew, and the ways of God and the things of the kingdom of God were forever put beyond the veil of his "knowing."

There can be no other first step! It is upon the spirit of man that God has stamped eternal, and that spirit shall experience eternity either in eternal death or eternal life. If the mind of man is to be renewed, it must once again have access to the things of eternal life as revealed by the Father through His Holy Spirit. The only window the soul of man has upon the things of eternity is the window of his own spirit. Until that spirit is made alive, is reborn, is born from above—until the spirit of man knows life anew there is no hope of receiving revealed knowledge.

I pause here once again, my reader friend, and say to you that the reason for the little interlude between chapters two and three was precisely for the purpose we are now addressing. If for some reason you picked up this book and began with this chapter out of curiosity, or if by some other strange circumstance you have come this far in this book and have not met Jesus Christ as your personal Savior, let me urge you to go back to the interlude and there pray with me the prayer which we have included at that point. My heart is filled with great love for you even now as I write, and the love of our heavenly

172

Father for you is infinitely greater. I can only press upon you this one reality: Until you come to the point where you humble yourself before God and accept Jesus Christ as your Savior and Lord, there is nothing in the rest of this chapter for you. Please establish this point once and for all in your own heart.

To the rest of you who read this point, let me add an additional comment. Some of you are still trusting a commitment you made very early in your childhood, and that is wonderful, for I, too, came to know my Lord at a very early age. Others of you will be trusting an act of baptism, a series of studies followed by an act of confirmation, or any of a dozen other processes that you were told made you a Christian. If there is any question in your heart and mind about your own stand before God, let me encourage you also to turn back between chapters two and three and reread those words and pray that prayer again as you accept Him into your heart. By faith reach out and receive Him afresh as if it were the first time in your life, and from this point on drive a stake and say, I know that I know that I know He is my Lord and my God!

I can almost hear someone say at this point: "But you can't get saved over and over again." I understand that. But I also understand two things: First, every one of us must be utterly certain about our salvation before the Lord; and secondly, we need to have the channel between our spirit and His Spirit absolutely clear of any sin. Now that you have reached out and received Him by faith and have driven a stake; now that you have determined that for all time and eternity you are going to serve the Lord, then know of a certainty you have established point one on this eight-point ladder: Your spirit has been reborn.

Parenthetically, let me call your attention to Charts 10 and 11, which present visually for you the steps which I am outlining. They are simply two complementary ways of portraying for you the steps in the process of renewing the mind.

Now, let's return to the matter at hand and examine a few more scriptures concerning the necessity for a reborn spirit. One more time, look with me at Paul's great word:

> *But a natural man does not accept the things of the*
> *Spirit of God; for they are foolishness to him, and he*

cannot understand them, because they are spiritually appraised. (1 Corinthians 2:14)

How better can we say it? The natural man, whose spirit is dead toward God, does not accept the things of the Spirit of God nor of His kingdom for two reasons: They are foolishness to him and he has no tools to grasp them if he chose to. As Jesus told Nicodemus, unless one is born again, he cannot see the kingdom of God.

On the eve of His crucifixion, Jesus is speaking to the disciples at some length about their need for receiving and knowing the Holy Spirit:

> *And I will ask the Father, and He will give you another Helper, that He may be with you forever; that is the Spirit of truth, whom the world cannot receive, because it does not behold Him or know Him, but you know Him because He abides with you and will be in you. I will not leave you as orphans; I will come to you.* (John 14:16-18)

Now Jesus is clearly speaking of the necessity of the disciples' coming to know the power of the Holy Spirit in their lives. As He does, He distinctly says that the world (read: natural man) cannot receive the Holy Spirit, nor can it see Him. However, Jesus calls the Holy Spirit the Spirit of truth. I propose to you that the ultimate "knowing" of the things of God's kingdom is totally dependent on the power of the Holy Spirit in our lives serving as our Teacher. This is a matter for a later point. At this time, however, notice that the natural man is totally cut off from truth no matter how vehemently he may profess his knowledge and wisdom. One may spend a lifetime studying every branch of knowledge and accumulate a half-dozen PhD's in the process; he will never get the first corner on truth until his spirit is reborn in Christ Jesus.

Let me illustrate again from the life of the disciples:

> *And He took the twelve aside and said to them, "Behold, we are going up to Jerusalem, and all things which are written through the prophets about the Son*

of Man will be accomplished. For He will be delivered up to the Gentiles, and will be mocked and mistreated and spit upon, and after they have scourged Him, they will kill Him; and the third day He will rise again." And they understood none of these things, and this saying was hidden from them, and they did not comprehend the things that were said. (Luke 18:31-34)

What a fascinating picture. Jesus is explaining to the twelve disciples the simple truths of the Old Testament prophets. Yet they understood none of it. What do you make of this? Jesus was explaining to them God's great plan of salvation, His own death on the cross and His resurrection from the dead. However, this is the very mystery of the ages: if the forces of hell had understood this mystery, they would not have crucified Jesus. Put simply, Jesus is explaining to them the central truths of the kingdom of God. These truths are spiritual. The twelve, on the other hand, could not possibly have had Renewed Minds for they did not have spirits that were reborn. It would be still some days or weeks until Jesus died on the cross, and until He did there was no hope of redemption from Adam's fall. The disciples indeed had natural minds at this point, and so it is recorded of them: "They understood none of these things, and this saying was hidden from them, and they did not comprehend the things that were said." Just in case you missed it, Luke puts it three different ways so you cannot possibly misconstrue it.

Luke 24 is a veritable gold mine on this subject. In this chapter Calvary is over, Jesus is resurrected from the dead, but Pentecost is still fifty days away. There are numerous instances of how far they are yet from a Renewed Mind, and we may well argue with many other scholars that they are not yet born again, that the first new converts came with the birth of the church on the day of Pentecost. However that may be, and however you interpret the state of the souls of men and women in that fifty-day period, Luke makes several fascinating observations in relationship to this chapter of our study. As the women visit the tomb early on Sunday morning and find the angels awaiting them, the angels remonstrate them by quoting the very same prophecies Jesus had so often given concerning Himself. It is almost as if the angels, coming from the heavenly viewpoint, say to the women: "Didn't you learn anything from what He taught you?" And then in those curious words: "And they remembered His words." It is almost as if the very first glimmers of that Sunday morning light brought the first rays of understanding to their own hearts and minds: "Ah, yes, He did say that, didn't He?"

The women rushed back to tell the disciples what they had discovered and what the angels said, but Luke records it again in verse 11: "And these words appeared to them as nonsense, and they would not believe them."

Later, Jesus appeared to the two men on the way to Emmaus, just as He seemed to have a habit of appearing and disappearing all through this fifty-day period. The men from Emmaus were still dependent on their natural eyes giving them rational information, and as Jesus appeared to them in His glorified body, Luke records in 24:16: "Their eyes were prevented from recognizing Him." As they walk the dusty road back to Emmaus that day, Jesus begins once again to open the Scriptures to them patiently with just a bit of loving chiding. And then out of His sovereign love for these two, Jesus reveals Himself to them in the breaking of bread.

But to me the most thrilling and glorious thing about this entire passage is verse 32: "And they said to one another, 'Were not our hearts burning within us while He was speaking to us on the road, while He was explaining the scriptures to us?'" Their minds certainly were not yet renewed. And we may well argue that their spirits had not yet been made alive in Christ. But Calvary had come and Jesus had paid the price for the redemption of man's spirit and soul. The new birth was now possible. What is more, the resurrection had come as well, and the same power that raised Jesus from the dead was just waiting in the form of the Holy Spirit to indwell everyone who believed. And in the midst of that strange and complex mix of circumstances came that familiar stirring you and I have recognized so many times: the burning of the heart! "Did not our hearts burn within us as we walked with Him and He spoke with us and He opened the Word to us on the way?"

Just a few more words from the apostle Paul as he wrote to the Corinthian people: "For the word of the cross is to those who are perishing foolishness, but to us who are being saved it is the power of God" (1 Corinthians 1:18). Then the following verses:

Having therefore such a hope, we use great boldness in our speech, and are not as Moses, who used to put a veil over his face that the sons of Israel might not look intently at the end of what was fading away. But their minds were hardened; for until this very day at the reading of the old covenant the same veil remains unlifted, because it is removed in Christ. But to this day whenever Moses is read, a veil lies over their heart; but whenever a man turns to the Lord, the veil is taken away. (2 Corinthians 3:12-16)

Therefore, since we have this ministry, as we received mercy, we do not lose heart, but we have renounced the things hidden because of shame, not walking in craftiness or adulterating the word of God, but by the manifestation of truth commending ourselves to every man's conscience in the sight of God. And even if our gospel is veiled, it is veiled to those who are perishing, in whose case the god of this world has blinded the minds of the unbelieving, that they might not see the light of the gospel of the glory of Christ, who is the image of God. (2 Corinthians 4:1-4)

Paul's words are so distinctive and clear that they require little comment. To the natural mind, the mystery of Calvary appears total foolishness, but to those who are alive in Christ it is the very power of God. Using the Jewish people's rejection of Jesus as an example, Paul holds them up as a model of the natural mind which has been hardened and blinded against the things of the kingdom of God. Once again, however, that veil of blindness is removed in Christ Jesus when a man turns to the Lord.

Briefly, on the road to a Renewed Mind there is no equivocating about the first step. Until one has experienced new life in Christ Jesus, everything else about the Christian walk, everything else about the kingdom of God, even God's ways and His thoughts, are as sheer foolishness. Man must have a reborn spirit and sequentially this act must come before every other step in the process of acquiring a Renewed Mind.

177

The Second Step Toward a Renewed Mind: Must Sacrifice the Body

By now you must have the opening verses of Romans 12 memorized, but return with me once again:

I urge you therefore, brethren, by the mercies of God, to present your bodies a living and holy sacrifice, acceptable to God, which is your spiritual service of worship. (Romans 12:1)

It is so easy to leap ahead to verse 2, isn't it? To fix our attention on the laudable desire for a Renewed Mind, and to miss Paul's systematic steps as you go.

The King James Version translates it: "Present your bodies as a living sacrifice." Williams states it: "Make a decisive dedication of your bodies as a living sacrifice." In our worst condition, our bodies ruled our minds and our spirits were dead. In our best condition, our minds had the control of our bodies at least half of the time. But if we are to get things back into God's divine order the steps are obvious: Our spirits must be made alive so they can once again rule our total being, and then the flesh must be brought into proper place in the total perspective of man. How the mind gets reoriented toward the Spirit and accepts its rightful position is the subject of this whole book.

A living sacrifice! In my mind I see an altar not unlike that prepared for the Old Testament sacrifice. To this altar we come, saying: "Lord, through my flesh I have been serving every evil and serving self. I've been lustful, prideful and ego-centered. I now present this body of flesh to You as a living sacrifice that I might turn to do Your will." And so as the Holy Spirit calls these things to my memory, I offer to Him my flesh, my desires, my lusts, my cravings and my passions. The thing that was dearest to me is the thing that most needs offering.

But there is more. For some of us (and I certainly include myself here) the more difficult sacrifice comes at the point of yielding the pride of the rational mind to the heavenly Father. My senses, my brain, my cleverness and all the knowledge gained thereby have to be yielded unto Him if I am ever to have hope of hearing His voice bringing me revelation knowledge.

Bringing the sacrifice in the Old Testament was certainly an act of worship. Sometimes it was an offering for the atonement for sin; at others it was an act of gratitude for the goodness of the Lord. However, it was an act of pure worship of the Lord. Note that Paul closes this first verse by saying that this act of presenting our bodies as a living sacrifice unto God is our spiritual service of worship.

Build an illustration in your own mind! You know the problems you face in the flesh. Now you come to the Lord desiring to worship Him in spirit, singing and praying in the Spirit, blessing His name. However, if the flesh is out of order and rebellious, you are keenly aware that your act of worship of the Lord in spirit is short-circuited. In this context the highest order of worship for the day is the sacrifice of the flesh. Once the fleshly matter that is gnawing at you is settled once and for all, then the spiritual worship takes on an entirely new dimension.

Just a little earlier Paul had penned these powerful words to the Romans:

> *Therefore do not let sin reign in your mortal body that you should obey its lusts, and do not go on presenting the members of your body to sin as instruments of unrighteousness, but present yourselves to God as those alive from the dead, and your members as instruments of righteousness to God. For sin shall not be master over you, for you are not under law, but under grace. What then? Shall we sin because we are not under law but under grace? May it never be! Do you not know that when you present yourselves to someone as slaves for obedience, you are slaves of the one whom you obey, either of sin resulting in death, or of obedience resulting in righteousness? But thanks be to God that though you were slaves of sin, you became obedient from the heart to that form of teaching to which you were committed, and having been freed from sin, you became slaves of righteousness. I am speaking in human terms because of the weakness of your flesh. For just as*

you presented your members as slaves to impurity and to lawlessness, resulting in further lawlessness, so now present your members as slaves to righteousness, resulting in sanctification. (Romans 6:12-19)

What a powerful choice of words. "Do not let sin reign in you mortal body." For if we are alive from the dead—our spirits have been reborn—Paul says then we ought to present ourselves unto God and our flesh as instruments of righteousness. Sin must no master us.

Then Paul gives us this insight: Whomever we obey, we are slaves of that one. We have a simple choice: Either we obey sin and death or we obey righteousness and life. Through Jesus Christ we have been set free from the bondage to sin and the flesh. Therefore, it remains our responsibility to present our bodies as a living sacrifice Paul has admonishing words for the Corinthians when he writes:

Do you not know that your bodies are members of Christ? Shall I then take away the members of Christ and make them members of a harlot? May it never be! Or do you not know that the one who joins himself to a harlot is one body with her? For He says, "The two will become one flesh." But the one who joins himself to the Lord is one spirit with Him. Flee immorality. Every other sin that a man commits is outside the body, but the immoral man sins against his own body. Or do you not know that your body is a temple of the Holy Spirit who is in you, whom you have from God, and that you are not your own? For you have been bought with a price: therefore glorify God in your body. (1 Corinthians 6:15-20)

Note with me two crucial observations. First, while our bodies must be brought into submission and their rightful position in God's order, we cannot disassociate ourselves from our bodies, nor can we say that so long as our spirits are serving the Lord it matters not what our bodies do. Paul simply says that our bodies are members of Christ. Again he says that our body is a temple or sanctuary of the

Holy Spirit.

Secondly, the acts of the body have strong reverberations and repercussions upon our spiritual relationship with God. Were one to join his body with a harlot, he would be corrupting that beautiful, God-given covenant relationship which God ordained between husband and wife. We have said before that God does not tolerate confusion and such adultery certainly brings about confusion, for man becomes one with the harlot even as he is one with his wife. Further, because our body is a temple of the Holy Spirit, any sins that involve the body become a great grievance against the Holy Spirit.

Paul closes these thundering words with the admonition that we not only glorify God in spirit, but that we glorify God in our bodies. Is that not really the same as giving our bodies as a living sacrifice, which is an act of worship of God? Concerning the sacrificing of the body, Paul has some very strong medicine to offer us. Note these two passages:

Therefore I run in such a way, as not without aim; I box in such a way, as not beating the air; but I buffet my body and make it my slave, lest possibly, after I have preached to others, I myself should be disqualified. (1 Corinthians 9:26-27)

So then, brethren, we are under obligation, not to the flesh, to live according to the flesh—for if you are living according to the flesh, you must die; but if by the Spirit you are putting to death the deeds of the body, you will live. For all who are being led by the Spirit of God, these are sons of God. (Romans 8:12-14)

Using the great model of the Greek and Roman races, Paul says, "I run toward a goal, not without aim." And if necessary, he says that he buffets, bruises or pummels his body and makes it his slave, lest having preached to others, he himself should be disqualified. Again to the Romans Paul says that if our flesh rules us, we are headed for death, but if we want to get victory over the deeds of the body, then by the power of the Spirit—God's Spirit—we put to death the deeds of the body.

One final passage from Paul to Timothy:

On the other hand, discipline yourself for the purpose
of godliness; for bodily discipline is only of little profit,
but godliness is profitable for all things, since it holds
promise for the present life and also for the life to come.
(1 Timothy 4:7-8)

Many use Paul's words here to defend a great program of physic
discipline. However, careful reading will show even this disciplir
is the discipline of the body for the purpose of godliness. Paul
saying very clearly that if you are going to discipline the body, k
sure that discipline brings about a system of godliness. Further,
you want to get your priorities straight, recognize that godliness
profitable for all things in this life and the next and must certain
supersede bodily discipline.

One of the surest ways of measuring the level of any culture is 1
know where its people fix their priorities. At the risk of alienatin
every exercise and fitness addict in the country, I want to say a fe
strong words. Over the weeks that I have been penning this bool
I have tried to hear a little world news mornings and evenings. I a
astounded at the number of advertisements that relate to the huma
body. Ads for fitness clinics, ads for every kind of food that
supposed to give us better health and longer life, ads for evel
conceivable product in the care of the body. Many of these adve
tisements are blatantly sensual, implying that if you follow th
advice offered you will be much more attractive to the opposite se
and far more successful in your romantic adventures, howeve
promiscuous those might be. One of the national television ne
works recently broadcast a three-week series on the matter
physical health and attractiveness. The underlying assumption-
occasionally verbalized—was that if you have your bodily healtl
you have everything.

Now someone is going to go away from this book and say th;
Gottier said that exercise is sinful. Again that is careless reading.
am simply saying this: We as Christians are very much in danger
letting the world establish our agenda. Paul does suggest that w

ought to care for the body—it is the temple of the Holy Ghost. But if you think I am overstating this, let me ask you to do one simple exercise for me. Take a pencil and tablet and spend fifteen minutes honestly jotting down how much time you spend in the care of your body, in the discipline of your mind, particularly in moving toward a Renewed Mind, and how much time in the care and feeding of your spirit in the course of one week.

I read not long ago a testimony of a man who has been a committed Christian for many years but who suddenly became concerned about his own health and began to jog. Now so far there is nothing wrong with this. However, he suddenly discovered that he was devoting over fourteen hours a week to jogging and would jog at the expense of every other aspect of his life. By his own confession his daily devotions stopped, he neglected his children and his wife, and he began to travel and enter races as a result of his jogging. When we get that excited about having Renewed Minds and becoming spiritual men, the kingdom of God will begin to change this world instead of being dragged down by it.

I have even heard two or three charismatic teachers who are well known through the national media come down hard in favor of having a beautiful body, reiterating the world's position on the matter. Again I say it: We are letting the world set our agenda, and we are absorbing its thinking almost by osmosis. If I am exaggerating all this, let me ask you one other question: Why is it that anorexia and bulimia are virtually as widespread among the young girls in our Christian homes as among those in the world? In the name of our precious Savior Jesus, I beg of us, let us get our priorities straight.

In summary, let us not lose the central issue. Paul admonished us to present our bodies a living sacrifice unto God, which is our rightful service of spiritual worship. This means bringing our body into God's order where our spirit rules our mind and together they rule our body. It certainly means sacrificing the flesh with all of its desires, lusts and passions. It also includes sacrificing our trust in the sense knowledge, which we have used to overrule revelation knowledge for years.

Let me say it all a different way: We are not our bodies. We are spirit, and to our spirits God has given the very precious tool of our minds with which to think, will, choose, emote and learn. To our spirits and minds God has given us beautiful, strong, sound bodies. That body ought to be properly fed, clothed, housed, exercised and cared for. Our bodies in the long run are a tool. If God provides us with an automobile to accomplish His purposes and to travel where we need to go, then we need to take care of that car by servicing it, tuning it and providing whatever maintenance it requires. But if we come to the point where that car is an end in itself and we worship the car, we have totally lost sight of its proper role in our lives. And I submit to you that we are not as Christians going to move on to a Renewed Mind until we have a proper perspective on our God-given bodies.

The Third Step Toward a Renewed Mind: Come to a Humbleness of Mind

Once again let us come back to Paul's great twelfth chapter as he writes to the Romans.

> *I urge you therefore, brethren, by the mercies of God, to present your bodies a living and holy sacrifice, acceptable to God, which is your spiritual service of worship. And do not be conformed to this world, but be transformed by the renewing of your mind, that you may prove what the will of God is, that which is good and acceptable and perfect. For through the grace given to me I say to every man among you not to think more highly of himself than he ought to think; but to think so as to have sound judgment, as God has allotted to each a measure of faith.* (Romans 12:1-3)

Did it ever occur to you to ask this question: If God renewed my mind, gave me great knowledge and understanding, and opened to me all of the wisdom of heaven, but I had not humility, what sort of man would I be? And therein is the context for our third step on the way to a Renewed Mind. Paul opens Romans 12 by addressing them as brethren, those who have come to a reborn spirit. Next he appeals to them for the sacrifice of the body. Paul then presses on to the request for the renewing of the mind, which is our subject here and is the result of these accumulated eight steps.

Paul goes on to say that one of the results of a Renewed Mind is knowing the good, acceptable and perfect will of God. Whenever any of us come to the point that we have been entrusted first with God's good will, then with His acceptable will and finally His perfect will, that is pretty heady stuff.

Paul follows this thought with his great exhortation of verse 3: "For through the grace given to me I say to every man among you not to think more highly of himself than he ought to think."

What a flood of thoughts surround that verse. If we know the will of God, even His perfect will, it is only because He has chosen to entrust us with that knowledge through the revelation of His Spirit. There is, consequently, no room for pride in that which is sovereignly given to us of God. Secondly, we are pursuing the mind of Christ if you will remember. How can anyone imagine that there is room for pride of mind in that beautiful and humble One that walked in Galilee? Third, Paul goes on to put this in the context of the fact that we are all members of one body. And in this body, no one particular part has any more honor or glory than another.

But why should this whole matter of humility of mind be third in the sequence of steps toward the Renewed Mind? Go back and look up the charts in the earlier chapters on the divine order for the nature of man. If that order is to be worked out, then first of all man's spirit must be made alive and put in a position to once again rule his entire being. Second, the flesh must be laid on the altar as an eternal sacrifice unto God and be ruled willingly by the mind and the spirit.

Now, where does that leave the mind? Things are happening all around it. In the old days before the spirit was reborn, the mind had the run of the place. In fact, the most obvious characteristic of every natural mind is arrogance. I hear you say, "Ouch! That is too strong." Is it really? Has not every human mind analyzed everything around it, taken in all the information, processed this through its little computer and arrived at the correct solution to every problem? When I was a small boy there used to be a radio program called the "Life of Riley," and one of Riley's favorite sayings was: "My head is made up." And isn't the mind? Small or great, young or old, having analyzed everything from my perspective and fed in all the relevant facts as far as I'm concerned, my head is made up. Say what you will, there is a basic unteachableness about the natural mind.

Given this scenario, there is really only one hope for a Renewed Mind. If our minds are ever to be reoriented from our senses to our spirits, from the things of the world to the things of God, then we are going to have to climb down off of our individual soap boxes and say "I have been wrong." In the last analysis I suspect there is no greater difficulty, no greater hurdle on the road to a Renewed Mind than for the mind that has operated in the natural for so many years to humble itself and say, "I need to be retrained before God."

Later in this same chapter Paul addresses the matter again:

Be of the same mind toward one another; do not be haughty in mind, but associate with the lowly. Do not be wise in your own estimation. (Romans 12:16)

Do not think more highly of yourself than you ought. Do not be haughty in mind. Do not be wise in your own estimation. What requirement! If you are like me, I suspect your very first question is "Is it even possible?" Well, it must be possible or Paul would not have made the requirement mandatory. What is more, I suspect the task is ours and ours alone. Peter wrote: "Humble yourselves, therefore under the mighty hand of God, that He may exalt you at the proper time" (1 Peter 5:6). If we can come to the point where we can admit the arrogance, we have the battle half won. But win the battle we must, for the Renewed Mind requires no less.

In that same verse of Romans, Paul adds this thought: "But associate with the lowly." At first glance this may seem to have absolutely nothing to do with the Renewed Mind. Yet I suggest to you that it has everything to do with it. One of our greatest temptations as Christians in the late twentieth century is to have a man fearing spirit. We are so impressed with the importance of being seen with the right people, being accepted by the right people; that certainly includes having the right people approve and sanction our thoughts and beliefs. Frequently these may be other Christian friends. They have an important title, a major position; they can even be seen on the right television programs. Now if the Lord begins to reveal to you a portion of truth that others have not yet grasped and they belittle the direction in which God is taking you, do you quickly etreat and say, "Oh no, I must have missed God"?

This was really the question of the Pharisees: How will it help my image? Jesus said they made long prayers, wore wide phylacteries, put large ornate fringes on their robes, chose the chief seats at banquets and dearly loved to be called "teacher."

The subject is humbleness of mind. Have we suddenly left the road and are going down a byway? I think not. As you start down the road to a Renewed Mind, I believe you will find two major stumbling blocks: One—how can I bring myself to admit that I have been wrong for so many years about all these matters? And the other—what will all my friends think when they find out that I am becoming a fanatic?

Jesus emphasized the importance of such humility on numerous occasions. One day He was pronouncing great judgment on Capernaum, Chorazam and Bethsaida. Suddenly in the midst of this He looked toward heaven and said:

> *I praise Thee, O Father, Lord of heaven and earth, that Thou didst hide these things from the wise and intelligent and didst reveal them to babes. Yes, Father, for thus it was well-pleasing in Thy sight.* (Matthew 11:25-26)

Thank You Father, You have hidden these things from the wise and intelligent and revealed them unto babes. What Jesus undoubtedly meant of course was that these things were hidden from those who thought they were wise and intelligent and were revealed unto those that were as humble as babes. I have always liked Kenneth Taylor's translation in The Living Bible of this verse, for he has it that Jesus says: "Thank you Father for hiding these things from the PhD's." And so it is.

One of the most powerful passages in the Word of God is in Matthew 16:

> *Then Jesus said to His disciples, "If any one wishes to come after Me, let him deny himself, and take up his cross, and follow Me. For whoever wishes to save his life shall lose it; but whoever loses his life for My sake shall find it. For what will a man be profited, if he gains*

187

the whole world, and forfeits his soul? Or what will a
man give in exchange for his soul?" (Matthew 16:24-
26)

The word translated life here is really soul-life, or the mind, the
self-image, almost the personality. If I may paraphrase, Jesus is
saying if anyone will come after Me, let him take up his cross—and
crosses are to die on: for pride, self-image and arrogance to die on.
For anyone who demands to save his own self-image, his own soul-
life, his own proud and arrogant self-view, will ultimately lose it. But
he who is willing to humble himself and lose that prideful self-image
for the sake of Jesus and His kingdom shall find his life.

Paul further illuminates this point in two key passages to the
Corinthians:

> *Let no man deceive himself. If any man among you*
> *thinks that he is wise in this age, let him become foolish*
> *that he may become wise. For the wisdom of this world*
> *is foolishness before God. For it is written, "He is the*
> *one who catches the wise in their craftiness."* (1 Corinthi-
> ans 3:18-19)

> *For I am jealous for you with a godly jealousy; for I*
> *betrothed you to one husband, that to Christ I might*
> *present you as a pure virgin. But I am afraid, lest as*
> *the serpent deceived Eve by his craftiness, your minds*
> *should be led astray from the simplicity and purity of*
> *devotion to Christ.* (2 Corinthians 11:2-3)

Once again the same basic theme: If a man thinks he is wise let
him become foolish, for it is only in becoming foolish that one may
hope to become wise in the wisdom of heaven. Further, Paul says
that the wisdom of this world is foolishness to God for He is the One
who catches the wise in their craftiness. Paul further points out in
the second passage that this is not really a once and for all battle. It
is an ongoing struggle as long as we live. For he says to the
Corinthians: I am afraid, lest as the serpent deceived Eve that you
too may be led astray from the simplicity and purity of devotion to

Christ. And that temptation is before every Christian at every moment. That somehow in my wisdom I have that which surpasses the Word of God and become estranged to the simple gospel of salvation in Jesus Christ.

I often comment in my teaching that I am convinced that the single greatest fear of Christians in this age is that someone will call them a fanatic. Once you have discovered that to every man the definition of a fanatic is someone who loves Jesus more than he does, you will no longer be intimidated by that word.

Every cult ever formed begins with some new, special, secret knowledge never before available and not available to the common man. Such pride in sensual, rational knowledge inevitably leads the cult and its members away from the centrality of the Lordship of Jesus Christ and soon into gross error.

Let me remind you once again that the final characteristic of the Renewed Mind is that we have the mind of Christ. With this thought before us, let me cite to you one of the most powerful passages in the Word of God:

> *If therefore there is any encouragement in Christ, if there is any consolation of love, if there is any fellowship of the Spirit, if any affection and compassion, make my joy complete by being of the same mind, maintaining the same love, united in spirit, intent on one purpose. Do nothing from selfishness or empty conceit, but with humility of mind let each of you regard one another as more important than himself; do not merely look out for your own personal interests, but also for the interests of others. Have this attitude in yourselves which was also in Christ Jesus, who, although He existed in the form of God, did not regard equality with God a thing to be grasped, but emptied Himself, taking the form of a bond-servant, and being made in the likeness of men. And being found in appearance as a man, He humbled Himself by becoming obedient to the point of death, even death on a cross. Therefore also God highly exalted Him, and bestowed on Him the name which is above every name,*

that at the name of Jesus every knee should bow, of those who are in heaven, and on earth, and under the earth, and that every tongue should confess that Jesus Christ is Lord, to the glory of God the Father. (Philippians 2:1-11)

Paraphrasing Paul: Do nothing from selfishness, contentiousness or empty conceit, but with humility of mind, let us each regard another as more important than self. Have the same mind in you which was also in Christ Jesus, Paul says, for though He was a very part of the God-head and spoke the worlds into being, yet still He did not think that the glories of heaven were something to be clasped to Himself. But laying aside all the privileges of heaven, Jesus took upon Himself the form of a bond-servant; He humbled Himself and became obedient even to the point of death on a cross.

If about this time you are ready to skip over this "lesser" point to get on to the good stuff, let me encourage you to read Philippians 2:1-11 several more times.

Once more, Paul wrote to the Colossians:

> *Since you laid aside the old self with its evil practices, and have put on the new self who is being renewed to a true knowledge according to the image of the One who created him,—a renewal in which there is no distinction between Greek and Jew, circumcised and uncircumcised, barbarian, Scythian, slave and freeman, but Christ is all, and in all. And so, as those who have been chosen of God, holy and beloved, put on a heart of compassion, kindness, humility, gentleness and patience.* (Colossians 3:9-12)

Once we have put on the new man (our spirits have been made alive), and our mind is being renewed to a true knowledge, then let us put on a heart of compassion, kindness and humility.
James gives a slightly different emphasis to this now familiar message:

> *But He gives a greater grace. Therefore it says, "God is*

190

*opposed to the proud, but gives grace to the humble."
Submit therefore to God. Resist the devil and he will
flee from you. Draw near to God and He will draw near
to you. Cleanse your hands, you sinners; and purify
your hearts, you double-minded. Be miserable and
mourn and weep; let your laughter be turned into
mourning, and your joy to gloom. Humble yourselves
in the presence of the Lord, and He will exalt you.*
(James 4:6-10)

God is opposed to the proud, but He gives grace to the humble.
Therefore submit yourself to God, resist the devil, the things of the
flesh, the things of the world and the things you learn solely through
the senses. Draw near to God and He will draw near to you.

But here is the key: We must purify our hearts and minds if we are
double-minded. Remember that being double-minded is trying to
be fixed on the things of rational knowledge and the things of revealed knowledge at the same moment, and it cannot be done.
Finally, once again He says that if we humble ourselves in the
presence of the Lord He will exalt us.

In January 1974, after many years of sinking deeper and deeper
into skepticism and rationalism, I came to the end of it all and fell on
my knees before the Lord. In a voice that seemed almost audible the
Lord began to outline for me the steps ahead if I were to come back
to serve Him. As clearly as any voice I have ever known, I heard the
Lord instruct me that the first step on my way back would be coming
to a point of humbleness of mind before Him. This entire book in
general, and this particular point specifically, was born deep in the
furnace of this struggle. I can only surmise that there are multitudes
of Christians out there in a position not unlike my own, for whom the
journey back to the Renewed Mind will rise or fall primarily on the
ability to overcome this hurdle: conquering one's own prideful self-
image.

Finally, once the spirit of man is reborn and he once again has
access to the things of the kingdom of God, and once man has
moved decisively in offering his body of flesh as a sacrifice unto the
Lord, the next major hurdle will be dealing with the arrogance of the
mind. Natural man has such a vested interest in his own ego, his own

mind and self-image. In fact, many of the personality systems developed in psychology are built almost solely around the defense mechanisms which the ego uses. Rational man is simply not prepared to admit on his own that he has made a mistake. I am fully confident that the step of taking one's ego by the nape of the neck and saying, "humble yourself under the mighty hand of God," will be the single biggest step for most of us in this journey toward a Renewed Mind.

Unfortunately, vast numbers of Christians will make this struggle and lose. Therein we have some of the great conflicts within the church of Jesus Christ. I make these comments in great love and compassion, but hear me clearly. I believe this is precisely the explanation of why on many occasions there has been a great outpouring of the Spirit of God calling the church to revival and renewal, but many—if not most—of the leaders of the great denominations are entirely bypassed. Men who have come to points of leadership and positions of prominence face several major problems. First, the possibility of losing their own position if they move into the flow of God. Secondly, many denominational leaders have spoken so often against the work of the Holy Spirit and the gifts of the Spirit that the cost of admitting they have been wrong all this time is too high. Thirdly, it is very difficult to be entrusted with positions of great responsibility and still maintain a teachable spirit within oneself.

Please don't read these comments as an attack on denominational leaders, but simply a stern warning that Satan's central appeal to the Christian again and again is to his ego and his mind. Remember this was the point at which Satan himself fell, for he said "I will exalt my throne above the throne of God" (see Isaiah 14:12-15). And many men who would never fall to immorality or greed succumb to the subtle appeal of pride and the rational mind.

I encourage you to read and reread the scriptures that we have cited here. If necessary, stop your forward progress in this book—put it down for three weeks while you deal with this matter. A breakthrough at this point will do more to further your own Christian growth than any other single battle in which you have ever engaged. Please, deal with the matter of coming to humbleness of mind now—your entire walk with Christ hinges on it!

The Fourth Step Toward a Renewed Mind: Be Determined to Be Transformed

Let's have one more look at Romans 12:

> *I urge you therefore, brethren, by the mercies of God, to present your bodies a living and holy sacrifice, acceptable to God, which is your spiritual service of worship. And do not be conformed to this world, but be transformed by the renewing of your mind, that you may prove what the will of God is, that which is good and acceptable and perfect.* (Romans 12:1-2)

In the King James Version these words read: "be ye transformed by the renewing of your mind." This imperative verb carries the definite connotation of intent and determination. Be ye transformed!

From the perspective of the mind—trapped between the spirit and the flesh, having no access to the outside world—all the ground rules seem to be changing. The spirit, which has never before been heard from, is suddenly alive and the gentle, sweet whisperings of the Holy Spirit seem ever to challenge the mind. The flesh, which has been the competitor, has suddenly been sacrificed on the altar of worship and adoration to the Lord. As if that were not enough, by an act of the will the arrogance of the mind has been struck down and those familiar words of Peter have been heard again and again: "Humble yourself under the mighty hand of God."

Now the mind faces the last line of defense. Oriented for many years to the things of the flesh and the senses, suddenly there comes this new command: "Be ye transformed—by the renewing of the mind." In fact, along with these words from Romans 12, there are other words that are constantly echoing through the mind:

> *If then you have been raised up with Christ, keep seeking the things above, where Christ is, seated at the right hand of God. Set your mind on the things above, not on the things that are on earth.* (Colossians 3:1-2)

Focus your mind on the things above, not on the things on the earth. This seems to be the whole choice for the mind. For so long all the things of this world have seemed so terribly important. Now through the whisperings of the Holy Spirit there is the desire to look up. And the mind has looked up again and again, thrilled at what it saw. However, the things of this life and this world are still as comfortable as an old shoe, so familiar, so utterly dependable.

In many ways this is the deciding step of the eight. When the spirit was reborn, the things of the knowledge of the glory of the Lord were once again available. When the flesh was laid on the altar the competing cries of lust and passion were silenced. When the mind was brought to humility before God, its arrogant rebellion was subdued. Now there seem only the two competing voices: the old, familiar things of earth, or the new, promising voice of heaven.

Having visited with a number of people who have heard me teach on the Renewed Mind, I believe that for most people the final step toward the Renewed Mind comes almost in a moment of crisis as certainly as the decision to accept Christ as Savior. Finally, one day after vacillating for perhaps days, months or even years like James' double-minded man, the individual says: "Enough! From this moment on I choose to trust the things of God no matter what it costs me." That is a great day in the life of any man and, in all fairness, some of us will probably make it a half-dozen times. Though we may start down this road and fail, each time it gets easier to trust the ways of the Lord.

I know that we have almost camped in Romans 8 throughout this book, but come one more time with me to a crucial passage:

> *In order that the requirement of the Law might be fulfilled in us, who do not walk according to the flesh, but according to the Spirit. For those who are according to the flesh set their minds on the things of the flesh, but those who are according to the Spirit, the things of the Spirit. For the mind set on the flesh is death, but the mind set on the Spirit is life and peace, because the mind set on the flesh is hostile toward God; for it does not subject itself to the law of God, for it is not even able to do so; and those who are in the flesh cannot please God.* (Romans 8:4-8)

194

Try as we may, we simply cannot escape it. This language of intent and determination seems to be everywhere we read. Let me paraphrase: Those who live according to the flesh set their minds on the things of the flesh. The mind set on the flesh is death, but the mind set on the Spirit is life and peace. The mind set on the flesh is hostile to God.

There seems no other way to state it now. All that remains to the mind at this point is a simple decision, a simple act of determination to be transformed. The alternative according to Romans 12:2 is to be conformed to this present world, or as J.B. Phillips would put it, to let the world squeeze us into its mold. But since that answer will never do for a man or woman of God, the simple decision is before us: We will be transformed by the renewing of our minds for we have set our every intention upon it.

There is a marvelous illustration of all this in the life of Peter as Mark records it. Following Jesus' query, "Who are people saying that I am?" and Peter's God-given insight, "You are the Messiah," Jesus begins to tell them of the cross ahead:

> *And He began to teach them that the Son of Man must suffer many things and be rejected by the elders and the chief priests and scribes, and be killed, and after three days rise again. And He was stating the matter plainly. And Peter took Him aside and began to rebuke Him. But turning around and seeing His disciples, He rebuked Peter, and said, "Get behind Me, Satan; for you are not setting your mind on God's interests, but man's."* (Mark 8:31-33)

Jesus responded to Peter with these crucial words: "Get behind Me, Satan; for you are not setting your mind on the things of God, but the things of man." The very fact that Jesus rebuked Peter in this situation suggests that Peter had an alternative. You do not reprimand a man for doing the only thing he is able to do. But Jesus' words are very stern and He is saying: "You had a choice, and you chose the wrong one." But notice once again the strong latitude for intent, as Jesus said, "You are not setting your mind."

Jesus gives us another powerful illustration in the Gospel of John:

195

Yet no one was speaking openly of Him for fear of the
Jews. But when it was now the midst of the feast Jesus
went up into the temple, and began to teach. The Jews
therefore were marveling, saying, "How has this man
become learned, having never been educated?" Jesus
therefore answered them, and said, "My teaching is not
Mine, but His who sent Me. If any man is willing to do
His will, he shall know of the teaching, whether it is of
God, or whether I speak from Myself. He who speaks
from himself seeks his own glory; but He who is seeking
the glory of the one who sent Him, He is true, and there
is no unrighteousness in Him." (John 7:13-18)

The Jews as usual were questioning everything about Jesus—His authority, His theology, His education and now His teaching. In the midst of this dialogue, Jesus gives us a profound insight into the things of heaven. If man is willing to do the will of the Father, he shall at once know the teaching—whether it is from God. Let me bring this into the context of the present chapter. We shall soon be emphasizing the role of the Word of God in the renewing of a man's mind. However, a crucial point needs to be made: The more we are willing to be taught, the more we are willing to do His will and be obedient, the more He is willing to open His Word to us and reveal Himself and His ways.

Now back to the business of setting our mind on the things above. If I am double-minded—with my mind set on the things above one moment and the things of this earth the next—it will be difficult for the Lord to entrust His Word to me. It will be difficult to even grasp the power of His Word in the first place. The Old Testament teaches us that God hates a mixture. If the revealed knowledge from above has to be mixed with rational knowledge from below every time the mind flip-flops, confusion results. On the other hand, to the extent that my mind is now determined—set on the things above—can the Father begin to entrust the Word to me.

The writer to the Hebrews picks up very nearly this precise thought:

Therefore leaving the elementary teaching about the

*Christ, let us press on to maturity, not laying again a
foundation of repentance from dead works and of faith
toward God, of instruction about washings, and laying
on of hands, and the resurrection of the dead, and
eternal judgment. And this we shall do, if God permits.*
(Hebrews 6:1-3)

The key concept here is one of pressing on toward maturity. Once again there is the same element of determination: Press on.

Parenthetically, there is the interesting parallel here that spiritual maturity is not only refocusing one's gaze from the things of this earth to the things of heaven, but a shifted focus from the things that are primarily external in orientation to an understanding of the deeper truths of His kingdom, as these come by revelation knowledge.

The apostle Peter uses still another imagery to make the point we are discussing:

*Therefore, gird your minds for action, keep sober in
spirit, fix your hope completely on the grace to be
brought to you at the revelation of Jesus Christ. As
obedient children, do not be conformed to the former
lusts which were yours in your ignorance, but like the
Holy One who called you, be holy yourselves also in all
your behavior.* (1 Peter 1:13- 15)

This translation from the NASB actually misses a portion of this beautiful picture. Peter quite literally says: "Gird up the loins of your mind." To understand the imagery here you have to know that in Jesus' day their clothing consisted of an undergarment and then a long outer tunic which reached nearly to the ground. This arrangement was fine for walking, but hardly conducive to running if someone were chasing you. At such a time you twisted the outer tunic into a coil. Then you would swing this between your legs, bring it up and tie it around your waist to form a type of pantaloon, leaving the legs free for running. Now if you can pick up the same imagery of the mind, Peter is saying: "Cut out this nonsense, maybe this, maybe that, maybe something else. Know what you believe, gird up the loins of your mind, and fix your hope completely on the grace that is brought to you at the revelation of Jesus Christ." The result, Peter says, is that we will no longer be conformed to our former lusts, but like Jesus who called us, our own behavior will be holy too.

By the way, I get amused at Peter's picture of this long tunic flapping in the wind as a man tries to run. When he translates this to the girding of the loins of the mind, I so want to blurt out: "I have a number of academic-type friends whom you just perfectly described!" I know men whose students have not pinned them down to one honest point of belief; they stand for not one thing after twenty years. They have played the academic game so long that no matter what side of an argument you take, they are delighted to take the other side. If that is not a mind flapping in the wind, then I misunderstand this whole thing.

And so, the fourth step toward a Renewed Mind: Be ye transformed by the renewing of your mind. Once again the sequence is absolutely mandatory. Man's spirit has been reborn, the body of his flesh sacrificed on the altar of divine worship, his mind willfully and intentionally brought to a place of humility before God. Now with all the old familiar tuggings and pullings subdued, the mind is confronted with the most significant choice it will make. For years it has been comfortable in trusting the things of the senses, rational knowledge as it is given through the flesh. But now the wooings and the promises of the Spirit of God keep calling with an ever stronger voice. This is no time for vacillation. This is a time for determination. Be ye transformed; set your minds; will to do His will; press on to maturity; gird up the loins of your minds.

As I have said before, let me repeat: I am convinced that you will never accidentally wake up one morning with a Renewed Mind. I believe that pressing on to a Renewed Mind and becoming a spiritual man requires a decision of nearly the same level of impact as accepting Jesus Christ as your personal Savior and Lord. In fact, in terms of the long-range impact on your ability to live a victorious overcoming Christian life, the former decision may be just as important as the latter. Am I demeaning the importance of the new birth by that comment? Not at all! I am simply saying that millions of Christians, apart from moving toward a genuinely Renewed Mind, will continue to live a Christian life of fits and starts—moving one step forward, sliding two steps back—ultimately to find themselves in Pilgrim's Slough of Despond.

The Fifth Step Toward a Renewed Mind: Be Filled With the Holy Spirit

Perhaps Paul's greatest sustained teaching on the Renewed Mind is found in the first three chapters of 1 Corinthians. Let me point you here once again:

> *Yet we do speak wisdom among those who are mature; a wisdom, however, not of this age, nor of the rulers of this age, who are passing away; but we speak God's wisdom in a mystery, the hidden wisdom, which God predestined before the ages to our glory; the wisdom which none of the rulers of this age has understood; for if they had understood it, they would not have crucified the Lord of glory; but just as it is written, "Things which eye has not seen and ear has not heard, and which have not entered the heart of man, all that God has prepared for those who love Him." For to us God revealed them through the Spirit; for the Spirit searches all things, even the depths of God. For who among men knows the thoughts of a man except the spirit of the man, which is in him? Even so the thoughts of God no one knows except the Spirit of God. Now we have received, not the spirit of the world, but the Spirit who is from God, that we might know the things freely given to us by God, which things we also speak, not in words taught by human wisdom, but in those taught by the Spirit, combining spiritual thoughts with spiritual words.* (1 Corinthians 2:6-13)

Note that Paul speaks here of revelation knowledge: He speaks of wisdom among those who are mature—a wisdom not of this age, a wisdom not of things that are passing away, but a wisdom which was conceived before the foundations of the earth. This wisdom includes the miracle of Calvary and God's eternal plan of salvation.

This revelation knowledge came to us, Paul says, through the Holy Spirit. For the Holy Spirit searches all things, the deep things of God, and knows the thoughts of the Father God; and He brings these truths to the spiritually mature.

In verse 12 Paul is very specific when he says: We have received the Spirit who is from God that we might know the things freely given to us by God. Even the words we speak are not the words of our human wisdom, but the words taught to us by the Holy Spirit. Then he gives us a powerful insight: The thoughts that we have from revealed knowledge and the words by which we express them are both the gift of the Holy Spirit who dwells within us.

And so we come to the fifth step toward a Renewed Mind: Be filled with the Holy Spirit! So absolutely crucial is this step that I am convinced those who neglect the matters of the Holy Spirit or openly mock or oppose the presence and gifts of the Spirit today can never fully come to understand the revealed truths in God's Word.

When a man faces death, his last words reveal the deepest feelings of his heart and the uppermost thoughts of his mind. The apostle John devoted five chapters of his Gospel to Jesus' last words on the night before He was crucified. There in the upper room, Jesus returned again and again to the matter of the Holy Spirit. Let's briefly consider these words of profound truth.

First, in John 14:

> *These things I have spoken to you, while abiding with you. But the Helper, the Holy Spirit, whom the Father will send in My name, He will teach you all things, and bring to your remembrance all that I said to you.* (John 14:25-26)

Of all the beautiful things Jesus could have told us about the precious Holy Spirit, He chose to focus primarily upon the role of the Holy Spirit in teaching us. In particular here He emphasizes two major functions of the Holy Spirit: First, it is the Spirit's responsibility to teach us *all* things. We already learned from Paul that the Holy Spirit understands the thoughts of God the Father. And the Spirit is charged with communicating His thoughts to us! If that doesn't astound you, it should! Not only that, He will bring to our remem-

200

brance everything Jesus said.

This promise undoubtedly has many ramifications: It certainly explains how the apostles and Gospel writers were able to recall the words of the Lord and put them down accurately, producing the New Testament as we have it today. But it promises even more: It includes all the times when we need to give a reason for the faith that is within us, and our precious Holy Spirit comes at just the right moment with the right Scripture passage, the right illustration, the right phrasing of the testimony.

Next, in John 15:

> *When the Helper comes, whom I will send to you from the Father, that is the Spirit of truth, who proceeds from the Father, He will bear witness of Me, and you will bear witness also, because you have been with Me from the beginning.* (John 15:26-27)

Jesus reveals a striking point: If the Holy Spirit has a second name, He is to be called the Spirit of truth. We have talked much about truth in this book. The word truth is thrown around haphazardly as a description for rational knowledge millions of times every day I suspect. But real truth, God-given truth, comes only by revealed knowledge. And here we have one more portrait of the Revealer of that knowledge, the Holy Spirit of truth.

Next, John 16:

> *But I tell you the truth, it is to your advantage that I go away; for if I do not go away, the Helper shall not come to you; but if I go, I will send Him to you. And He, when He comes, will convict the world concerning sin, and righteousness, and judgment; concerning sin, because they do not believe in Me; and concerning righteousness, because I go to the Father, and you no longer behold Me; and concerning judgment, because the ruler of this world has been judged. I have many more things to say to you, but you cannot bear them now. But when He, the Spirit of truth, comes, He will guide you into all the truth; for He will not speak on His own ini-*

tiative, but whatever He hears, He will speak; and He will disclose to you what is to come. He shall glorify Me; for He shall take of Mine and shall disclose it to you. All things that the Father has are Mine; therefore I said, that He takes of Mine, and will disclose it to you. (John 16:7-15)

Jesus tells the grieving disciples, who were troubled at their Master's leaving, that it is best that He go away. For He must first go away in order that the Holy Spirit, the Helper, can come. In what I consider to be a golden text on the subject of understanding revealed knowledge, Jesus explains to them: "But when He, the Spirit of truth, comes, He will guide you into all the truth." What a fantastic promise—yield to His leading, listen to His voice, stick around long enough and He will tell you all the deep truths of the kingdom of God. Paul's statement is confirmed as Jesus goes on to say that He will not speak on His own initiative, but whatever He hears He will disclose to you.

As if to disavow those today who say, "We worship Jesus, but you worship the Holy Spirit and ignore Jesus," our Lord goes on to say, "He shall glorify Me." What a beautiful truth that so many miss: The more power of God's Holy Spirit that indwells you, the more you will glorify Jesus. And then for the third time in the Word, we have the very same concept: The Holy Spirit takes the things of Jesus and reveals them to us; but Jesus got the things He had from the Father; therefore the Holy Spirit is taking the things of the Father as spoken through Jesus and revealing them to us.

If our minds are to know as God knows, if we are to be taught by revelation knowledge, we must have the Teacher of revelation knowledge dwelling within our spirits, and that is our precious Holy Spirit. He has direct access to the Father's heart and the things taking place in heaven at every moment; and it is His business to reveal that to us. The Spirit of truth communicates to us the Father's love, the Father's concern and care for us, and now and again the frown from the Father when we have grieved Him. He is always taking the things from the kingdom of God, the very heart of God Himself, and teaching us. How much stronger could we say it? He is the very Spirit of truth who leads us into all truth.

You would expect Paul to address this subject in Romans 8 wouldn't you? And he does not disappoint:

> For the mind set on the flesh is death, but the mind set on the Spirit is life and peace, because the mind set on the flesh is hostile toward God; for it does not subject itself to the law of God, for it is not even able to do so; and those who are in the flesh cannot please God. However you are not in the flesh but in the Spirit, if indeed the Spirit of God dwells in you. But if anyone does not have the Spirit of Christ, he does not belong to Him. (Romans 8:6-9)

We begin in the context of this familiar passage. The mind set on the flesh is death, but the mind set on the Spirit is life and peace. Paul reminds us that the mind set on the flesh is hostile against God. But then he goes on to give us the test of not being in the flesh—the Spirit of God must dwell in you. So the mind that has been focused on the flesh and the senses for so long must be reoriented to focus on the reborn human spirit and on the Holy Spirit, who now indwells that spirit.

Paul writes in his letter to Titus a few words of relevance to us here:

> But when the kindness of God our Savior and His love for mankind appeared, He saved us, not on the basis of deeds which we have done in righteousness, but according to His mercy, by the washing of regeneration and renewing by the Holy Spirit, whom He poured out upon us rightly through Jesus Christ our Savior. (Titus 3:4-6)

Paul clearly summarizes our salvation here: We are saved, not on the basis of our deeds, but according to the mercy of God by two basic steps—the washing of regeneration and the renewing by the Holy Spirit. And it is this infilling of the Holy Spirit which I urge upon you as so critical at this point.

Just one more passage on this:

And as for you, the anointing which you received from Him abides in you, and you have no need for anyone to teach you; but as His anointing teaches you about all things, and is true and is not a lie, and just as it has taught you, you abide in Him. And now, little children, abide in Him, so that when He appears, we may have confidence and not shrink away from Him in shame at His coming. If you know that He is righteous, you know that every one also who practices righteousness is born of Him. (1 John 2:27-29)

You have an anointing from the Holy One, and you all know. Some manuscripts add, "you know all things," but that really doesn't change the impact of the meaning here. Because we have the anointing from the Holy One, we can know. Further, John says that because we have the anointing from the Holy One and He abides in us, we have no need for anyone to teach us. This is an extremely important point. Many people submit themselves to teachers who do not know the infilling of the Holy Spirit and, in fact, are in open opposition to the gifts of the Spirit. According to John, the much better course is to know the power of the Holy Spirit within your own life, and then ask Him to teach you the deep things of God and His Word. John carries it still further: Because His anointing rests upon you and teaches you all things, you can trust the teaching that comes from the Holy Spirit because it is truth and not a lie.

I mentioned earlier my encounter with the Lord in January 1974, and His call for me to return to the truth of His Word. Out of His sovereign goodness, and for reasons which I do not fully understand to this day, God chose to speak to me very directly that day. I mentioned earlier that His first words were that I must come to a point of humility of mind toward Him. His second statement was equally direct: "You must be filled with the Holy Spirit."

Receiving the fullness of the Holy Spirit was most difficult for me. I had accepted Jesus as my Savior at age nine and had grown up under very strict teaching that the gifts of the Holy Spirit were not for our day. However, I made a covenant with God that afternoon that I would reaffirm the authority of the Word in my life and would never again question its authenticity. God in great love patiently taught me hour after hour, day after day, in the things of the Word. Months later the day came when I finally looked up and said, "Father, I am sorry for all the times I have opposed You and the things of Your Word. I see clearly that the infilling of Your Holy Spirit is taught consistently and systematically throughout the New Testament. Now I give myself to You utterly and ask that You give me all that You have for me." And what a blessed experience it was that day. I tell you this to just make one point: From that day on, the Word of God came alive in my heart in a dimension more powerful than I had ever known it before.

And so I say to you once again, my reader friend, that I fully believe the Lord is calling you to a totally Renewed Mind—to being a totally spiritual man. However, I believe there is a depth of understanding of the Word of God and of revealed knowledge about the kingdom of God that will never be fully revealed to you until you accept the Holy Spirit as your primary Teacher.

It is beyond the scope of this book to go in depth about the infilling of God's Holy Spirit in our lives and the operation of His gifts in the body of Christ; however, I would refer you to the following passage:

> *Now suppose one of you fathers is asked by his son for a fish; he will not give him a snake instead of a fish, will he? Or if he is asked for an egg, he will not give him a scorpion, will he? If you then, being evil, know how to give good gifts to your children, how much more shall your heavenly Father give the Holy Spirit to those who ask Him?* (Luke 11:11-13)

There are many other wonderful passages in the Word of God, but this is all you need to know. If you and I, in our own evil condition compared to God, will always bless our own children with good gifts, how much more will our heavenly Father give the Holy Spirit to those who ask. I can't make it any clearer. I would encourage you to find a quiet place by yourself and pour out your heart to Him. Ask Him to cleanse all sins that are there—not only the sins of the flesh, but the sins of your own attitudes, ego and pride. When you have done this, ask Him to fill you afresh. Receive it by faith just as you received your salvation and begin to pour out your adoration and praise for the Father, the Son and the Holy Spirit. Your life will be changed from this moment on.

I have been mentioning throughout this chapter the sequential nature of these eight steps. You may legitimately be asking: Why must the infilling of the Holy Spirit come precisely here? Let me give you a few words of perspective. For many years a number of groups pictured receiving God's Holy Spirit as an event for which one had to pray and tarry and beg for hours, if not nights, on end. I see nothing in the Word of God that confirms that. In fact, I know hundreds of friends to whom God has graciously given His Holy Spirit at the very moment they reached out in faith. I further believe that if we were properly taught, we ought to move immediately from the point of accepting Jesus as Savior to asking the Father to fill us with His Holy Spirit. If that has been the case in your life and you have known the fullness of the Holy Spirit, then simply praise God with me and thank Him that you have already passed this step before we got to it.

My reason for putting it fifth in these eight sequential steps is that I believe it is the last possible moment at which you can receive the infilling of the Holy Spirit and still go on to a Renewed Mind. I am fully aware that the presence of the Holy Spirit would be a great aid at several of the earlier steps. However, we may concede these four points: You come to receive Jesus as your Savior and your spirit is made alive. You may, as an act of your will, lay your body of flesh on the altar of sacrifice before God, and God will honor it. I believe that you may somehow take your mind by the nape of the neck and determine to be humble before God, though certainly the power of His Spirit would be of great help at this point. Further, you may, by an act of your will, set your mind on the things above. At this point, however, the whole process comes to a grinding halt.

Some mature Christian out there may say: "But you need the power of the Holy Spirit in steps two, three and four." And I totally agree. I am simply saying I am convinced that this is the outside limit of self-effort, and that one simply will not go on to a deep understanding of the Word of God or the miraculous apart from the power of the Holy Spirit indwelling him.

The Sixth Step Toward a Renewed Mind: Feed on the Word of God

Pause with me for a moment at this juncture to review the plight of the carnal mind. You will remember that the carnal mind is simply a natural mind with one distinguishing feature—a window has been opened on heavenly things through the rebirth of the spirit. Now the most distinctive thing one can say about the natural mind is this: It consists of the accumulated wisdom of this age and of all its past experiences as it has been taught through the five senses.

In the carnal man, since his spirit has been made alive, his mind begins to hear the first whisper of spiritual things. However, reality for the carnal mind is still defined in terms of the wisdom of this world and this age. Though he may have an occasional glimpse of the possibilities of life lived on a higher plane, his efforts at achieving such dreams still are carried out at the rational level. In the midst of these sincere efforts, he still finds himself waging war with unbelief.

Stated bluntly, the mind of the carnal man has had a lifetime of bad teaching. He needs nothing in the world now as much as a new education. He needs to go to Holy Spirit school and be retaught in the ways of God. In fact, all further growth in his spiritual life and his progress toward a Renewed Mind will hinge almost one hundred percent upon how well his mind and spirit are fed in the pastures of God's truth.

If you have followed the first five steps on this path to the Renewed Mind, you are now ready for a veritable explosion in your growth in the Christian life. With your spirit reborn and your fellowship with the heavenly Father restored, you now have a clear channel to receive His course-correcting revelation knowledge. The battles which you once waged with the flesh have been put behind you as you placed the body of flesh on His altar as a living sacrifice. The old problems of arrogance of mind and proudful self-image have faded away as the ego was crucified on the cross. In their place has come a humbleness of mind toward the Lord. Further, against the competing wisdom of this age, you have with conscious determination set your mind on the wisdom from above. Finally, having received the fullness of God's Holy Spirit, you now have your own Teacher indwelling you. He is ready to open the Word and instruct you in dimensions you never before believed possible.

You are now ready for a spiritual growth spurt the extent of which is governed by the amount of spiritual food you feed your mind and spirit. The Word of God is a pasture of such proportions that it has never yet been over-grazed by any Christian of which I know. In the Word you will find His ways, His thoughts, His principles and the laws of the kingdom of God. If the carnal mind's most pressing need is a thorough re-education, then the textbook is the Word of God and the Teacher is the Holy Spirit.

The final factor in this equation is the amount of discipline you bring to this reschooling process. I have always been fascinated with the fact that in the Greek language discipline and teaching are intimately bound up in the same word-stem. Jesus instructed His own disciples to spread out and make disciples or literally "taught ones" in all nations. Even in the universities of this country we still speak of the various schools or fields of study as "disciplines." So what I urge upon you is no randomly chosen word. It will be literally the discipline that you bring to the school of God that determines the pace of your spiritual growth.

Remembering once again that last words seem always to carry special significance, in Moses' great valedictory to Israel he gave us a model for all that I have been saying to you:

> *Now this is the commandment, the statutes and the judgments which the Lord your God has commanded me to teach you, that you might do them in the land where you are going over to possess it, so that you and your son and your grandson might fear the Lord your God, to keep all His statutes and His commandments, which I command you, all the days of your life, and that your days may be prolonged. O Israel, you should listen and be careful to do it, that it may be well with you and that you may multiply greatly, just as the Lord, the God of your fathers, has promised you, in a land flowing with milk and honey. Hear, O Israel! The Lord is our God, the Lord is one! And you shall love the Lord your God with all your heart and with all your soul and with all your might. And these words, which I am com-*

manding you today, shall be on your heart; and you shall teach them diligently to your sons and shall talk of them when you sit in your house and when you walk by the way and when you lie down and when you rise up. And you shall bind them as a sign on your hand and they shall be as frontals on your forehead. And you shall write them on the doorposts of your house and on your gates. (Deuteronomy 6:1-9)

What a passage filled with profound insights! The very purpose of studying the commandments and statutes of the Lord is that you and your children may properly fear the Lord. And in this call for obedience to the Word of God, Moses suggests a variety of ways in which this discipline be carried out. These words are to be stored in our heart (spirit). We are to teach them diligently to our children— talk of them whether we are walking by the road or sitting in our home, when we lie down and when we rise up. The Word of God is to be the central focus of our every waking moment. Everywhere we turn there should be a reminder of the Word: bound to our hands and our foreheads, written upon our gateposts and the lintels of our doors.

Only a few days after Moses spoke these words, the Lord spoke to Joshua, his successor, in like fashion:

No man will be able to stand before you all the days of your life. Just as I have been with Moses, I will be with you; I will not fail you or forsake you. Be strong and courageous, for you shall give this people possession of the land which I swore to their fathers to give them. Only be strong and very courageous; be careful to do according to all the law which Moses My servant commanded you; do not turn from it to the right or to the left, so that you may have success wherever you go. This book of the law shall not depart from your mouth, but you shall meditate on it day and night, so that you may be careful to do according to all that is written in it; for then you will make your way prosperous, and then you will have success. (Joshua 1:5-8)

Few men have ever been entrusted with greater responsibilities than was Joshua. He was to take several million people across the Jordan and there clean out a dozen or more hostile nations and prepare God's people for living in the promised land. In this context God calls to Joshua for great strength, great courage and for a constant focus on the Word of God. Specifically, Joshua was to meditate on the Word day and night and keep the principles of the kingdom of God perpetually on his lips.

The King James translators rendered Psalm 119:11 thus: "Thy Word have I hid in mine heart, that I might not sin against Thee." However, I am particularly fond of the NASB translation: "Thy Word I have treasured...."

I believe it is significant that the Old Testament passages constantly refer to the Word being stored in the heart and not in the mind, and I will comment on this a bit later.

Following Jesus' forty-day temptation in the wilderness, the tempter came to Him in an effort to get Him to use His divine powers to meet the needs of His hungry flesh. Jesus responded with the words of Deuteronomy again: "Man shall not live on bread alone but on every Word that proceeds out of the mouth of God" (Matthew 4:4).

Paul wrote to the Colossian people:

> *And let the peace of Christ rule in your hearts, to which indeed you were called in one body; and be thankful. Let the word of Christ richly dwell within you, with all wisdom teaching and admonishing one another with psalms and hymns and spiritual songs, singing with thankfulness in your hearts to God.* (Colossians 3:15-16)

If one is to live by the Word of God, meditate on the Word of God be taught by the Word of God, it must first be stored up so that it is available for the Holy Spirit to call forth in this instruction process. In this light there is such a wealth of truth in the Colossian passage we just read: "Let the word of Christ richly dwell within you." The Word is not simply stored as in the memory bank of a computer, but once the Word takes up residence deep in our minds and spirits i becomes a living thing—dwelling there, alive, ready to be called forth at the beckoning of the Holy Spirit at the proper moment.

The writer to the Hebrews must have had this matter of spiritual maturation and the re-education of the mind clearly before him when he wrote:

> *Concerning him we have much to say, and it is hard to explain, since you have become dull of hearing. For though by this time you ought to be teachers, you have need again for some one to teach you the elementary principles of the oracles of God, and you have come to need milk and not solid food. For every one who partakes only of milk is not accustomed to the word of righteousness, for he is a babe. But solid food is for the mature, who because of practice have their senses trained to discern good and evil.* (Hebrews 5:11-14)

Note carefully that the word of righteousness is for the mature who because of practice have their senses trained to discern good and evil. Here the matter of re-educating the mind, of moving on from the things of this age to the things of righteousness, is clearly a matter of process—a matter of constant training, a matter of practice, if you will. It is interesting to note that the central agenda of man through the ages has not changed. When Adam and Eve rebelled by eating of the tree of knowledge of good and evil, they got exactly what they asked for—an understanding of evil as well as good. Now that every natural man has a superabundant knowledge of evil, the very mark of the mature, spiritual man is the ability to discern between good and evil as noted here.

While I have spoken of discipline in this retraining process of the mind, there ought to be an element of excitement and adventure that draws us to the Word constantly. Peter taught this in the following words: "Like newborn babes, long for the pure milk of the word, that by it you may grow in respect to salvation" (1 Peter 2:2).

Long for the Word, or like a newborn infant cry out for the things of God so you may grow in respect to things related to righteousness.

Finally, just one example of the emphasis the Word of God places on "spiritual knowing." Follow John's emphasis on "we know" carefully:

> These things I have written to you who believe in the
> name of the Son of God, in order that you may know
> that you have eternal life. And this is the confidence
> which we have before Him, that, if we ask anything
> according to His will, He hears us. And if we know that
> He hears us in whatever we ask, we know that we have
> the requests which we have asked from Him. If any one
> sees his brother committing a sin not leading to death,
> he shall ask and God will for him give life to those who
> commit sin not leading to death. There is a sin leading
> to death; I do not say that he should make request for
> this. All unrighteousness is sin, and there is a sin not
> leading to death. We know that no one who is born of
> God sins; but He who was born of God keeps him and
> the evil one does not touch him. We know that we are
> of God, and the whole world lies in the power of the evil
> one. And we know that the Son of God has come, and
> has given us understanding, in order that we might
> know Him who is true, and we are in Him who is true,
> in His Son Jesus Christ. This is the true God and
> eternal life. Little children, guard yourselves from
> idols. (1 John 5:13-21)

Now let me touch upon a point which I have intentionally left for our present discussion. Note that in this whole process of reading the Word, feeding upon it and storing it, I have intentionally used the words "mind and spirit." After much study in the Word of God, I have come to the conclusion that the ideal storage place for the Word of God is deep in our spirits and not in our minds. You may ask me if this is not really a distinction without a distinction—I think not. Remember, the mind can never really be its own teacher. It was designed only to receive information, store it, bring it forth, process it and act upon it. In chapter one we talked about created man and the fact that his mind was trapped between his spirit and his body. From that vantage point, the mind has the possibility of two teachers: either the mind is instructed by the senses coming in through the flesh or by the revealed knowledge of God coming in through man's spirit.

The Word stored deep within man's spirit has the further advantage of being immediately available to the ministry of the Holy Spirit in teaching the mind. Further, I believe that the heart (spirit) of man is a more trustworthy repository of the Word than is his mind. The mind of man has a strong tendency to force the truths of the Word of God into the mold of the rational knowledge which he has accumulated over the years. If the Word of God does not conform to man's definition of reasonableness, then it is either rejected or reshaped to fit his rational knowledge. On the other hand, the Word stored deep in the spirit can dwell there in all of its natural beauty until called forth by the Holy Spirit.

The Old Testament is filled with passages on this subject (for example, Jeremiah 31:33, Ezekiel 11:19), but let me refer you to just one New Testament passage:

> *For this is the covenant that I will make with the house of Israel after those days, says the Lord: I will put My laws into their minds, and I will write them upon their hearts. And I will be their God, and they shall be My people.* (Hebrews 8:10)

The writer of Hebrews does suggest that the laws will be placed upon the mind, but also written upon the hearts. The Old Testament prophets clearly understood that when the heart of stone within man could be replaced with a heart of flesh, the law of the Lord could be written upon that heart. This is the picture we have here.

Now the question may arise, "How, then, do I get the Word into my heart?" There are available today a number of excellent programs of Scripture memorization, and I do not want to detract from any of these. However, I believe in the economy of God there may be a better way. The Lord's word to Joshua was that he should meditate on the Word day and night. As you approach the Word each day, prayerfully ask the Lord to open the Word to you, to make it come alive, and that as you read it, to store it deep within your spirit. I am certainly not wise enough to fully understand how God accomplishes this whole process, but I can tell you from personal experience that it works. Further, I find that when the Word is stored deep in my spirit, the meaning goes beyond the obvious meaning of the words written on the page into a deep understanding of the principles and truths of God.

Let me see if I can illustrate. I have had the experience hundreds of times of pondering and meditating on a particular problem before me in prayer. As I discussed it with the Lord and sought His mind on the matter, the Holy Spirit would suddenly begin to quote to my own mind several passages of Scripture that I had never before seen as related to the issue at hand. Sometimes in a matter of a few seconds the Lord has given me a richness of understanding about a subject that I would not have dug out with Bible and concordance in several hours.

Frequently I will ask the Lord questions in prayer and find the Holy Spirit giving me an astonishingly clear answer as He quotes two or three verses of Scripture. Further, often as I am teaching before a group of people the Holy Spirit enables me to quote literally dozens of verses I have never consciously memorized.

Undoubtedly someone will ask if this is not the lazy way out of Scripture memorization. If it seems so to you then so be it. I can only tell you that after hundreds of hours of reading the Word of God, meditating on it, and having had the Holy Spirit open it to me, I find a richness of understanding which could never be gained otherwise.

Let me offer you just one other argument. In the course of my lifetime I have met perhaps a half-dozen people who were very proud of the fact that they had memorized large portions of the Word of God; in several cases they were able to quote entire books without stopping. However, in many instances there seemed to be no accompanying evidence of a Renewed Mind—no evidence of the fruit of the Spirit, of a transformed or victorious life, or characteristics of the spiritual man. The rational mind has such a vested interest in wresting the Word of God and causing it to agree with its own preconceived notions that it is not a trustworthy repository of the Word of God.

Finally, I must touch on one further matter before we leave this point. Remember James told us that a fountain ought not to issue both sweet water and bitter at the same time. And yet Jesus told us that it is out of the abundance of the heart that the mouth speaks. Put those two together for a moment, and let me offer you one of the strongest warnings I can. Anyone who aspires to a Renewed Mind and to become a spiritual man before the Lord must guard with all the heavenly arsenal at his command the "stuff" he puts into his mind and spirit. I am appalled when I see a Christian brother or sister who claims to spend an hour or two in the morning in the Word of God and in prayer and meditation, and then turns around and feeds his mind and spirit on the trash of this world. I intentionally use the word "stuff" here, for the array of garbage that the enemy would get us to place in our minds and spirits seems almost limitless. What comes to your mind as you read? Pornography, novels, soap operas? For years I looked askance at Christians who were so self-righteous and holy that they thought no Christian ought to own a television set in his home. However, I am now convinced that apart from a few national news events, there is virtually nothing on network television that is fit to put into a Renewed Mind.

My Christian friends, I believe we stand on the threshold of both the final and greatest battle with evil that the church has ever imagined. In the midst of that battle the Holy Spirit can only call forth for your defense that which you have stored deep within your spirit. If that is hundreds of hours of meditation on the Word of God, then your arsenal is strong. If it is mixed with the confusing signals of this world's filth and nonsense, then that final battle will be less than victorious.

As Israel camped at Kadesh-Barnea, they could not go into the promised land for another thirty-eight years because the spirits of the people had been tainted as they gave heed to the discouraging majority report of the ten spies upon their return (Numbers 13-14). Had they filled their spirits with the words of Joshua and Caleb, they would have gone into the land a generation sooner and avoided a great deal of heartache.

The Seventh Step Toward a Renewed Mind: Accept Revelation as the Lord Gives It

If you have been earnestly following the path to a Renewed Mind up until this point, then on the authority of the Word of God I can assure you that you are beginning to hear the voice of the spirit—the voice of your spirit, but even more the voice of God's Holy Spirit as He indwells you and speaks through your spirit to your mind. Even though this is the very thing you long for, and as much as you may have expected it to happen, it is still a traumatic event.

Remember that a few steps back we said we would set our minds on the things above. We made a conscious decision that we would pay attention to the things of God. Suddenly, we began to hear the voice of the Holy Spirit. What He has to say is frequently at such odds with our past rational knowing that the prior decision to set our minds on the things above seems almost academic by comparison.

As you have received the fullness of the Holy Spirit, you are meditating on the Word of God and suddenly the Spirit speaks a beautiful truth into your heart. Or what is more likely, He may give you an instruction that seems contrary to everything you have ever known in the rational world. Your first reaction is, Was that the Lord or Satan or me? Your first step, if you have not already done so, is to ask the Lord to give you the gift of discernment as Paul promised to the Corinthian people (1 Corinthians 12:10). Then when you test the "word"—discerning its origin by the power of the Spirit and checking to see if it agrees with God's Word—you find the voice that you have heard passes every test.

You are now confronted with a simple reality: God has spoken and He expects you to accept it. As you begin to receive these early revelations, act upon them. Return to hear the voice of the Lord again, being always obedient. Jesus taught us that if we were willing to do the will of God, we would know whether or not the teaching was from God; in other words, we would have a discerning spirit (John 7:17).

As you begin to trust the voice of the Holy Spirit, hear His word again and again, and flow in the things of God, it will be one of the greatest assurances that you are edging closer to a Renewed Mind.

Let me pause here for a personal observation. I am deeply concerned that the most glaring weakness in the church of Jesus Christ today is in the lack of discernment. I urge you to learn to accept revelation knowledge and act upon it. I am absolutely convinced it is important to a Renewed Mind. At the same time, however, there are untold numbers of Christians running around the world asking: "Do you have a word from the Lord for me?" And they are vulnerable to every passing deception. Why? Simply because they have been unwilling to pay the price of time, discipline, submission and effort to know the voice of God. On the other hand, I remain firmly convinced that God will not give the earnest seeker a serpent when he asks for a fish.

Note for a moment what the Word of God has to say about revelation knowledge. First, the words of Paul to the Galatians:

> *For I would have you know, brethren, that the gospel which was preached by me is not according to man. For I neither received it from man, nor was I taught it, but I received it through a revelation of Jesus Christ.*
> (Galatians 1:11-12)

Here our beloved Paul states unequivocally that the gospel he preached—and that certainly must include the thirteen or fourteen books he wrote in the New Testament—did not come through rational knowledge from man, nor from a human teacher, but through the divine revelation of Jesus Christ.

You may respond: "But that was Paul and he was an apostle called of God. I could never hear from the Lord." Note Paul's words in his letter to the Ephesians:

> *For this reason I too, having heard of the faith in the Lord Jesus which exists among you, and your love for all the saints, do not cease giving thanks for you, while making mention of you in my prayers; that the God of our Lord Jesus Christ, the Father of glory, may give to you a spirit of wisdom and of revelation in the knowledge of Him. I pray that the eyes of your heart may be enlightened, so that you may know what is the hope of His calling, what are the riches of the glory of His*

217

inheritance in the saints. (Ephesians 1:15-18)

Paul specifically mentions the strong faith of the Ephesian people and their love for the Lord, but goes on to pray for them that they might receive the spirit of wisdom which comes by revelation and brings a knowledge of the Lord. Again, using almost the very language of our book, Paul prays that the eyes of their spirit may be enlightened so that they may know the hope of Christ's calling, the riches of the glory of His inheritance among the saints and more. In the simplest English possible, Paul prays that the eyes of their heart will be opened that they may understand the deep truths of God's kingdom. That is revelation for the common man—available to every Christian.

Just one further passage from the pen of Paul:

> *But we speak God's wisdom in a mystery, the hidden wisdom, which God predestined before the ages to our glory; the wisdom which none of the rulers of this age has understood; for if they had understood it, they would not have crucified the Lord of glory; but just as it is written, "Things which eye has not seen and ear has not heard, and which have not entered the heart of man, all that God has prepared for those who love Him." For to us God revealed them through the Spirit; for the Spirit searches all things, even the depths of God.* (1 Corinthians 2:7-10)

This is a portion of one of Paul's elaborate sentences, but he speaks of receiving the wisdom of God, mysteries, hidden wisdom, the things which none of the men of this age—not even the rulers of this age—understand. The natural eye cannot see it, the natural ear cannot hear it, and yet Paul says it was revealed to him through the Holy Spirit because the Spirit searches the deep things of God and in turn tells us.

As you begin to hear the voice of the Holy Spirit and receive revelation knowledge, you are once again confronted with a major decision. In fact, in many ways this decision will be one of the most crucial decisions of your entire Christian life. You may receive the revealed truths of God as the Holy Spirit speaks to you and treasure them in a neat compartment, while the things you have learned by sense knowledge are stored in another compartment.

You may make the conscious choice: "I think I will keep those two compartments separate and never mix the two." Sadly, many Christians who start down the road to a Renewed Mind stop at this point. This is a painful decision—particularly for highly educated people and those who teach others the knowledge they have accumulated. There is an enormous price to pay once one begins to let the revealed knowledge of God seep into the box of his rational knowledge. Unfortunately, I number many among my friends who have started down this road, glanced ahead and seen something of the price to pay, and have retreated to the comfort and convenience of worshiping Christ on Sunday while teaching humanism on Monday.

Happily, there is an alternative to this decision as well. Once we consciously open our minds to the white light of His searching and allow the Holy Spirit to instruct us—not only in the things of the kingdom of God, but to bring course correction to our rational knowledge—we will find opening before us vistas of truth that we never dreamed possible. Soon we will realize how foolhardy it was to put the label "truth" upon our meager reasonings.

Let me put this whole matter of accepting revelation knowledge in a slightly different context. The Lord spoke through Isaiah:

> *"For My thoughts are not your thoughts, neither are your ways My ways," declares the Lord. "For as the heavens are higher than the earth, so are My ways higher than your ways, and My thoughts than your thoughts."* (Isaiah 55:8-9)

Visualize with me for a moment two very discrete entities: Above us, a great source of "knowing" which we will label His ways and His thoughts; about us, another great source of knowing which we will label our ways and our thoughts. Our rational knowing is constantly bringing in information from around us, from the wisdom of our ways and this age. On the other hand, through our spirits the Holy Spirit is constantly revealing new truths about His ways and His thoughts. What I am suggesting here is that we must constantly choose to receive that revelation knowledge as it comes.

One of the most beautiful facts about all this is that the more you accept revelation knowledge, the more it becomes part of your normal thought processes. As His ways and His thoughts saturate your thinking, you will discover one day that you are quite at home in the midst of revealed knowledge. That is the day that you cry: "Praise God! A Renewed Mind may be possible after all."

Let me give you an illustration from my own experience: A couple of years after my wife and I had fully returned to the Lord and received the infilling of His Spirit, we were seeing the power of God move in our lives in many ways. A friend of mine asked if I would share my testimony with his Bible class one evening. This class was comprised primarily of people from a highly sophisticated academic community, but there was a good deal of openness toward the things of the Lord.

As I shared my testimony that evening, I told the group about miracles we had experienced in recent months and noted frequently how the Lord had spoken to us. As I concluded, one man raised his hand and responded: "If I could ever see just one miracle—just one person healed—from that point on I would believe." In my enthusiasm, I opened my mouth to argue with this man, whom I later learned was a medical doctor. But before I could utter a word the voice of the Lord spoke clearly: "He will never see a miracle." In that split second the Holy Spirit gave me an education worth half a lifetime: The individual who has decided that the miraculous does not exist will always have a rational explanation for anything he observes—even if it is a remarkable demonstration of the power of God.

Just a few weeks before our town had been visited by a well known Catholic priest with a powerful healing ministry. A paraplegic who had been confined to a wheelchair for many years was miraculously healed. Our local newspapers picked up the story and carried it with pictures as a front-page article. That evening as this young doctor chided me about my belief in miracles, the Holy Spirit reminded me of this paraplegic. I mentioned to the group assembled this very evident healing in our midst. The doctor's only response was: "It simply was his time to get well." That kind of reasoning will never accept revelation knowledge.

Let me refer you one more time to Paul's words to the Galatians:

> *But I say, walk by the Spirit, and you will not carry out the desire of the flesh. For the flesh sets its desire against the Spirit, and the Spirit against the flesh; for these are in opposition to one another, so that you may not do the things that you please. But if you are led by the Spirit, you are not under the Law.* (Galatians 5:16-18)

The things of the flesh and the things of the Spirit are at enmity with one another. Rational knowledge and all of its arrogance will always reject the things of revealed knowledge until it is broken in submission to God.

Since you have humbled your mind before God and set it on things above, the Holy Spirit will begin to illumine the Word that you are storing up in your spirit and as He speaks you will have clear revelation knowledge. This seventh step requires that as we hear the Lord giving us revealed knowledge, we humbly reach out as a little child and accept it. It begins as an act of faith, but our loving heavenly Father soon confirms it to us in many ways.

The Eighth Step Toward a Renewed Mind: Come to Grips with the Miraculous

If you have accomplished the seven previous steps in the journey toward a Renewed Mind, then you are a candidate for a miracle. In fact, I can tell you without hesitation, you are about to run headlong into a miracle. Whether it is in direct answer to prayer or simply a beautiful love gift from God confirming His revelations, you will soon find that the miraculous is inescapable.

Undoubtedly about this time a remnant of the old rational mind will rear its head and complain: "All this is entirely too mystical. This smacks of the supernatural. You will soon be labeled a fanatic for sure." You thought you had the mind fixed on heavenly things some time ago, but there are parts of the old rational mind that are still rebelling.

Part of the old nature is going to complain: "Won't you look pretty

221

silly when you tell your best friend that the Lord spoke to you?" or "How can you possibly stand and testify that the Lord touched you?"

Knowing that the rational mind will revolt when confronted with the supernatural, what are you going to do when you actually experience a real-life miracle?

That is why I urge upon you this eighth step on the road to a Renewed Mind: Come to grips with the miraculous. If the miraculous bothers you and you are among those who testified for years that God's intervention in the lives of men stopped in the first century, then you will have a particularly tough time with the miraculous. However, the moment you looked into the face of Jesus and cried out for forgiveness you were dealing with the miraculous. And every step along the way since then has been fraught with the miraculous.

But maybe I can help clear the air with a fresh definition of the miraculous. I hear far too many definitions today that border on the mystical, the mysterious, even the occult. Very simply, the miraculous includes every event that operates on the principles of God and is in agreement with the laws of God's kingdom. Any event that is in line with His ways and His thoughts, that agrees with revealed knowledge, fulfills His original intent and purpose for man, is a miracle. There are His ways and there are our ways. When an event begins to agree with His ways and fulfills the highest principles of the kingdom of God, I would call it a miracle. Simply because an event fulfills and is obedient to rules which our eyes cannot see and our ears cannot hear is no reason to be fearful of it. God is Spirit, His kingdom is a spiritual kingdom, His laws are spiritual laws, His ways are spiritual ways, and events that take place in that realm will be knowable only to our spirits—not to our fleshly senses. Once and again God breaks through from His kingdom into our earthly realm and reveals Himself by fulfilling His principles in our realm. Because these do not fit our normal expectations of the way things ought to operate, our rational minds tend to be skeptical if not fearful.

Let me illustrate: God created Adam perfect in every way. This included a perfectly healthy body which was designed to live forever as long as he lived by the rules of God's kingdom. Because of Adam's willful sin and rebellion, his entire being was subjected to the laws of destruction in the kingdom of Satan. The Father sent His Son into the world to die on behalf of our sins and to undo all the work of the Fall in Eden. I believe there is potential in Calvary for the full restoration of this earthly kingdom to God's once-intended ideal. Because Satan is still the ruler of this world and prince of the power of the air and multitudes choose to follow him, we will not see in earth's reality the total restoration of God's creation until our Lord returns and puts Satan in his well-deserved place. However, here and there about the face of the earth, a few committed Christians are rediscovering the ways of God's kingdom, coming to the point of a Renewed Mind, and operating in terms of the principles of the kingdom of God. To that extent God is free to restore the principles of His kingdom in that microcosm. If we lay hands on a brother and pray for his healing and God sovereignly restores him, we cry, "Praise God for the miracle!" The Father is simply releasing the principles of His kingdom into a small microcosm of His kingdom here on earth because we have trusted in Him and brought our heart, mind and being into agreement with His Word.

That was a long excursion into a little-known world. However, the moment you can grasp the important truth that there are two separate kingdoms in which we operate as Christians, and can understand that our rational minds and senses grasp only the things of this earth, then it is evident that our Renewed Minds deal with the kingdom of God that operates on a set of principles utterly different from anything we have understood before. It should not be a fearful matter to accept that miracles do occur. Simply put, miracles are operating in the realm of His divine kingdom. Now if by the processes outlined in this chapter you and I can come to a fully Renewed Mind and begin to see into that kingdom as clearly as we used to see into the kingdom around us, it ought to be no great thing to experience the miraculous in our lives. In fact, I fully believe that life in the miraculous ought to become the commonplace, the norm for us.

Let me go on. If you have received Jesus Christ as your personal Savior, then any skepticism about miracles in the Christian life is incongruous. Everything about your Christian life is a miracle. You trusted in Jesus as your Savior, and everything about Him was a miracle—His birth, His life, His ministry, His death and certainly

His resurrection. He walked in the realm of the miraculous, pe
forming miracles regularly. He was so supremely conscious
being a part of the kingdom of God that He often paused mi
sentence as He addressed the crowds to turn and say a word to H
heavenly Father. Ultimate reality for Him was the reality of th
kingdom of God.

Further, the church of Jesus Christ is a miracle. The Bible itse
is a profound miracle. The new birth is a miracle. Pentecost is
miracle. God's provision for our lives is a miracle.

In the Old Testament, the kingdom of God had not yet come i
our midst as Jesus said, and yet the Old Testament is filled wit
miracles. God's leading Abraham, the birth of Isaac, the preserva
tion of Moses at his birth—all were miracles. The list goes o
crossing the Red Sea, God's care for Israel in the wilderness, th
Shekinah glory on the tabernacle. Read the lives of Elijah, Elisha
Isaiah and Daniel. Life in the miraculous was commonplace fc
them.

Turn with me to the words of Jesus as John records them:

> *"Do you say of Him, whom the Father sanctified and
> sent into the world, `You are blaspheming,' because I
> said, `I am the Son of God'? If I do not do the works of
> My Father, do not believe Me; but if I do them, though
> you do not believe Me, believe the works, that you may
> know and understand that the Father is in Me, and I
> in the Father." Therefore they were seeking again to
> seize Him; and He eluded their grasp.* (John 10:36-39)

Jesus was simply saying to the Jewish leaders who were skept
cal: "If you are having trouble believing in Me, then believe th
works that you see Me do. Once you believe the works, you ca
begin to know and understand that I am from My heavenly Father
In other words, the miraculous validates the presence of the kin
dom of God in our midst. Let me go on and say that I believe th
miraculous validates the Word of revelation knowledge which w
hear through God's Holy Spirit and our own moving toward
Renewed Mind.

The Lord has privileged me on a number of occasions to shar

extensively with some of the most hardened rationalists and skeptics in this country. As an outcome of many such hours of conversation, I fully believe that the most hardened skeptic way down deep craves miracles—to know the reality of the living God. Far too often the skeptic has been offered packaged religion rather than living reality, and rightfully so he has become disabused about the things of God. However, once he sees the living reality of the Holy Spirit speaking through us, a tenderness comes over him and he begins to open to the real possibility of a God we can know.

As Mark records Jesus' final words to His disciples, the Lord says: "These signs will accompany you." The margin says literally: "These attesting miracles shall follow you." Whether it is authority over demons, speaking with new tongues, being untouched by deadly serpents or poisonous drinks or healing the sick; these attesting miracles are to be the validation of the fact that we are living in the kingdom realm.

You might wonder why this strong emphasis on the miraculous comes at the close of a chapter outlining the steps to a Renewed Mind. The Lord has allowed me to share this series rather widely, and it is not unusual for someone to come up with this statement: "I am really excited about the possibility of having a Renewed Mind, but I don't want to get involved in the miraculous." First, I am certain that this is a rational mind speaking. But second, this person is saying they want all the fruit of living in revelation knowledge but they want to accomplish it by rational means. At the very beginning of these chapters when we left the comfortable shoreline of the rational, you were getting into the deep waters of revelation knowledge. Just as the beautiful river of Ezekiel 47 got deeper and deeper, so our journey toward the Renewed Mind increasingly plumbs the depths of the miraculous.

I urge you to renounce fear for what it is—the enemy's attempt to keep you from moving on in the things of God. Then turn and quickly embrace the miraculous for what it is: the revelation of the principles of God's kingdom spilling over into your present world.

Conclusion

This is a difficult chapter for me to close. There is so much that

I want to say on each of the eight steps toward a Renewed Mind. There are times when I feel that an entire book on each would not cover all that is in my heart. However, I fully trust the teaching of the Holy Spirit to your heart and to mine, and I know that He will open to you the truths that are especially important for where you are at this moment in your spiritual development. If you choose to take this chapter as a plan for your own spiritual growth, I encourage you to follow the steps sequentially. I believe they are divinely ordered, and if you begin to skip around, there is always the danger that the earlier steps will be slighted and you will be confronted with a lusting body or an arrogant mind long after both should have been dealt with.

Let me close this chapter as we began it, with Paul's majestic verse to the Romans: "Do not be conformed to this world, but be transformed by the renewing of your mind, that you may prove what the will of God is, that which is good and acceptable and perfect' (Romans 12:2). To understand increasingly the will of God, to yield increasingly to the will of God, to conform increasingly to His will for the laws of His kingdom to become more real than the law of gravity holding you to your chair—that is to know a Renewed Mind (see charts 10 and 11 on page 121)

As you diligently pursue these eight steps, I want to leave you with ten expectations you might reasonably anticipate in your spiritual life:

1. The power of the flesh will lose its hold on your life.
2. The driving ego, pride and self-centeredness will fade
3. Circumstances will lose their power to control you.
4. The fear of men's opinions will diminish.
5. The reality of His ways will increase.
6. The power of His Word will saturate your every thought
7. The voice of the Holy Spirit will become clearer than ever before.
8. The miraculous will become commonplace.
9. Knowing His will and His leading will be easier every day.
10. Your mind will become renewed!

CHAPTER SIX

THE RENEWED MIND: BASIC TO PRACTICAL CHRISTIANITY

It has been well over a dozen years now since the Lord first began to deal with me about the possibilities of a Renewed Mind. The principles developed herein have been born out of many hours spent meditating on the Word. Yet I still find that not a day goes by that the Lord does not reveal one more application of these precious truths to my life. Therefore, when I consider the applications that grow out of the concept of a Renewed Mind, the breadth of material available seems to preclude even undertaking the task.

In fact, as the Lord provides the time, I am now committed to an entire volume related solely to the implications of the Renewed Mind for our educational system. The subject matter of virtually every academic discipline must be totally rewritten from a Christian understanding of truth. Our process of education needs rethinking from kindergarten through the PhD. There also needs to be a book uncovering both the roots and the tentacles of humanism and a strategy laid out for turning the tide against that satanic end-time religion. In fact, there is virtually no aspect of our modern lives that would not be revolutionized by the applications of the Renewed

Mind and the leadership of truly spiritual men. One can readily imagine a book outlining the impact of the Renewed Mind on our business and economy, another on the ways in which we govern ourselves, another on our cultural and entertainment world and so forth. The structure of Christian homes could be totally transformed if only Christians had truly Renewed Minds and submitted their family relationships to such divine wisdom.

In the pages remaining I can only raise a few issues and sketch some ideas that may serve to direct your own devotional and prayer life on various subjects, as well as to give guidance for courses of action.

As we begin please note Chart 12 (on page 123), in which I am offering a first version of a model for a Renewed Mind. There are no surprises here, for each point has been covered in the preceding chapters. However, once you understand the principles involved, each new issue that is raised can be brought to this model for guidance and insight.

I Long to Live a Victorious Christian Life

Very frequently I meet Christians who have had enough teaching to know that living an overcoming Christian life is a very real possibility, but for a combination of reasons these people always seem to be defeated. My first response is to applaud the desire, for a victorious Christian life is certainly one of the central evidences of the Renewed Mind. However, let us agree on the definition of victorious Christian living.

When most Christians are pressed for an answer, they define the overcoming Christian life in terms of a rather nebulous concept of "always feeling good and nothing ever going wrong."

Before I give you my definition of victorious Christian living, let me remind you that as Christians we have been introduced to another kingdom that is open and available to us. First, there is the kingdom of this world, the realm of evil and rebellion against God that is the only type of existence available to natural man. But to you and me, Jesus came to reveal the kingdom of God, the spiritual realm of righteousness and blessing.

Now a two-part definition of victorious Christian living: First, it is life lived according to the principles of the kingdom of God; and second, it is life lived in dominion over the principles of this present evil age. With a clearly focused definition, we have available to us all the resources of the Word of God and the power of His Holy Spirit to reveal the principles of His kingdom. Basically, the entire context of this present book is a focus on the principles of the kingdom of God.

Perhaps we can discover where most well-meaning Christians go wrong. Someone has encouraged them to memorize a great many promises of God from His Word, and this is a wonderful foundation for a victorious life. However, when it comes to bringing these promises to bear on the circumstances of life, the eyes of the Christian are so much upon this present age that there is no real impact of faith behind the quoting of the promises. In fact, in many instances this dichotomy serves only to heighten the frustration of the Christian. On the one hand are the enormous possibilities of God's promises, could they only be realized; but on the other hand is a day-by-day reality that seems only to hold defeat.

Now let me add to this mix of problems a vitally important but often misunderstood word: *faith*. Untold numbers of books and sermons have been devoted to this crucial word, and yet how little is understood of it. Nevertheless, we receive absolutely nothing from the kingdom of God apart from faith. Our very salvation came by faith in the Son of God. It is impossible to overemphasize the extent to which Jesus underscored faith. With adequate faith, trees are uprooted and mountains are cast into the sea (Mark 11:23). A woman with an issue of blood is healed because of her great faith (Mark 5:25-34). A centurion astounds even Jesus because of the amount of faith he exhibits (Matthew 8:5-10). In fact, all things are possible to him who believes (Mark 9:23).

In terms of this book, let me give you a simple definition of faith that I believe will transform both our understanding and our behavior. I have repeatedly emphasized that there are two realities available to the Christian mind: the reality of this present age, which has been experienced by the rational mind from the day of one's birth, and the reality of the kingdom of God, which is known only through the revealed knowledge of God's Word and His Holy Spirit. Faith is simply the overwhelming confidence that the reality of the things of God's kingdom is far more powerful and enduring than the reality of the things of this present age. I remind you once again o: Paul's powerful statement that "the mind set on the flesh is death but the mind set on the Spirit is life and peace" (Romans 8:6).] believe it is not an oversimplification to state that faith is ultimately the focus of the Renewed Mind on the things of the Spirit and o: God's kingdom.

In the case of the struggling Christian who longs to live ɑ victorious life but seems destined to fail, he may hear the words o: God's promises, which he has stored in his spirit, but when the time for application comes, the things of the senses and reason seem sɩ much safer that the mind remains set on the flesh. Once again the plight of the carnal Christian is this: He longs for revelation results but seeks to accomplish them through the tools of the flesh and the senses.

Note if you will that great definition of faith found in the first verse of Hebrews 11: "Now faith is the substance of things hoped for, the evidence of things not seen" (KJV). Substance, evidence, reality— these are the terms that define this world, this age, for all natural minded people. But here the Word is teaching us that faith is the real, enduring substance and evidence. Faith is of the spiritual realm; faith is the mind set on the spirit—not the flesh. Put simply the writer of Hebrews is saying, "The enduring evidence and substance is to be found in faith, and that faith is anchored in God': kingdom."

On Sinai the Lord instructed Moses to build an earthly tabernacle following very carefully specified plans. The great attention to detai] required by God revealed the importance of an enduring highe: model—a model in heaven not made with human hands. To the natural-minded Israelite, the planks and skins and sockets com prised reality. To Moses, who had seen the true model revealed by the Father, the real substance was in the kingdom of God. We coun it as evidence when we begin to see our prayers answered and God' promises fulfilled in this present world. However, the Hebrews 11: definition suggests that by faith the evidence in the heavenlies is th greater reality.

Let me say it once again: Faith is the overwhelming confidenc that the reality of the things of God is far more powerful an enduring than the reality of this present age. This may appear to be a circuitous route to victorious Christian living, but every revelation of the power of God in our lives—in these natural lives—is a direct result of faith. Until we have a clear grasp of the definition of faith, we will miss its implementation. No matter how many times we hear the call of God's voice through His Word, if we persist in keeping the focus of the mind on the flesh—on the circumstances around us— the end product is always the same: death.

I may have memorized every passage in the Word of God on physical healing and know that by Jesus' stripes I am healed. Yet if my mind is fixed on the fact that for as long as I can remember I have had bronchial flu three times every winter, then that reality overwhelms the possibility of His promised healing. By definition, I do not have faith. I have said that the reality of this present age is greater than the reality of the things of the kingdom of God.

I know of a dear pastor who will preach much about the matters of faith, but whose mind always seems focused on the dangers of this present world. He built a new home and I commented to him that it was a difficult place to find, for he had not put his name on the mailbox. His response was instructive: "Oh I could never do that— that is how thieves find out your name and call on the phone to see if you are home. If you are not, they come in and rob you." There seemed to be no comprehension of the possibility of divine protection, of an angelic guard around one's home; worse, there seemed to be no realization of the incongruity between the words he taught on faith and what was lived out in reality.

Even worse, this whole dilemma is greatly exacerbated today by the fact that the vast majority of professing Christians, even in evangelical and charismatic groups, live under these spiritually schizophrenic conditions. Peer pressure is so intense that if you and I focus on the things of the Spirit and begin to see victory in our lives, we are perceived as fanatics if not heretics. Simply put, the carnal mind has been the norm even in the church for so many years that the spiritual mind is a threat to the status quo.

Out of all the principles we have outlined in chapters four and five, I suspect most Christians will succeed or fail right here. In the early spring of 1974, all five members of our family (my wife, Carol, and I along with our three teenage daughters) came into the fullness of

231

the Holy Spirit. We began to see many powerful miracles in our home. However, in a few short months we realized there were tremendous pressures within the church to maintain the status quo. At that point the five of us made a literal covenant with one another to accomplish three things. First, we determined to individually and collectively spend much time storing the Word of God deep in our spirits so that we would hear the voice of the Spirit teaching us His promises. Second, we made a firm covenant to individually and collectively set our minds on the things of the Spirit—the things above. Third, we agreed to accept no confessions confirming the reality of this present age from each other in all of our daily conversation.

This last point of agreement was by far the most difficult to accomplish in reality. Our lips confess the experiences of our minds, and we are so ego-involved in the things we believe and say that when another—even a dear friend—corrects a statement we have just made and suggests it is committing us to things of this age, feathers can get ruffled. However, we were so united in the agreement that the end result was worthwhile, and we stuck it out. Within a few days there was a marked change in the tone of our conversation. In six months the focus of our minds and conversations was so transformed that not one of us would have dreamed of going back to the old ways. At least in part as a result of that decision and that six-month period, all three daughters are today married to God-fearing men, and their homes are built around the principles of God's kingdom. Miracles and victories are the daily norm in their lives as well as our own.

Jesus gave us some very familiar but often misunderstood words in Luke's Gospel:

> "And his master praised the unrighteous steward because he had acted shrewdly; for the sons of this age are more shrewd in relation to their own kind than the sons of light. And I say to you, make friends for yourselves by means of the mammon of unrighteousness; that when it fails, they may receive you into the eternal dwellings. He who is faithful in a very little thing is faithful also in much; and he who is unrighte-

ous in a very little thing is unrighteous also in much. If therefore you have not been faithful in the use of unrighteous mammon, who will entrust the true riches to you? And if you have not been faithful in the use of that which is another's, who will give you that which is your own? No servant can serve two masters; for either he will hate the one, and love the other, or else he will hold to one and despise the other. You cannot serve God and mammon." (Luke 16:8-13)

Remember the two ages? The two realities? Jesus said that the sons of this age are more shrewd in relation to their own kind, or their own age, than the sons of light. At least the sons of this age faithfully pursue reality as they see it, and they work at it with a vengeance. Yet we, the sons of light, have been offered a view into the things of eternity, and at least the spirit within us knows that this is ultimate reality. Nevertheless, when our minds are set on the flesh, we are denying the very reality we have embraced.

In summary, if you have pursued the eight steps outlined in chapter five with great diligence, then for you the Renewed Mind is certainly a reality and the miraculous has become the norm rather than the so-called reality of everyday sense knowledge. For you this section on victorious Christian living may be superfluous. However, if you are still struggling over this great gulf between the possibility of what could be and the reality of what you are experiencing, then I send you back to an earlier point. Once and for all choose between the reality of this age and the reality of the kingdom of God, and then set your mind on the things of the Spirit. Only that kind of an unshakable determination will produce the fruit of an overcoming Christian life.

Why Did I Lose My Healing?

Again and again I hear the plaintive cry: "I know that God healed me. I was perfectly fine for several days, but now the affliction is back, worse than ever before. Why did I lose my healing?"

Let me offer you a parallel illustration. I have talked with hundreds of people who are born-again Christians. Virtually one hundred percent of them will agree, if asked to stop and think about it for a moment, that in the days and weeks following their original conversion to Jesus Christ, the enemy of their souls came to them on several occasions, saying: "Oh, nothing really happened to you. You simply imagined that." However, if you are like those individuals and you are still serving the Lord today, it is for only one basic reason: Your salvation was and is important to you, and when Satan tries to make you give up your faith and doubt the reality of that salvation, you simply say, "In the name of Jesus, be gone, Satan." In other words: You kept your salvation exactly like you got it—by faith!

In like fashion, you keep your healing the same way you got it— by faith! Just because you have had the faith to trust God for a great miracle in your life doesn't mean that Satan will roll over and play dead. In Ephesians 6, the apostle Paul admonishes us to resist the enemy and stand our ground against his attacks: "Take up the full armor of God, that you may be able to resist in the evil day, and having done everything, to stand firm" (verse 13).

Satan will offer you the same symptoms you had before and you will find yourself losing your healing again and again until you learn to stand against him. I retain God's miraculous gift in my life, whatever it is, as I first received it—by standing in faith. This means that I continue in my unshakable confidence that the reality of the principles of the kingdom of God are far more powerful and enduring than the reality of this present age.

We praise God for many miracles in our own family, but one particular instance fits perfectly here. A number of years ago my wife, Carol, found on her wrist a ganglion cyst approximately half the size of a filbert nut. We began to take authority over that cyst and rebuke it in the name of Jesus. Each time we thought about it we simply laid hands on it, rebuked it and thanked the Lord for His healing of it. One day as we were riding in the car Carol cried out: "Look, it is absolutely gone!" There was no trace of the cyst. We praised God and thanked Him for His healing and went along with our business. Approximately three months later, Carol looked down one day and that cyst was back as big as ever. With one voice we cried: "Satan, you cannot do that. In the name of Jesus take it away." And almost as quickly as the prayer was out of our mouths that cyst was gone and has never returned. I am fully confident that as certainly as Satan would put any kind of evil on us originally, he will offer it back to us; the only way we can retain the miracle is the way we got it—by faith.

I need to offer you one further caution. I have known people who have been healed primarily through another person's faith, perhaps in a healing service with some great evangelist like Kathryn Kuhlman. If they have been inadequately taught and do not understand the principle of standing by faith, they invariably yield to Satan when he comes along and offers them back the same symptoms and the same disease. I would underscore two matters for you: First, the urgency of your own in-depth understanding of the Renewed Mind and your need to stand in faith. Second, the importance of a family being united in this standing, for Jesus is quoted in Matthew 18:19 as saying, "If two of you agree on earth about anything that they may ask, it shall be done for them by My Father who is in heaven."

In every great miracle from God, there are three witnesses. First, there is the witness of the Word of God revealing the reality of His kingdom. Second, there is the reality of this world and its circumstances, evidenced by pain, symptoms, etc. In between is the focus of the mind, choosing to trust either the reality of the kingdom above or the reality of this age. The Renewed Mind, set on the things of the Spirit of God, knows the power of God to act and trusts the heavenly Father to manifest the reality of His kingdom in this present earthly reality.

One further caution at this point. Occasionally an innocent new Christian, virtually untaught in the Word, will say to me: "Is this view not very close to that of Christian Science?" The answer is a resounding, "No!" The position of Christian Science basically is the power of mind over matter—the power of the mind over the flesh. If in your mind you deny long enough that something exists, it will simply go away.

Our Christian view is entirely different: The essential nature of man, created in the image of God, is the spirit. The Renewed Mind, ruled by the Spirit-controlled spirit, reaches out and appropriates the power of God's kingdom—all that was accomplished by Jesus through Calvary and His resurrection—and brings that great power to bear upon the things of earth.

In the instance of Christian Science, the glory for any results must go back to the mind which accomplished such great things. In the Christian view, all the glory goes to God who, out of His infinite riches in glory, bestows upon us the manifold blessings which we need.

Circumstances Entangle Me

I frequently hear the almost pleading cry: "I do want to be free from the circumstances around me and keep my feet from being entangled in the web the enemy seems always to be weaving." The solution to this problem has been covered in the section on living the victorious Christian life, but I want to discuss one special aspect of this problem. It is once again a matter of the mindset. Many years ago an elderly poet wrote: "It is the set of the sail and not the gale that determines the direction of the ship." And this is precisely the answer: If the mind is set constantly on the circumstances around it, then those circumstances will inevitably entangle it.

However, I believe there is one additional point to be made here. When someone comes to me about their entangling circumstances, I usually question them rather carefully. I often discover the root of the problem is a severe case of a man-fearing spirit. What we so often call circumstances boils down many times to what other people think about my reaction in this situation. In fact, I would go so far as to say that the greatest liberty you will ever discover in the Christian life will be finally breaking the bondage to one question: "What will other people think if I do this?"

I don't mean that we should come to the point in which we have no sensitivity to the feelings of others. Rather, I am speaking of being so attuned to the Father's voice that the opinions of other people fade into insignificance. In reality, I suspect that this too is the result of a final set of the mind. Once our minds are utterly and completely set on the things of the Spirit, the circumstances and the people around us begin to fade more and more.

Just one further thought on the entangling circumstances: They very often hinder our reaching out and receiving the blessing God has for us. When I meditate on this matter, I visualize a scene something like the following. A large group of committed Christians is sitting in concentric circles around an altar. They are sharing together about the goodness of God, the beauty of His promises and how wonderful it is to serve Him. Suddenly the Lord Himself appears, standing behind the altar. He places a beautiful blessing right in the middle of the altar. He says: "I have come to bring this blessing to you tonight. It is for you." And then He leaves.

The conversation goes on: "What a beautiful blessing. My, I wish I could receive that blessing. I know He really didn't intend it for me, it is for those of you here who are worthy." For several minutes this conversation goes on. Suddenly a brash young Christian, who has just been saved two weeks ago and has been observing all this, comes running forward. "Pardon me, my brothers and sisters," he cries, "but this is mine; God promised it to me." And off he goes with the blessing.

Now the conversation changes: "That's not fair. Who does he think he is to come in and take my blessing? Why, I have been serving the Lord thirty-five years."

So the well-meaning Christians who are so entangled with their own circumstances, trapped by the web of their own unworthiness, their own false modesty and the lack of understanding of eternal reality, miss God's very best for them.

I Long to Be More Spiritual

More often than not the individual who longs to be more spiritual harbors a rather muddled definition of spirituality in which the "truly spiritual person" is comprised of three parts sentimentality, two parts external image and four parts the opinions of other men.

I believe a clear understanding of the Renewed Mind automatically gives us a biblical understanding of true spirituality. We outlined such a definition in chapter four. Spiritual man is man restored to God's intent and order for him. His spirit has been made alive and it rules the rest of his being. His mind has been renewed and set on the things of the Spirit. Together the spirit and the mind rule the flesh. Such a restored man is submitted to the authority and lordship of Jesus Christ in his life and is indwelt by God's Holy Spirit. Being Spirit-ruled and Spirit-led is to be spiritual!

Adam was undoubtedly the most spiritual of all created men. His spirit was alive and he was in constant fellowship with his heavenly

Father. Until the day in which he rebelled, Adam was fully obedient to God's will and was constantly receptive to God's way of knowing as revealed to him through his spirit. By most prevailing standards of spirituality today, we would not have quickly discerned that Adam was truly spiritual, yet he is the exact model of spiritual man.

Jesus, the second Adam, was also a fully spiritual man. The things of the kingdom of God were far more real to Him than the things He saw about Him. To anyone who would listen, He would announce: "The kingdom of God is come among you." In various ways He would say again and again: "I do only the things I see My heavenly Father doing. I tell you only the things I hear from My heavenly Father." He was truly a Spirit-led and Spirit-ruled man. Yet the Pharisees, applying their external definitions of spirituality, called our Lord a glutton, a drunkard and a friend of sinners (Matthew 11:19).

One of the beautiful truths about the life of Jesus is that since He chose not to cling to the things of His glory in heaven, but, as Paul teaches us, laid aside that glory, then He was in all forms like unto us as men, except that He was not sinful. The encouraging thing for us is that the same resources available to Jesus are available to us. We too can know the mind of the Father, be in fellowship with the Holy Spirit, be instructed in the Word, know the power of God and exercise dominion in the world around us and so on.

I want to convey two things here: First, I want to disabuse you of the rather gooey notions of spirituality we have entertained most of our lives, based largely on externals. Secondly, I want to help you understand that if you have a genuinely Renewed Mind and are obeying the Father and trusting Him implicitly, then you are spiritual.

I believe the most spiritual thing a spiritual man can do is come into the presence of his Lord and offer Him full worship, praise, adoration. At the point of Jesus' death, the veil before the Holy of Holies that separated us from God was torn in two (Luke 23:45). Now the Father bids us to come boldly into His presence to worship and enjoy Him. As the two sisters in Bethany were entertaining their Lord one day, Martha was highly critical of Mary for sitting at the Lord's feet and not helping with household chores. Jesus responded that Mary had chosen the better part.

If you long to be more spiritual, pursue a Renewed Mind with all your being. Then in constant fellowship with your Lord, learn to worship Him, praise Him and enjoy Him as you were created to do.

Reading the Word Is Tough-sledding for Me

I frequently meet individuals who give every appearance of pressing on toward a Renewed Mind, but who seem to be genuinely struggling with the reading and understanding of God's Word. This ought not to be. I sought the Lord in prayer about it, and I believe He has revealed one or two central stumbling blocks.

When we approach the Word of God, we must constantly remember that we are dealing with revealed knowledge. Paul reminds us repeatedly that these spiritual truths are not available to the natural mind and are veiled to the mind that has rejected Jesus. You may rightly counter that you have come to know Christ as Savior and that veil has been lifted in Christ Jesus.

However, I believe that precisely here is the point. Even as Christians, when we come to the Word of God we tend to subject the revealed knowledge found in His Word to the familiar skills and tools of the rational mind. There is a strong tendency to leap in with our powerful analytical skills and try to dissect and understand what we are reading in God's Word. I am not suggesting that this is intentional or even conscious. It is simply the way we have learned to approach all new knowledge out of the background of our experience. I find this to be especially true of those who are highly educated.

There are three paragraphs from Paul's writings that are worth noting here:

> *I wish that you would bear with me in a little foolishness; but indeed you are bearing with me. For I am jealous for you with a godly jealousy; for I betrothed you to one husband, that to Christ I might present you as a pure virgin. But I am afraid, lest as the serpent deceived Eve by his craftiness, your minds should be led astray from the simplicity and purity of devotion to Christ.* (2 Corinthians 11:1-3)

O Timothy, guard what has been entrusted to you, avoiding worldly and empty chatter and the opposing arguments of what is falsely called "knowledge"— which some have professed and thus gone astray from the faith. Grace be with you. (1 Timothy 6:20-21)

But refuse foolish and ignorant speculations, knowing that they produce quarrels. And the Lord's bondservant must not be quarrelsome, but be kind to all, able to teach, patient when wronged. (2 Timothy 2:23-24)

Though Paul stated it differently in each of the three books, the principle is ever the same: No matter how close we may come to the Lord in spiritual matters, there is always the temptation that an argument will appeal to our "clever minds" and to the "rightness of our own thinking." There is always the temptation to be led astray from the simplicity of the truth in Christ Jesus, to be fascinated with opposing arguments and new knowledge, or to be caught up in foolish and ignorant speculations.

I believe that in the vast majority of cases there is no malicious intent to be rebellious, nor even an awareness that we are using the tools of the rational mind. However, I want to offer you what I believe is a better solution.

I believe there are two basic steps that will transform your Bible study and bring the Word alive to you. The first is based on Paul's words in Colossians 3:16: "Let the Word of Christ richly dwell within you." Second, know that only by the Holy Spirit's gentle teaching will you ever come to an in-depth understanding of God's Word. Specifically, this means that as you begin to read the Word of God, you do not try to analyze every word and phrase in an attempt to grasp its immediate meaning for you. Rather, as you read the Word and meditate upon it, ask the Holy Spirit to store it deep in your spirit. You may find that under the Holy Spirit's tutelage, new truths seem to leap off the pages of the Bible.

As you read the Bible, remember that you are studying it for the long-term advantage. What I mean by this is that after many days and weeks and months of storing the Word in your spirit and the

Holy Spirit teaching you constantly, perhaps you will be confronted with a question you have never focused on before. As you wait before the Lord, you find that the Holy Spirit brings to the front of your attention four or five different passages of Scripture from widely selected areas in the Word of God, which you may have stored in your spirit over a period of many months or years. But the Holy Spirit in His infinite wisdom brings together these truths and illumes them to your mind and He is indeed your Teacher. Suddenly your perplexing question fades away into resolutions.

For myself, I have found that a rather strict regimen at the beginning of my daily devotions has proved highly useful over the years. First, I ask to be filled afresh with God's Holy Spirit for that day. Second, I set my mind against all distractions and take authority over anything that would keep me from the Word. Third, I consciously open my heart and mind to the voice of God's Spirit. Next I invite the Holy Spirit to be my Teacher, to cause the Word to be alive in me. In particular I ask for wisdom and understanding, that the Lord through His Holy Spirit would teach me His ways that I might know Him. You may comment that the Lord knows ahead of time that I need all those things, so why bother Him daily with them? The Word of God says we do not receive because we do not ask (James 4:3). I am simply confessing before the Lord each day my own inadequacy at understanding His Word, my strong desire to be taught of Him and covenanting with Him afresh each day that He should be my Teacher.

One of the beautiful byproducts of such an in-depth study in the Word on a regular basis is that when it comes to living a victorious Christian life, you will soon discover that the Word of God and the words of God are gaining ascendancy over the words of men around you. This means that faith—confidence in the principles of the kingdom of God—becomes increasingly a more natural response of your heart.

How Can I Know the Will of God for My Life?

Let me first comment that this question is of such vital importance and of such intense interest in the Christian community today that it deserves an answer well beyond the scope of this chapter. In fact, the Lord has dealt with me on this subject for years, and if He permits, I want to set down my thoughts in another book.

However, let me offer you a few guidelines at this point as they grow out of the Renewed Mind.

I am appalled by some of the things being written today by sincere Christian people on knowing the mind of the Lord. Again and again the answers fall one hundred percent into the category of sense knowledge. People are advised to read the circumstances around them, observe where God seems to be opening and closing doors, and go through the open ones—to put out fleeces as Gideon did on the threshing floor (Judges 6:36-40). This calls for reliance upon sense knowledge and puts the source of our information in the world where the enemy of our souls can manipulate it.

I do not question that God shapes the circumstances of our lives, nor that He opens and closes doors. However, those things should only be confirmation of what we have already heard from Him otherwise.

In His great discourse on shepherds, Jesus said:

> *"But he who enters by the door is a shepherd of the sheep. To him the doorkeeper opens, and the sheep hear his voice, and he calls his own sheep by name, and leads them out. When he puts forth all his own, he goes before them, and the sheep follow him because they know his voice. And a stranger they simply will not follow, but will flee from him, because they do not know the voice of strangers."* (John 10:2-5)

> *"My sheep hear My voice, and I know them, and they follow Me."* (John 10:27)

Herein in the crux of the matter. As Paul said, "All who are being led by the Spirit of God, these are sons of God" (Romans 8:14). This means one of the surest marks that a man is a son of God is that he is being led by the Spirit of God. As Jesus put it, His sheep follow Him because they know His voice. In every other area of life, you can be open to deceit. If you trust circumstances, you risk the possible deceit of your enemy. If you ask the wisdom of another person—no matter how close that individual is to the Lord—you cannot be certain that he has heard directly from the Lord for you. His responsibility is for his own soul, and he does not carry the same depth of responsibility for you.

Once again you understand why all through this book I have insisted that our spirits must gain ascendancy over our minds and our flesh. Every area of life is influenced by this—every question, every decision, every issue before us. Only as we come to the point where we are fully comfortable with discerning the voice of the Holy Spirit and being led by Him can we be absolutely certain of following the Lord's will.

Once we have heard His voice, our loving heavenly Father may raise the comfort level several degrees by giving us several confirming promises in His Word. He may even go further and send a dear brother in the Lord with a confirming word from the Holy Spirit. Finally, you may very well see the circumstances of life beginning to take shape with what God has promised you; in fact, you can expect them to if you have heard from the Lord. However, the moment we begin to reverse this process by analyzing the circumstances about us and then rushing to God for His blessing on our decisions, we are in deep trouble.

How Can I Retrain My Mouth?

This is another of those topics that deserves far broader treatment than we can give it here. There are many powerful verses of Scripture on this subject, such as this one: "He who guards his mouth and his tongue, guards his soul from troubles" (Proverbs 21:23).

But you say to me: "I know the warning. I know the consequences. But how do I change my confessions?" Every action in a man's life begins first with a thought; in the same way, the words of a man's mouth are born out of his thoughts. Given that understanding, let us look again at Paul's words to the Corinthians:

For though we walk in the flesh, we do not war according to the flesh, for the weapons of our warfare are not of the flesh, but divinely powerful for the destruction of fortresses. We are destroying speculations and every lofty thing raised up against the knowledge of God, and we are taking every thought captive to the obedience of Christ, and we are ready to punish all disobedience, whenever your obedience is complete. (2 Corinthians 10:3-6)

Follow Paul's reasoning here. We are in spiritual warfare, and the weapons God has entrusted to us are not of the flesh but spiritual—divinely powerful for the destruction of that which opposes our spiritual lives. Specifically, we are destroying speculations, casting down imaginations and taking every thought captive to the obedience of Christ. If there is that which rises up in disobedience, we are ready to punish that as well.

Harsh as it may seem, I believe that most of us as Christians need to take great heaping doses of casting down our imaginations and taking every thought captive. Paul clearly suggests that the matter of what we think about is within our control. The enemy, or even our own flesh, may quickly flash an image on the screen of our minds that we recognize to be incompatible with the pure things of the kingdom of God. At that point the option is ours—we can either entertain the thought and enjoy it, or we can dismiss it in the name of Jesus.

Now psychologists know enough about the human mind to know that you will talk about what you think about. Therefore, if the question is one of restructuring our words or retraining our mouths, then the responsibility is an inner one, taking every thought captive.

Let me hasten to add that we are not left to our own resources alone here, though we do have the ability to choose what we think about. To the extent that the Word of Christ dwells in us richly and permeates both our spirit and our thoughts, then these words from Hebrews take on very special importance:

> *For the word of God is living and active and sharper than any two-edged sword, and piercing as far as the division of soul and spirit, of both joints and marrow, and able to judge the thoughts and intentions of the heart.* (Hebrews 4:12)

Note that the Word is so sharp that it is able to judge the thoughts and intentions of the heart. What does this mean? First it means that God has given you the power to choose what you think about. Second, it means that if there is any question whatsoever about the rightness of that thought, the Word of God is immediately able to judge it.

The psalmist tells us: "The Lord knows the thoughts of man" (Psalm 94:11). If we could always live aware that God has constant viewing rights to our every thought, this in itself ought to encourage us to judge a thought clearly and promptly.

I had the privilege some time ago to join a group of men on an inside tour of a vast new urban bank that was in the process of opening. Deep in the heart of this skyscraper, we were shown a control room where security guards could sit in front of television monitors, dozens of screens, and observe every important activity going on in the bank. From this one spot they could monitor every exit, stairway and hallway, the vault, the cashier's desk, and determine if anything untoward was occurring in that building. This is only a feeble illustration of our Lord's ability to know the thoughts and intents of our heart, but I was deeply impressed that day with the extensive amount of information that was coming to a central spot for one man to monitor.

Have we left the subject completely? I trust not. I believe a great many sincere Christians recognize correctly that the greatest task before them is the retraining of the mouth. I am suggesting that the wellspring for our words is deep within the heart and mind of man. As our thoughts are brought into captive obedience to Christ Jesus, our words will quickly follow.

But let me go on. If my mind is truly becoming renewed and I have set it on the things which are above, then the matters of the kingdom of God are forming for me a reality far more authentic than the reality of the circumstances about me. Since my mind is set on this reality, it follows that my thoughts concern the reality of this kingdom. Suppose that my physical body is suddenly attacked with every symptom of flu or cold. At this point my lips have the choice of confessing one of two major realities. From the natural perspective I may say, "Oh, I feel so very sick, I believe I am taking the flu"; or from the spiritual perspective I may say, "No thanks, Satan. By

Jesus' stripes I am already healed and I'll have no part of the flu you are offering me."

I have a friend who cannot grasp this at all. He will argue that since for the moment my body still feels the pain and symptoms the enemy is offering me, I am lying to say that by Jesus' stripes I am healed. The point I am making is simple: My lips will confess one reality or the other and the question is, Which is the higher reality, and which pleases my God most?

Let me illustrate from the life of Jesus. The call comes to our Lord to visit the home of Jairus, where his little daughter has just died. As Jesus takes Peter, James and John with Him, they encounter those who are weeping and wailing at the home. Note the words on Jesus' lips: "The child has not died, but is asleep" (Mark 5:39). They laugh at Him in ridicule, but Jesus does not confess the lower reality. He confesses that, by looking into the kingdom of God, He sees the little girl alive—which she is very shortly.

Of course all of this assumes that we have known the voice of the Lord and His Holy Spirit and know what the will of the Father is. However, in such matters as our health and well-being the Word is very explicit on God's intent. We have the mind of the Lord for our health and our lips may safely agree with that higher reality.

Other Problems Related to Our Words

In James 3 we are told that if anyone does not stumble in word, he is a perfect man (verse 2). He goes on to say that the tongue is a fire, the very world of iniquity, and defiles the entire body, setting on fire the course of our lives (verse 6). There are a number of matters centering around the fruit of our lips which ought to be the natural product of the Renewed Mind. I can only touch on each of these.

In the decalogue which God gave to Moses on Sinai, the third commandment states unequivocally: "You shall not take the name of the Lord your God in vain" (Exodus 20:7). Let me approach this matter on two levels. First there is the individual who has been rescued by the Lord from a life of gross sin in the world. It has been almost second nature to curse when with his friends. Now as his mind is being renewed and brought into fellowship with the things of the Spirit—both the spirit of man and the Holy Spirit—and a new and intense love relationship is established with his Lord, then any word that would mock His name cuts like a knife to his heart. Such a habit is usually corrected almost at once.

But I want to mention another related matter that I find even more grievous. In many circles of Christians in the United States there is what I call "polite cursing" that has become almost a way of life. The names "Lord" and "God" are tossed into sentences totally apart from any indication of praise or worship or even a discussion of the Lord. One well-known evangelist in particular laces his sermons with the phrase "my Lord, my brothers and sisters." I can only recall God's words to Moses that He must be treated as holy in the sight of the people (Numbers 20:12).

There is yet another area of language I can only label as obscenities. Off-color jokes, off-color words, off-color comments—call them what you will—they are totally unbecoming to a mind that claims to know the mind of Christ. To anyone who is sincerely pursuing a Renewed Mind, walking into the midst of such comments touches his soul and spirit much as pouring coal dust on a white suit. I am far more distressed, however, when these words come from the same lips that only moments before witnessed to the power of Jesus Christ. The fact that such words can flow forth from his mouth tells us what kind of food that man has been feeding his spirit.

Just one more matter of the mouth. This entire business of gossip, ridicule, undercutting and backbiting really turns out to be the destruction of a brother or sister. Jesus warned us that "all those who take up the sword shall perish by the sword" (Matthew 26:52) and that we should be careful how we judge, for by our standard of measure, it shall be measured to us (Matthew 7:2). The end-time army of our Lord Jesus needs a Renewed Mind for many reasons, but certainly one of the most crucial must be the manner in which we treat one another.

We have talked much about the mind set on the Spirit and the mind set on the flesh. Jesus has told us that Satan's agenda is to steal, kill and destroy; our Lord's is to give life and that abundantly. There is simply no place in the life of spiritual man for words which hurt, cut and destroy. Much less is there place for words that intentionally demean and assassinate the name and character of a fellow Christian. I would recommend that every sincere Renewed-Mind Christian frame these words and place them on the desk in front of him: "Consider that remark—what spirit does it reflect?"

Dealing With Temptation

Will having a Renewed Mind affect my ability to deal with temptations as they come? Let me answer that question with an illustration from the life of Jesus. In chapter four we have already pointed out that the finest thing you can say about spiritual man when he has come to a Renewed Mind is that he has the very mind of Christ. Now what do we know about our Lord? We know that while He was the Son of God, He was at the same time fully man. He walked the same roads and byways and met the same people, and must certainly have been exposed to the same temptations as you and I. In fact, the writer to the Hebrews says that Jesus was in all points tempted even as we are tempted, and yet was without sin (Hebrews 4:15). Since every one of us has known something of the scope of temptations that can come to a new Christian and of the internal battle that rages in the attempt to get victory over those temptations, then it is highly encouraging to know that if we truly have the mind of Christ, we have the potential of living above sin.

Much of what I want to say here has already been covered in the section of this chapter titled "How Can I Retrain My Mouth?" Jesus reminded us that out of the abundance of our hearts our mouths speak, and we concluded in that discussion that the ability to bridle our tongue hinges directly upon our capacity to take every thought captive.

Similarly, every sinful act in the external realm of this world was first born in the inner recesses of the mind. In fact, I believe the Word teaches us that Satan would have no power to tempt us to sin in the external, visible realm if he could not first appeal to our inner thoughts. Remember that the central mark of the Renewed Mind is that it has been reoriented, refocused, set on the things which are above, the things of the Spirit, the things of the kingdom of God, the things of life. Only when the mind is focused on the things of the senses and the flesh do the thought processes lead to death. Now every sin which is known to mortal man such as murder, adultery, theft, violence, greed, anger, was born first in our thoughts as the enemy appealed to our fleshly minds.

The short answer to the question of temptation is very simple: If we at all times have a Renewed Mind and our every thought is fixed on the things of the kingdom of God, then temptations will roll off our minds and our flesh as the proverbial water off a duck's back. Incidentally, this is the explanation for Jesus' ability to be subjected to the same temptations as we are, yet be without sin.

To those who heard Jesus teaching day after day, His words must often have appeared to be harsh and demanding—even impossible at times to the natural mind. For instance, Jesus said harboring an evil picture in one's mind is adequate to convict the person of great sin.

Let me illustrate: In Matthew 5, during Jesus' sermon on the mount, He said that under the old law adultery was forbidden. However, Jesus goes on to say that looking "on a woman to lust for her" means that the individual has already committed adultery with her in his heart (verse 28). Further, as Jesus discussed the sinfulness of murder, He said that to be simply angry with one's brother is to be equally guilty (verse 22). Much later, John took up the same theme: "Every one who hates his brother is a murderer" (1 John 3:15).

To the natural mind, or even to a casual reading by a Christian, it may well appear that these words of our Lord have made battling temptation infinitely more difficult. However, the Renewed Mind will recognize that exactly the opposite is the case: As the natural mind battles each new temptation in the flesh, it seems always to be losing the battle and even the war. James understood this weakness in the flesh and the powerful role that our thoughts play before the act of sin is carried out: "When lust has conceived, it gives birth to sin, and when sin is accomplished, it brings forth death" (James 1:15).

Conversely, the Renewed Mind understands the power of the mind set on the flesh or the mind set on the Spirit. With the apostle Paul, the spiritual man understands the strategy of destroying speculations, casting down imaginations, by taking every thought captive (2 Corinthians 10:5).

In the book of Proverbs we read: "For as he [a man] thinks within himself, so he is" (Proverbs 23:7). Paul extended the implication of these words when he wrote:

> *Finally, brethren, whatever is true, whatever is honorable, whatever is right, whatever is pure, whatever is lovely, whatever is of good repute, if there is any excellence and if anything worthy of praise, let your mind dwell on these things.* (Philippians 4:8)

My grandmother taught me that an idle mind is the devil's workshop. While it may not be scriptural, it certainly is in agreement with Paul's teaching that the mind set on the flesh is death.

Spiritual man with his Renewed Mind is not taken out of the world, and it is inevitable that temptations will come as Jesus taught us. However, the Renewed Mind has three basic tools in the face of temptation: the authority to cast down evil imaginations when the enemy presents them; the strength to refuse evil thoughts and harbor them in the heart; the presence and strength of the Holy Spirit to refocus the mind on those things which are pure, holy and virtuous.

Knowing spiritual man, knowing that his ongoing victory over temptation will be the result of his refocused mind, we are not surprised that these words are his constant prayer: "Let the words of my mouth, and the meditation of my heart, be acceptable in thy sight, O Lord, my strength, and my redeemer" (Psalm 19:14, KJV).

The Impact on Our Marriage and Home

My wife and I have discussed many times and agree fully that the first twenty years of our marriage were beautiful and excellent. However, as we received the fullness of the Holy Spirit, began to grow under His instruction in the Word and saw the first fruit of the Renewed Mind, both our marriage and our family life moved to an entirely new plane.

How can people who love each other quarrel so much? Or why do people abuse, both physically and emotionally, the ones who mean the most to them? Still more serious—how can these things take place in Christian homes?

Review with me the basic characteristics of both the natural man and the carnal man: Their unrenewed minds are basically egocentric, viewing things only from their own selfish vantage points. The basic cry of the unrenewed mind is: "Be reasonable, see things my way." The central demand for each one having his own way and the arrogance about one's own self-worth are a blueprint for strife between individuals when life is lived on an intimate level.

On the other hand, the Renewed Mind—seeing things from God's vantage point—understands the needs of others. Having received the power of the Holy Spirit, the first fruit of His presence is an abundance of *agape* love—the selfless and enduring divine love that the apostle Paul describes in 1 Corinthians 13. This makes that individual self-giving, others-centered.

There is an abundance of good books on Christian marriage, and it is not the purpose of this present text to resketch all these matters. However, I want to make two or three important points. Much of the writing being done on the home today assumes that if both partners are born-again Christians marriages are going to be automatically wonderful. I believe there are several additional prerequisites for a loving, giving marriage. Two I would emphasize as mandatory: First, I believe the power to love with *agape* love is beyond our grasp until we receive the indwelling presence of God's Holy Spirit. Secondly, only as our minds are renewed—reoriented from the flesh and self to the things of the kingdom of God—can we grasp the needs and desires of our partner fully.

I am convinced that many Christian people miss these facts to their own hurt. For many years I counseled individuals as a Christian psychologist. I have found that the amount of heartache within so-called Christian marriages is at least as great as in those outside Christ. A number of years ago our daughter was a high school student in a fundamentalist Christian school. One day her English teacher assigned a paper on the topic "Why My Family Quarrels." Our daughter pondered this for awhile and asked her if she might have a different topic. When asked why, our daughter answered that she had really never seen her family quarrel. The teacher was so incredulous she treated the matter as humorous. When she was finally convinced that our daughter was serious, she allowed her to write on the topic "Why My Family Does Not Quarrel." I am delighted to report that she got the highest possible grade, writing on the power of the Holy Spirit in peoples' lives and His ability to change the way we love, the way we think and the way we treat each other—even in our most intimate relationships.

One further word of caution. In recent years Satan has launched attacks on the home in general and the Christian home in particular with greater ferocity than perhaps at any other time. Today's casual attitudes toward sexual relationships, widespread divorce and open mockery of the sacredness of the home are horrifying enough in this world. But as we see these trends invading the church on every side (including widespread infidelity even among the clergy of our evangelical churches), we realize what a broadside Satan is firing against us. If I may take the comments made on handling temptation in the previous point along with those in this present section, I would speak to every sincere Christian who reads these words. If the cost of pursuing a Renewed Mind was solely for the purpose of solidifying our marriages and homes and giving us victory over temptations, it would be worth every second of the time spent. So great are the deceptions of the enemy today that it seems even the most sincere Christian falls prey to his lies. Only as we have a Renewed Mind and as we yield ourselves moment by moment to the leading of His Spirit are we going to see victory in our families.

The Effectiveness of Our Local Church

Nothing withers the hand of effectiveness of any church as does internal strife and quarreling. Simple observation will tell us that no group is exempt—fundamentalists, evangelicals, Pentecostals or charismatics. Internal bickering results in church splits. Even new Christians recognize that these things ought not to be.

Is there a simple explanation for this enigma? Yes—the absence of a Renewed Mind. If you restudy the characteristics of a Renewed Mind and the steps by which one attains them, you will find that there is no place for this kind of divisive behavior.

Watchman Nee often wrote of what he called "soulish men"— men who are sense-ruled, fleshly, carnal and, in some cases, even mean-spirited. Does the church attract the likes of these? Not particularly. In the natural, all men are sense-ruled, fleshly, carnal and, in some instances, mean-spirited. The problem is not that the church has attracted more than its share of "soulish" men, but rather, without adequate teaching, men have come to the Lord and joined the church and brought with them all the baggage of their carnal natures. Such brothers and sisters have the uncanny ability to find the speck in a brother's eye. Frequently there is unusual sensitivity to petty theological differences. Criticism and blaming others flow freely. A brother appears to stumble and we impute the worst possible motives to him.

The reason people quarrel in church is the same reason they quarrel at home with their families—they are still self-centered, egocentric, proud, selfish, demanding that everyone else understand their personal point of view.

Without extensive elaboration, let me say that our churches are going to continue to be grossly ineffective and inefficient until they are composed of men and women who have genuinely Renewed Minds. We need Renewed Minds in pastors, every staff member, every officer, every teacher and every member of the congregation.

Our churches are really the larger extension of our families. In the Old Testament a man taught his family at home. When a village contained a dozen such families, they could have a synagogue and gather to study and worship together. That is really the model for our churches—our families ought to be taught at home and then assembled together for the larger purposes of worship, ministry and teaching. But exactly at this point is one of the great problems of our churches: If our families are characterized by soulish, fleshly minds, then our churches will bear a similar hue. Family members cannot scream at one another for an hour and a half as they prepare for church on Sunday morning and then gather in church expressing great love for one another moments later. If no one else sees through this facade, our kids will in a hurry.

In Jesus' final words to His disciples, He set forth a strict standard on this matter:

> *"A new commandment I give to you, that you love one another, even as I have loved you, that you also love one another. By this all men will know that you are My disciples, if you have love for one another."* (John 13:34-35)

"This is My commandment, that you love one another, just as I have loved you. Greater love has no one than this, that one lay down his life for his friends." (John 15:12-13)

In every instance the Greek word translated love here is *agape*. This very highest form of God-given, self-giving love is far more deeply concerned about the welfare of others than one's self. This ability to love as Jesus loved, to bear one another's burdens, to strengthen and encourage each other and to labor together for the glory of the Lord without fighting over who gets the credit—this is *agape* love.

As hopeless as this may leave many churches, I am convinced that Renewed Minds are the first prerequisite for effective churches. Carnal minds must be refocused on the things of God. Self-centered thoughts must yield to hunger for His mind and His will. After Paul's great appeal for a Renewed Mind in Romans 12, he begins to identify some of the expected outcomes: "Be devoted to one another in brotherly love; give preference to one another in honor" (Romans 12:10). Here Paul's words suggest that we ought to outdo one another in showing honor to one another. Then we shall have an effective church.

The Witnessing Christian

Most of us have heard dozens of messages on the imperative of Christian witnessing. In fact, if you have been in a denominational church, such messages were probably accompanied by elaborate programs and clever gimmicks for "winning people to Christ." Such a message brings a picture to my mind of the great Socrates grasping his victim by the lapel of his cloak and grilling him with questions until he wearies of the game and goes off to quiz someone else.

This is but a slight exaggeration of many so-called witnessing programs. Undoubtedly some people will come to Jesus Christ under such an approach, but I fear that many more will be alienated in the process. Further, if you are alert to the principles in this book, you may recognize that such a strategy for witnessing capitalizes upon fleshly, soulish methods.

I believe the Lord has a better approach. We have already seen that one of the characteristics of the Renewed Mind is that the spiritual man is led by the Spirit of God. The Renewed Mind is in tune with the things of the Holy Spirit at every moment, and because he takes his every cue from the leading of the Holy Spirit, he has a decided advantage in his witnessing.

As an analogy, any good salesman may resort to "cold calls" on occasion and may actually sell some of his products once in a while. On the other hand, nothing is more valuable than an inside tip that a particular person is already shopping for precisely the product he represents. His task is to represent his product well and close the sale.

Without being irreverent, let me suggest that the Renewed Mind goes about its witnessing in a similar fashion. At the beginning of each new day, spiritual man includes in his prayers a petition that says: "Father, You know every step I will take today. You know every life that I will touch. Quicken my spirit to recognize the hungry heart—the one You have been preparing by the power of Your Holy Spirit. Give me the spirit to represent Jesus well—to explain the aspects of the Christian life that will most meet the need of this person. Give me the courage to lead him to You."

The Christian and Material Possessions

A couple of years ago the Lord told me that I must address the whole matter of prosperity teaching that is abroad today. I must confess this did not bring any joy to my heart, for I was not anxious to get caught up in such a divisive matter. However, after several weeks of searching the Word of God, I had the great thrill of discovering that man's relationship to the material world around him and his own material possessions is very much a matter of the Renewed Mind. I am further convinced that there is significant error not only in much of the so-called prosperity teaching, but also in the teaching of those who are trying to refute it.

There is space here for only a brief look at this vast subject. Remember that the Renewed Mind is focused on the things of God, the things of eternity. However, we still live in a body of flesh which has many needs. Are these needs important or are they not? And if they are, what should be the stance of the Renewed Mind regarding them?

Jesus has answered this question for us:

> "No one can serve two masters; for either he will hate the one and love the other, or he will hold to one and despise the other. You cannot serve God and mammon. For this reason I say to you, do not be anxious for your life, as to what you shall eat, or what you shall drink; nor for your body, as to what you shall put on. Is not life more than food, and the body than clothing? Look at the birds of the air, that they do not sow, neither do they reap, nor gather into barns, and yet your heavenly Father feeds them. Are you not worth much more than they? And which of you by being anxious can add a single cubit to his life's span? And why are you anxious about clothing? Observe how the lilies of the field grow; they do not toil nor do they spin, yet I say to you that even Solomon in all his glory did not clothe himself like one of these. But if God so arrays the grass of the field, which is alive today and tomorrow is thrown into the furnace, will He not much more do so for you, O men of little faith? Do not be anxious then, saying, `What shall we eat?' or `What shall we drink?' or `With what shall we clothe ourselves?' For all these things the Gentiles eagerly seek; for your heavenly Father knows that you need all these things. But seek first His kingdom and His righteousness; and all these things shall be added to you. Therefore do not be anxious for tomorrow; for tomorrow will care for itself. Each day has enough trouble of its own." (Matthew 6:24-34)

As in all other matters related to the kingdom of God, the correct response here depends on the focus of the mind. If the mind is carnal and pursues the material possessions of this world as an end in themselves, then it is clearly wrong. Spiritual man keeps his attention constantly focused upon the things of God, fully confident at every moment that his heavenly Father will provide every need of his flesh. In fact, Jesus was as specific as He could possibly be when He said that it is impossible for any of us to serve God and money at the same time. For this reason, Jesus goes on to say that we are not to be anxious at all about what we eat or drink or put on, for when we are, we have focused our mind again on the things about us and have become soulish.

Matthew 6:33 literally says: "Continually seek first the kingdom of God and His righteousness; and all these things will be added unto you." Once you get hold of this truth—or perhaps better, this truth gets hold of you—you will understand at once that this is very much a matter of a Renewed Mind. Even better, you will have great peace about your heavenly Father's provision for the needs of your life every moment.

The Educational Process

It was at this juncture that the Lord first began to reveal Himself to me in the matters of the Renewed Mind. Since I have spent a lifetime in the world of academe, I will always carry a special burden for the academic mind. In fact, I was so enthralled at the possibilities for the rebirth of the academic, sense-ruled mind that it was a couple of years before it began to sink in that the process of a Renewed Mind is for all Christians and transforms life itself.

If I let myself start down this road very far, this book will double in length and the manuscript will never be completed. If the Lord grants the time and the wisdom, there are a number of topics that must be explored in the years ahead. For one, the clever deceitfulness of humanism as it holds the educated, rational mind captive. Second, the nature of the human mind and the implications of the Renewed Mind for the entire educational process from kindergarten through the most advanced degrees. Third, the structure of the university system and various disciplines to a view of bringing a Christian perspective to bear on each. And again there is the almost limitless possibility of many Renewed Minds interacting with each other and integrating the complex fields of knowledge. What a fantastic thrill it would be if Jesus, during His millennial reign, would allow many Renewed Minds to come together and discover not only the complexities of the created universe, but God's goodness and principles for accomplishing the welfare of man.

In lieu of any extensive discussion of the four mentioned topics, let me offer you four very simple points, almost truisms.

First, since our heavenly Father has a plan for each of our lives, then one of the first responsibilities of a Renewed Mind is to know the mind of the Spirit and thus of the Father and discover that purpose and call. Conjointly, we will ask the question of what preparation, academic or otherwise, is needed to carry out God's purposes in our lives, and how this should be accomplished. We are such creatures of this present age that we often assume that we need certain academic degrees to pursue certain goals. God may very well choose otherwise for us. On the other hand, we may become so suspicious of the academic establishment that we avoid a particular course of study when that would be the Lord's most efficient means of preparing us for His work.

Second, virtually all of what we study needs to be rethought and seen through revelation knowledge. This being the case, no matter what you are studying—and no matter if the teacher professes to be a Christian—ask the Holy Spirit always to teach you what agrees with His Word and His will.

Third, no matter what we are studying—either the Word of God or any academic discipline—the Holy Spirit can greatly enable our own learning abilities. He can give us greater creativity, increase our recall, grant us insight, heap wisdom and understanding upon us and, in general, improve the whole efficiency and effectiveness of the educational process.

Fourth, while God has created us with different intellectual capacities, I believe the Holy Spirit can make all Renewed Minds genuine scholars. He can stretch your mind to its fullest capacity and in the process reveal to you great spiritual truths which He has entrusted to no one else.

The Workplace

From our discussions of the relationship between the Renewed Mind and material possessions, you are aware that the Renewed

Mind will require a whole new constellation of principles concerning the workplace. Spiritual man is constantly seeking first the kingdom of God and His righteousness, so he approaches everything that has to do with riches and mammon as a steward appointed by God. This stance will obviously color his reasons for working, who he works with, what he does, how he relates to others in the workplace and the ultimate product of that work.

If you ask the average individual why he works, he will say: "To make money." Spiritual man knows that his heavenly Father is going to meet his every need one way or the other, and thus his motive for working is entirely different. This is not an excuse to be indolent and lethargic, but is an understanding that with God's call upon one's life, there are many purposes to be served other than simply making money.

First, consider our vocation or the work we do. If God has a plan for our lives and we spend more hours in our vocation than in any other single matter, then He certainly has a preference for what He wants us to do. Properly understood, every honorable task on the face of the earth is a Christian vocation. Spiritual man has only one question: "What is God's highest purpose for my life?"

Secondly, you might well argue that the task to which God has called you does not pay enough to provide for the needs of your family. If you are confident you have heard the voice of the Lord, then continue to seek His kingdom and His will for your life and it is His responsibility to provide for you—He has promised it. God has available the unlimited resources of heaven, and He can provide for you and bless you in ways beyond your wildest imagination. My wife and I have just been through several years of this exact experience and I can testify that, beyond all question, God does meet every need.

Consider the question of whom we should work with. The apostle Paul wrote: "Do not be bound together with unbelievers; for what partnership have righteousness and lawlessness, or what fellowship has light with darkness?" (2 Corinthians 6:14). As Paul writes, do not be bound together, or unequally yoked, with unbelievers, for righteousness and lawlessness will not mix. I recognize that for years the church has applied this statement to marriage with good reason. However, the context does not uphold this limitation. Next to our wives, our most enduring and long-term relationships are likely to be in the workplace; Paul strongly argues that we ought not be bound together with unbelievers. This is especially crucial in business partnerships, for if you were to sit down and try to create a statement of purpose for your business with an unbeliever, you would find you were at opposite ends of the continuum on most issues. Further, matters of honesty and integrity will be almost impossible to manage in an unequally yoked relationship. I recognize that not all employees will work for Christian companies and Christian partnerships might not always employ born-again believers as employees. However, because spiritual man's reasons for working go beyond the matter of making money, I believe Paul's ideal stands.

Fourth, personnel relationships—the way we treat fellow workers, including our superiors and subordinates—provide one of the most important tests of a Renewed Mind. The unrenewed mind has but one objective in employee relationships—to use the other individual to the fullest extent for his own personal gains. But the renewed mind recognizes that he is a steward of the other person's welfare and he treats him with compassion, understanding and love. This doesn't mean the employer tolerates shoddy work practices or that the employee feels he can get away with less than his best because his employer is a Christian. Nor does it mean employees and their talents can be consumed until the last ounce of life is wrung out of them then tossed aside, broken and in despair. Sad to say, some Christian ministries in our nation have proved to be the worst role models of all when it comes to living by the standards of a Renewed Mind. For spiritual man, the principle is always the same: How can I be the best steward of the lives and talents entrusted to me.

Fifth, honesty and integrity are hallmarks of the spiritual man. Somewhere along the line the great American dream of free enterprise and the opportunity to create a new business has deteriorated into a headlong rush to maximize the profits. Greed has replaced integrity and misleading advertising has replaced the quality product. Spiritual man cannot tolerate this. With his focus on the kingdom of God, the man with the Renewed Mind will insist upon a quality product honestly described and trust God to take care of the profits.

Sixth, I believe God will give the creative energy and the creative mind necessary to the spiritual man so he may honestly compete in the world to which God has called him. Note that I did not say in any random business of the person's own choosing, but as spiritual man has heard the call of God and is doing what God has called him to do, I believe He will give creative energy to do it well. Whether this involves product design, production or marketing, the Renewed Mind has the mind of the Lord and He cares about everything that concerns us and certainly about the way we serve Him in our work.

Finally, I believe God grants favor in ways that are beyond our understanding. The Word of God is filled with illustrations of humble, God-fearing people who were granted favor so that they might fulfill God's call upon their lives: Joseph received favor with Pharaoh, Esther with Ahasuerus, and Daniel with several of the kings of Babylonia and Media-Persia. I believe that if spiritual man is fulfilling God's call upon his life, though he may be competing with children of this age working in a world under Satan's control, our heavenly Father is loving enough and powerful enough to grant him favor at every required point.

The Priorities of Life

The chief characteristic of the man with the Renewed Mind is that he is now a spiritual man. Once a natural man, more recently a carnal man, he is now spiritual in his very essence and nature. Restored to the potential of a created Adam with the mind of his Lord Jesus Christ, he truly is a new creature.

Because man is spiritual, his number one responsibility is the care and feeding of his reborn spirit and his Renewed Mind. This includes adequate time to be taught in the Word of God, to worship and praise his heavenly Father, to hear the voice and leading of the Holy Spirit, to know the mind of the Father and His will for his life. This goes well beyond what we have traditionally called "having our devotions" and recalls the pleasure of Adam and Eve in Eden's garden as they walked with the Father in the cool of the day. Spiritual man's consuming passion is his fellowship with the Father and His Son, Jesus Christ. Out of this fellowship is born joy, love, peace and the sustenance of life itself. This is not a matter of catching five minutes here or there to read a verse of Scripture and say good morning to the Lord. This is a matter of structuring one's life in such a way that fellowship with God and hearing His voice is paramount; every other activity must be arranged around that time and considered secondary in importance.

Second, note that following this fellowship, God's first assignment to Adam and Eve was to be fruitful and to multiply. This powerful emphasis upon family life and its centrality in the life of spiritual man is certainly God-given.

Man's second responsibility is to assume his role as prophet and priest in the home—to love and care for his wife and children, to instruct them in the things of God as he has been taught by the Holy Spirit and to speak the mind of God to his family. With his God-given authority, he will protect the family against the onslaught of the enemy and, in many senses, he will be pastor and shepherd to his family—a microcosm of the church of Jesus Christ. Further, he will shepherd them to the house of God and see that they are joined to the larger family of believers on a regular basis, so that their worship, ministry and instruction in the things of the kingdom of God is strengthened.

God's next charge to Adam was that he should rule and have dominion over the entire creation. God does have a plan for every man's life. Whether this includes a call to a Christian ministry or to a secular task, the inescapable fact is that God has called and our responsibility is clear.

One of the most significant concepts of the Old Testament is God's call to possess the land (for example, Numbers 33:53). For Christians today, the land represents that place of blessing and service He has promised to each of us. However large or small, however important or unimportant this assignment from the Lord may appear to us, there can be no higher calling on the face of the earth. Perhaps now it will be clear why I emphasize so strongly that we do not work for the purpose of making money. Our vocational assignment is the outworking of God's master plan for our lives, and our task is to go and exercise dominion in the land to which He calls us. Whatever our task, it is our responsibility to see that the rule of God comes to pass in our promised land, our corner of His calling

262

and kingdom.

As I understand the Word of God, these three central responsibilities overshadow all other concerns for spiritual man. Certainly other rightful responsibilities will be included. Proper rest, care, exercise and feeding of the physical body is an obvious one. There must be frequent occasions to fellowship with other believers in the body of Christ.

My Christian friend, can you grasp one thing? If we could keep our hearts and minds set on these three central priorities as God fixed them for us, it would free us from the tyranny of all the other things that the world thinks are urgent. What peace to know that the majority of activities that occupy the time of natural man are not in the economy of God.

Conclusion

Undoubtedly, a dozen different areas have occurred to you where we could have applied the principles of the Renewed Mind. You may find yourself with numerous questions concerning this whole maturation process as the carnal man becomes the spiritual man as a result of renewing his mind. I wish we had time to discuss all of these issues at great length.

However, as you press on day by day and follow the steps to a Renewed Mind, you should find yourself growing in confidence and learning to trust the Holy Spirit's instruction to you directly.

I trust that in the reading of this book you discovered there is no other task of greater urgency in the Christian life than developing a Renewed Mind. If so, you may find yourself reading and rereading different portions of this book to refresh your understanding. At a minimum, let me urge you to review very prayerfully chapters four and five until they are a part of your Christian understanding. The eight characteristics of the spiritual man or the Renewed Mind, and the eight steps to accomplish this spiritual growth, will be central to your own Christian maturation.

As you face new issues in your Christian life and new questions arise, learn to ask yourself one question repeatedly~~: How will I handle this matter differently if my mind is set on the things of the Spirit rather than on the things of the flesh and this world? I trust that

Chart 12 (on page 123) will help in resolving this question in your mind. Further, let our heavenly Father's words to Joshua, as he prepared to lead Israel in to take the land, reverberate in your own heart daily:

> *This book of the law shall not depart from your mouth, but you shall meditate on it day and night, so that you may be careful to do according to all that is written in it; for then you will make your way prosperous, and then you will have success.* (Joshua 1:8)

Let me leave you with another of those majestic passages from the pen of Paul. If Romans 12 is Paul's clarion call to abandon our carnal and fleshly thoughts for a Renewed Mind, then Ephesians 4 is his portrait of the end result—the spiritual man:

> *Until we all attain to the unity of the faith, and of the knowledge of the Son of God, to a mature man, to the measure of the stature which belongs to the fulness of Christ. As a result, we are no longer to be children, tossed here and there by waves, and carried about by every wind of doctrine, by the trickery of men, by craftiness in deceitful scheming; but speaking the truth in love, we are to grow up in all aspects into Him, who is the head, even Christ, from whom the whole body, being fitted and held together by that which every joint supplies, according to the proper working of each individual part, causes the growth of the body for the building up of itself in love. This I say therefore, and affirm together with the Lord, that you walk no longer just as the Gentiles also walk, in the futility of their mind, being darkened in their understanding, excluded from the life of God, because of the ignorance that is in them, because of the hardness of their heart; and they, having become callous, have given themselves over to sensuality, for the practice of every kind of impurity with greediness. But you did not learn Christ in this way, if indeed you have heard Him and*

have been taught in Him, just as truth is in Jesus, that, in reference to your former manner of life, you lay aside the old self, which is being corrupted in accordance with the lusts of deceit, and that you be renewed in the spirit of your mind, and put on the new self, which in the likeness of God has been created in righteousness and holiness of the truth. Therefore, laying aside falsehood, speak truth, each one of you, with his neighbor, for we are members of one another. Be angry, and yet do not sin; do not let the sun go down on your anger, and do not give the devil an opportunity. Let him who steals steal no longer; but rather let him labor, performing with his own hands what is good, in order that he may have something to share with him who has need. Let no unwholesome word proceed from your mouth, but only such a word as is good for edification according to the need of the moment, that it may give grace to those who hear. And do not grieve the Holy Spirit of God, by whom you were sealed for the day of redemption. Let all bitterness and wrath and anger and clamor and slander be put away from you, along with all malice. And be kind to one another, tender-hearted, forgiving each other, just as God in Christ also has forgiven you. (Ephesians 4:13-32)

What a litany of the culminating characteristics of the Renewed Mind! The unity of the faith, the knowledge of the Lord, a mature man in the stature of the fullness of Christ, no longer double-minded or tossed here and there by every wave and wind of doctrine, alert to the enemy's ways, discerning his deceit and lies, speaking the truth in love. The spiritual man has grown up into the very mind of Christ. His walk, his thoughts and his words have been purified. Since the Renewed Mind refuses to entertain Satan's wicked thoughts, he no longer gives the devil an opportunity. Or as Kenneth Taylor states it so beautifully: He does not "give a mighty foothold to the devil" (Ephesians 4:27, The Living Bible). He presses on to the very mind of Christ!

EPILOGUE

I am keenly aware that the burden of this book is not an easy message, but spiritually demanding. However, if God has spoken to your heart and you are still with us, then I have a very personal word and request of you, my reader friend. The Lord has impressed upon me repeatedly for several years that the call to a Renewed Mind will provide the foundation for all of the other training for God's end-time army. As the Lord moves on your spirit, I would ask that you join with me in intercessory prayer for the ministry of this book, and beyond that, for the purification of Christ's church and for a great sweeping move of the Holy Spirit that will bring believers from carnal minds to spiritual. Specifically, I would encourage you to pray daily for the following ten critical needs of this last day:

1. Pray that millions of carnal, lethargic Christians will awaken to the need for a Renewed Mind.
2. Pray that as the Lord continues to shake the foundations of the church, Christians will understand that this is not an attack of the enemy but rather the Lord calling them to be spiritual people.
3. Pray that the message of righteousness, purity and holy living will saturate the church of Jesus Christ.

4. Pray that the church will become a witnessing church — not by programs and gimmicks — but by yielding to the power, anointing and leading of God's Holy Spirit.

5. Pray that the Lord will quickly raise up His end-time army, comprised of overcoming, victorious Christians with Renewed Minds.

6. Pray that this end-time army will rediscover its God-given authority and exercise its rightful dominion in this age.

7. Pray that the church of Jesus Christ will be restored to a position of pure worship and adoration of our Lord and so fulfill our created purpose.

8. Pray that the tide of the satanic, end-time religion of humanism will be turned back.

9. Pray that Christians everywhere will be awakened to the deceptions of the so-called New Age movement and that the power of truly Renewed Minds will prevail.

10. Pray that as the end-time army marches forward and becomes articulate in the principles of the kingdom of God, "the knowledge of the glory of the Lord shall cover the earth as the waters cover the sea" (Habakkuk 2:14).

Finally, I want to share with you one of the most thrilling victories the Lord has given me in the last several years. In the midst of an in-depth presentation of the messages contained in this book to a Christian university family, I began to experience greater spiritual attack from the enemy than at perhaps any other point in my life. The attack was so great that I would find myself sitting bolt upright in bed in the middle of the night waging spiritual warfare deep in my spirit. Over and over I heard the words: "The Renewed Mind is not possible — abandon the idea!" I earnestly sought my heavenly Father on this matter. He clearly instructed me to set aside a weekend of prayer and fasting specifically for the matter of the Renewed Mind. During that time of being shut up with the Lord, on three successive mornings the Holy Spirit led me to a specific passage of Scripture each morning. Near the end of my period of prayer on the third morning, the Lord very clearly spoke to me: "I have just given you My full strategy for the defeat of the enemy, and My full promise for the fulfillment of Habakkuk 2:14."

I trust that these three divinely given promises will thrill your heart as they have mine again and again.

On the first morning, the Holy Spirit led me to the first chapter of Daniel. Nebuchadnezzar had instructed his chief officials to select several of the Jewish exiles to train for service in the Babylonian court. Daniel and his three friends refused the king's offered diet of delicacies and wine, choosing rather to trust the Lord for His favor and instruction. At that period of testing it is recorded:

> *As for these four youths, God gave them knowledge and intelligence in every branch of literature and wisdom; Daniel even understood all kinds of visions and dreams. Then at the end of the days which the king had specified for presenting them, the commander of the officials presented them before Nebuchadnezzar. And the king talked with them, and out of them all not one was found like Daniel, Hananiah, Mishael and Azariah; so they entered the king's personal service. And as for every matter of wisdom and understanding about which the king consulted them, he found them ten times better than all the magicians and conjurers who were in all his realm.* (Daniel 1:17-20)

The Lord's message to me was very specific. "Although the end times are virtually a carbon copy of the corruption of this Chaldean kingdom, I will raise up My army of men and women who have a thorough understanding of the kingdom of God and its principles, who are led by My visions and dreams, and who will thunder unapologetically: 'Thus saith the Lord.'"

In other words, I believe the Lord is telling us that it matters not how overwhelming the tide of humanism seems to be today, nor how entrenched the forces of the Antichrist appear — God will have an army that is fully equipped with the necessary understanding of His ways and the courage to say: "Thus saith the Lord."

The second morning, the Holy Spirit gave me the following passage:

269

For though we walk in the flesh, we do not war according to the flesh, for the weapons of our warfare are not of the flesh, but divinely powerful for the destruction of fortresses. We are destroying specula- tions and every lofty thing raised up against the knowledge of God, and we are taking every thought captive to the obedience of Christ, and we are ready to punish all disobedience, whenever your obedience is complete. (2 Corinthians 10:3-6)

The interpretation is clear: In this age we are engaged in spiritual warfare more certainly than at any other time since the creation of the world. The ultimate outcome of this battle depends not upon our flesh, not upon our rational knowledge, but upon the Holy Spirit of God. Our divinely appointed task is to destroy speculations, cast down imaginations and take authority over every lofty thought and word that are raised up against the knowledge of God. We will then have the authority to take captive every thought not only of our own mind but of those that vaunt themselves against Christ. And when our end-time army is completely obedient to its Lord, then and only then shall we have the power to punish all other disobedience. Hallelujah! My spirit soars every time I read this promise.

The Lord had shown me some years before that present-day hu- manism and the New Age movement are actually the old Babylo- nian-Chaldean religions resurrected. The rejection of God, the worship of the occult, and the glorification of Satan and his ways are involved in each instance. On the third morning, the Lord led me very miraculously to the following two verses:

The word which the Lord spoke concerning Bablyon, the land of the Chaldeans, through Jeremiah the prophet: "Declare and proclaim among the nations. Proclaim it and lift up a standard. do not conceal it but say, 'Babylon has been captured, Bel has been put to shame, Marduk has be shattered; Her images have been put to shame, her idols have been shattered,'" (Jeremiah 50:1-2)

If the end-time army is faithful — and we have absolutely no alternative, we must be — then God's final judgment on Babylon is foreordained. Proclaim it abroad: Babylon has fallen! Humanism has met its end! Its godless images have been shattered! The battle is the Lord's!

There is much intercessory prayer to be offered. There are many minds to be renewed. There are many soldiers to be trained. But rejoice with me once again! The battle is inescapable, the victory is inevitable, and the knowledge of the glory of the Lord shall fill the earth as the waters cover the sea!

For additional copies of this book, inquiries concerning teaching seminars, or other questions regarding this ministry, write to:

Dr. Richard F. Gottier, President
Zion Ministries of the East Coast, Inc.
P.O. Box 737
Kitty Hawk, N.C. 27949